Planning and Governing
the Metropolis

PRAEGER SPECIAL STUDIES IN
U.S. ECONOMIC AND SOCIAL DEVELOPMENT

Planning and Governing the Metropolis

THE TWIN CITIES EXPERIENCE

Stanley Baldinger

**Foreword by
Victor Jones**

**PRAEGER PUBLISHERS
New York • Washington • London**

The purpose of Praeger Special Studies is to make specialized research in U.S. and international economics and politics available to the academic, business, and government communities. For further information, write to the Special Projects Division, Praeger Publishers, Inc., 111 Fourth Avenue, New York, N.Y. 10003.

PRAEGER PUBLISHERS
111 Fourth Avenue, New York, N.Y. 10003, U.S.A.
5, Cromwell Place, London S.W.7, England

Published in the United States of America in 1971
by Praeger Publishers, Inc.

Library of Congress Catalog Card Number: 74-131946

Printed in the United States of America

To Judith

FOREWORD

Charles E. Merriam wrote, in his preface to my book <u>Metropolitan Government</u> (1942), that "the adequate organization of modern metropolitan areas is one of the great unsolved problems of modern politics." It is still an unsolved problem.

None of our large metropolitan areas is governed by a single entity called a metropolitan government, but each is governed in varying degrees by a congeries of single-function metropolitan governments--and the thrust toward the metropolitanization of urban problems has been intensified in recent years. As each urban problem becomes recognized as metropolitan, the usual organizational reaction has been to isolate it from the general political process by creating another special district or authority to plan a program to meet the problem, to adopt a program, and to finance and administer the program.

The question is not whether we need or should have metropolitan government. The questions are: What kind of metropolitan government do we want? Can we get what we want?

There is increasing recognition that our large multi-county, sometimes multi-state, metropolitan areas cannot be governed as if each was a single medium-sized urban county. In fact, the large, complex metropolitan area is likely to become even more complicated. And so we find concomitant thrusts toward both regional and neighborhood planning, decision-making, and administration. Both thrusts have to be accommodated, as has been done in large measure in some of our metropolitan areas

through the incorporation of very small urban municipalities and the creation of a multitude of
"neighborhood" special districts. There is, however, a major disparity between suburbia and the
large inner-core cities, in the kinds and degrees
of neighborhood influence exerted over those who
make urban policies and administer urban services.

But there are further complications. Both national and state governments are responding to the
demands generated by the metropolitanization of
American life by taking the initiative in formulating the broad, national intergovernmental urban
programs under which metropolitan America will be
governed during the rest of the century. These programs even now influence the governance of metropolitan areas significantly, and their influence will increase. Normally, however, each state and federal
agency acts autonomously and seeks a metropolitan
agency of equal autonomy as a counterpart.

The immediate prospect of greatest promise is
the creation of a formal system of linkages among
the federal, state, municipal, county, special district, and neighborhood governments that constitute
the intergovernmental complex of metropolitan governance.

One structure created to solve this problem,
the Metropolitan Council of the Twin Cities Area,
whose origin and early activity is described in
this book, has its own special meaning for the
people and institutions of that major metropolis.
Part of that meaning is unique, but an understanding of the establishment of the Council, its accumu-
lated experiences, and its adaptations are, and
will be, invaluable to people working to reorganize
other metropolitan areas. The Council is an effective, comprehensive, and viable reorganization of
the governance of a large metropolitan area. As an
organizational model, it is a strong competitor of
metropolitan councils of government; of limited,
multi-purpose metropolitan agencies that may evolve
from, or be created to replace, metropolitan

councils of government in some of the large metropolitan areas; of autonomous metropolitan districts; of directly elected metropolitan governments; and of city-county consolidations in the South and Midwest.

Even though the Metropolitan Council of the Twin Cities Area is in no respect a council of government, it operates in an intergovernmental context. The manner in which it establishes linkages-- sometimes mandatory, sometimes advisory, and undoubtedly at times negotiated--will test and help make concrete the feasibility and utility of a metropolitan "umbrella agency."

Despite the substantial promise of the Metropolitan Council, based on its leadership and accomplishments to date, there has not yet been time for observers to benefit fully from the lessons to be drawn from its experiences. Perhaps the most important lesson so far is that the deed was done: the governance of a major metropolitan area was reorganized; the Metropolitan Council was created, and it works. The way the need was done has great meaning for the future of metropolitan America, and Mr. Baldinger is fully aware of these implications, though in view of the short life of the Council to date, he is appropriately careful in drawing conclusions from his case study. Students and practitioners of metropolitan governance, as well as other citizens of metropolitan America, are indebted to him for the data he has collected and analyzed and for the fascinating story he has told.

Victor Jones
University of California

PREFACE

Every day we encounter articles, studies, and
reports on the condition of our urban crises. Our
cities and metropolitan areas seem to be falling
apart. The air is unfit to breathe. Sewage fouls
our rivers and streams. Traffic crawls through
our cities, strangling them; inner city residents
protest against freeways that carry suburban traffic and destroy their homes. Inadequate transportation and closed housing opportunities separate
people from jobs. Trash piles up faster than we
can dispose of it. Municipal competition for
development dollars distorts our urban economies,
creating "have" and "have not" communities. Val-
uable open land is consumed too rapidly and unwisely.
Each of these problems is the product of the growth
occurring throughout our metropolitan areas and of
the inability of our fragmented governmental structure to deal effectively with it. This fragmentation, in turn, has helped create an atmosphere
of despair about resolving most of the problems
of our urban crisis in the foreseeable future.

Over the years, various proposals have been
made to reorganize the structure of urban government, hoping to enable it to contend with the
sundry problems facing it. These have ranged from
direct state intervention, by the simple, voluntary
cooperation of councils of governments, to metropolitan government. Only in the last several years
have a few isolated attempts at metropolitan government been successful. The consolidation of Nashville with Davidson County, Tennessee; Jacksonville
with Duval County, Florida; Indianapolis with
Marion County, Indiana; and the urbanization of

MAP 1

LOCATION OF THE TWIN CITIES METROPOLITAN AREA
IN MINNESOTA

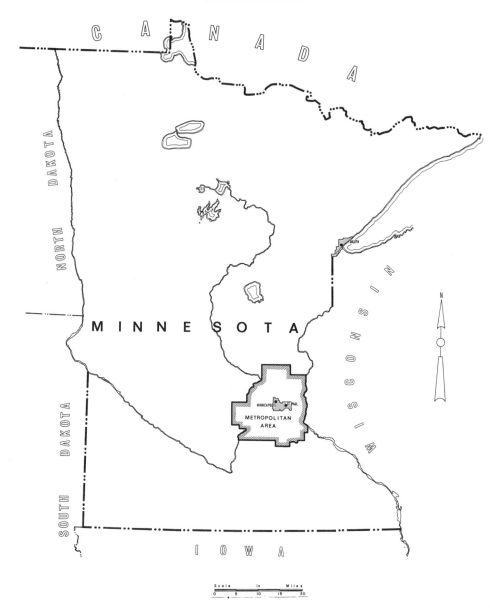

Source: Metropolitan Council of the Twin Cities
Area, "Sewerage and Water Planning Report" (by
Metcalf and Eddy), 1968.

Miami and Dade County, Florida, constitute a select group of areas, out of over one hundred attempts, that have been able to reorganize. These communitoes were helped in their efforts by two factors that all but one area shared in common. First, three of them are wholly or largely confined within single counties that contain relatively few units of local government.* Second, each utilized the county, a familiar and accepted unit of government, as the basic building block for reorganization. Because of this somewhat simpler structural context in which metropolitan reorganization was achieved, these areas have had only minimal value as precedent for the possible reorganization of other major metropolitan areas, most of which encompass two or more counties and hundreds of communities and special districts and possess a more extreme variety of urban ills.

In 1967, for the first time in this century, a major multi-county metropolitan area was re-organized along different lines and through different means from those previously mentioned. The Twin Cities of Minneapolis and Saint Paul, Minnesota, with seven counties, hundreds of suburbs, and a score of area-wide or intermunicipal special districts inaugurated a metropolitan council to deal with a variety of area-wide problems and concerns that each unit could not deal with adequately alone. The metropolitan council is a hybrid unit of government, combining aspects of both a true metropolitan government and a state agency and possessing a wide range of powers that, hopefully, should enable it to plan, coordinate, control, and direct the extensive growth taking place in the area. There has been considerable interest throughout the country over the Council and how it could be of value as an example to follow in reorganizing our more complex metropolitan areas.

---

*The Indianapolis SMSA (Standard Metropolitan Statistical Area) contains eight counties and 282 units of local government (1967). The consolidation of Indianapolis and Marion County involved only one county with sixty units of local government.

MAP 2

POLITICAL BOUNDARIES
OF THE TWIN CITIES METROPOLITAN AREA, 1970

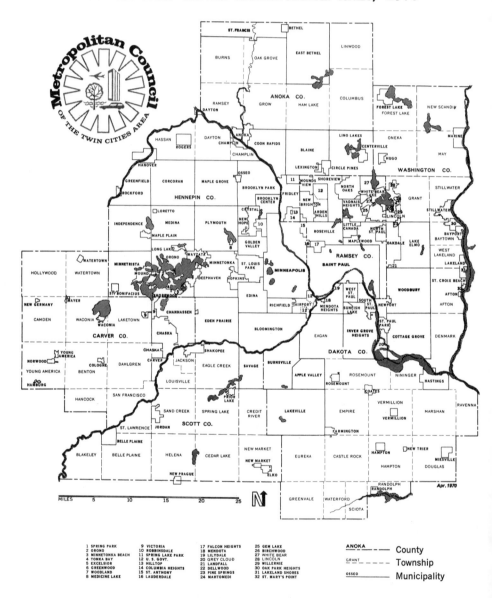

Source: Metropolitan Council of the Twin
Cities Area.

This case study has been undertaken for four reasons: (1) to ascertain exactly what the Metropolitan Council is and how effective it has been, (2) to learn why and how it came about, (3) to determine how useful it might be as an example to reorganize other metropolitan areas, and (4) to determine what, if anything, planners, political leaders, and the public in general can learn from the experiences of the Council and its proponents in planning and governing the metropolis. No attempt is made to propose specific means or strategies whereby areas may successfully reorganize based on the Twin Cities experience. Neither is the claim made that the Twin Cities Metropolitan Council is the only answer to our many metropolitan problems. There are a number of approaches, the study notes, that can satisfactorily meet metropolitan needs, as determined and required by local, area-wide, and state considerations. Rather, the hope has been to provide evaluations from the experiences of the Twin Cities Council and its supporters that may prove useful to planners and political leaders in taming the metropolis.

In carrying out this study, I am grateful to many people and organizations for their help and cooperation. James Hetland, Jr., and Reynold Boezi of the Metropolitan Council, Ted Kolderie of the Citizens League (of the Twin Cities area), and James Pickford of the Advisory Commission on Intergovernmental Relations were particularly helpful in opening their files and giving their views about the Metropolitan Council and other approaches to metropolitan reorganization. These gentlemen, along with William Cassella, Jr., of the National Municipal League, Richard T. Anderson of the Regional Plan Association, and Annmarie Hauck Walsh of the Institute of Public Administration, reviewed and commented on portions of the manuscript. I am especially thankful to S. J. Schulman, Adjunct Professor of Urban Planning at Columbia University, and Victor Jones, Professor of Political Science at the University of California (Berkeley), for their criticism, suggestions, and help in bringing this study about and making it a work of pleasure as well as knowledge. In addition, to the Twin Cities area community leaders, local officials, and business-men too numerous to mention and without whom this study could not have been made, I extend a simple but heartfelt thank you.

CONTENTS

LIST OF TABLES, CHARTS, AND MAPS

LIST OF ABBREVIATIONS

ACIR   [U.S.] Advisory Commission on Intergovernmental Relations

BPR   Bureau of Public Roads [U.S. Department of Transportation]

CML   Commission on Municipal Laws [Minnesota]

COG   Council(s) of Governments [voluntary cooperative intergovernment area-wide organizations]

DFL   Democratic-Farmer-Labor Party [in Minnesota]

FHA   Federal Housing Authority [U.S. Department of Housing and Urban Development]

HHFA   Housing and Home Finance Agency

HUD   [U.S. Department of] Housing and Urban Development

LMM   League of Minnesota Municipalities

MAC   Metropolitan Airports Commission

MHD   Minnesota Highway Department

MICC   Metropolitan Inter-County Council [of the Twin Cities area]

MMC   Minnesota Municipal Commission

MPC   [Twin Cities] Metropolitan Planning Commission

MSSD   Minneapolis-Saint Paul Sanitary District

MTC   [Twin Cities] Metropolitan Transit Commission

NSSSD   North Suburban Sanitary Sewer District

PCA   Minnesota Pollution Control Agency

PL   [U.S.] Public Law

SSSC   Suburban Sanitary Sewer Commission

SMSA   Standard Metropolitan Statistical Area

UMRDC   Upper Midwest Research and Development
        Council

GLOSSARY

1. Metropolitan Government. There are various
kinds of metropolitan government, ranging from incorporation of an adequately large geographic jurisdiction, through the urban-county and city-county
consolidation, to federation and special purpose
districts. The major attribute they share in com-
mon--one that makes each kind metropolitan--is
their complete or substantial coverage of the entire metropolitan area. The definitions used in
this study follow those of the U.S. Advisory Commission on Intergovernmental Relations (ACIR) in its
publication, Alternative Approaches to Governmental
Reorganization in Metropolitan Areas. (See Chapter
1, pp. 8-16.) The Twin Cities Metropolitan Council
closely approaches the concept of metropolitan federation as defined by the ACIR:

> The federation or borough plan approach
> to governmental reorganization involves
> the division of local government func-
> tions in the metropolitan area between
> two levels of government. Area-wide
> functions are assigned to an area-
> wide or "metropolitan" government,
> with boundaries encompassing the units
> from which the functions are assumed.
> The local type functions are left to
> the existing municipalities, which are
> sometimes enlarged in territory and
> called boroughs.[1]

2. Local Government. Classes of local government, as used in this study, follow the definitions
established by the U.S. Bureau of the Census: "A
government is an organized entity which, in addition

to having governmental character, has sufficient discretion in the management of its own affairs to distinguish it as separate from the administrative structure of any other governmental unit." Units of local government include: counties, municipalities, townships, independent school districts, and special districts. Special districts include single-function and multiple-function districts, authorities, boards, commissions, agencies, public corporations, "and other entities that have varying degrees of autonomy."[2]

NOTES

1. Alternative approaches to Governmental Reorganization in Metropolitan Areas (Washington, D.C.: Advisory Commission on Intergovernmental Relations, June, 1962), p. 75.

2. U.S. Bureau of Census, Census of Governments, 1967, Volume 1, Government Organization (Washington, D.C.: U.S. Government Printing Office, 1968), pp. 1-14, passim.

Planning and Governing the Metropolis

PART I

THE SETTING FOR CHANGE

CHAPTER **1** INTRODUCTION:
THE METROPOLITAN
PROBLEM

The Metropolitan Council of the Twin Cities area
has been characterized as the most promising and innovative governmental mechanism yet designed to direct
and cope effectively with the problems of metropolitan growth.[1] The Council, created in 1967, plans,
coordinates, and controls the comprehensive development of an urban region containing 1.9 million
people, seven counties, two large central cities,
and some 300 units of local government (including a
score of special purpose districts); it covers an
entire metropolitan area of almost 3,000 square
miles, of which over 500 are urbanized. This area
is the largest and most politically fragmented to be
so organized in America this century. The Council
is responsible for, among other things, the region's
sewage and solid waste disposal, pollution control,
comprehensive transportation planning process, and
regional parks and open space. In carrying out
these responsibilities, it possesses a broad range
of powers that include the indefinite veto of unacceptable plans and projects of all area special purpose districts; membership on all area special purpose district governing boards; review of all comprehensive plans of local governments; mediation of
intermunicipal conflicts over the provisions of
local government plans; participation in state proceedings on area government boundary changes; and
the levying of property taxes and bonding authority
to finance its operations and services.

This case study has been undertaken to explore
the basis for the statement made at the opening of
this chapter and to describe the nature and origins
of the Twin Cities Metropolitan Council. It traces

and seeks to explain the factors which contributed
to the establishment of the Council, focusing on the
reasons and events which brought it about. It dis-
cusses the possibility of its replicability elsewhere
and the lessons that planners and political leaders
may extract from the Twin Cities experience in meeting the challenge of metropolitan growth.

METROPOLITAN PROBLEMS: MYTHS AND REALITIES

There has been a great profusion of books,
articles, talks, studies, discussions, and other dis-
courses by a multitude of experts, students, commen-
tators, and other observers of the urban scene, each
expressing views and opinions on just what constitutes our metropolitan problems and the implications
they have for the planner and politician. Much of
the discussion is myth and confused. We encounter
words and pictures daily showing cars bumper-to-
bumper in rush hours, racial strife in the ghettos,
smoke-filled air and debris-filled rivers, garbage
dumps infested with rats, endless sprawling suburbs,
crime in the streets, inadequate electric and tele-
phone service, welfare and school disturbances, and
other dislocations of our society. They are presented to us as being substantially the same for
most of America's metropolitan areas. In fact, they
are not. Except for our biggest cities, these problems vary considerably from area to area and may not
be serious at all in many places.

Daniel Elazar, in a recent paper, points out
that there are great differences in the modes of
living in most cities in the country. Geographic
location and climate, proximity to major centers,
and differences in "life styles" are important determinants of urban environment that may make cities
of the same magnitude significantly different. Water
pollution may be a serious problem in New York or
Chicago, but it is not necessarily so in Los Angeles
or Atlanta. Crime may be increasing markedly in
Washington, but it is not in Indianapolis. Traffic

jams during rush hours may cause considerable delay
in New York or New Rochelle, but they "hardly add
ten minutes to the total travel time of motorists"
in Minneapolis.[2] Bernard J. Frieden similarly
points out the significant variations between the
public's image of central city-suburban differences
and "existing realities." Central cities purported-
ly are the homes of the poor, the minorities, the
unskilled and unemployed, the undereducated, and the
poorly housed. The suburbs, in contrast, are the
homes of the prosperous, the well-educated, the
healthy, and the middle-class. Reporting on a study
of the social and economic characteristics of the
190 largest Standard Metropolitan Statistical Areas
(SMSAs), he notes that "racial disparities are large
everywhere, but that "the other elements of the
dichotomy--education, income, employment, and hous-
ing--fit the stereotype consistently only in the
large metropolitan areas and those located in the
Northeast."[3] It does not generally fit the majority, or 110 metropolitan areas. In some areas,
elements of high and low economic status are distributed about equally in the central city and suburbs. In certain parts of the South and West where
a high portion of the total population is Black,
the typical pattern is reversed, with social and
economic status high in the cities and low in the
suburbs.[4]

Another myth involves the degree of urbanization in the country. According to the 1960 census,
70 percent of the American people live in urban
places, and almost two-thirds of the entire population live in metropolitan areas or SMSAs.[5] The
trouble with these figures lies in the definition
of "urban places" and "SMSA." An "urban place,"
the Census Bureau defines, is any settlement of
2,500 persons or more; an "SMSA," briefly, includes
at least one city of 50,000 persons or more, together with adjacent counties that are socially and
economically integrated with the urban center.[6]
Noting this, Elazar has pointed out that the 1960
census figures also showed that 58.3 percent of the
United States population lived in cities of under

50,000 or rural areas; only 10 percent lived in the
five cities of 1 million or more. And three-fourths
of all SMSAs had less than 500,000 inhabitants. The
trend since 1920, he goes on, has been the increase
in the number of urban places having populations between 10,000 and 50,000, with the percentage of
people living in cities of over 500,000 barely increasing.[7] What we have then is a nation of widespread, low density, small cities, each with a different character and a different set of problems.

A further myth concerns the resultant political
fragmentation of our governmental structure as a
consequence of building a nation of small cities.
Many advocates of political reform have long attri-
buted a major portion of our urban ills to this development and have proposed a variety of solutions,
notably consolidation.[8] The lack of an integrated
system supposedly frustrates the real will of the
people, leading to a variety of dislocations and
diseconomies. Their concept of what the American
city should be is apparently drawn from a highly
idealized European model, despite its development
in a political, economic, and social environment
different from the American.[9] Edward C. Banfield
and Morton Grodzins and, to a somewhat lesser extent, Luther Gulick, have pointed out clearly that
the present fragmented political structure essentially is the one American people prefer. People
seek the variety of choice and proximity of government, despite the problems generated.[10] Evidence of
this lies in the fact that out of more than one hundred attempts at metropolitan reorganization in recent years, only in Miami, Jacksonville, Nashville,
and Indianapolis have the electorates of major metropolitan areas voted in favor of it.

THE METROPOLITAN PROBLEM DEFINED

Traffic congestion, pollution, inadequate local
revenues, slums and the shortage of housing, inadequate public services, crime, lack of playgrounds,
and the cost and control of education are often

cited as examples of metropolitan problems. To understand them and their relationship to the metropolitan community, it is necessary to distinguish
between those "'problems which exist in metropolitan
areas' and those 'which exist by virtue of the inadequacies of governmental structure in the metropolitan areas.'"[11] While crime and the lack of
playgrounds may, indeed, be problems in metropolitan areas, they are not necessarily problems which
require area-wide governmental reorganization for
their solution. To be sure, all of these problems
have both local and metropolitan implications, and
whether a specific program or service is best
handled locally or on a metropolitan basis will vary
from area to area. Those problems that are recognized as being essentially metropolitan in character and that may require the reorganization of an
area's pattern of government, however, constitute a
relatively small portion of the sum total of problems which our metropolitan areas face.[12]

Another distinction should be made to have a
clear understanding of metropolitan problems. An
analysis of them will show that they vary qualita-
tively as well as governmentally. Problems such as
pollution, congestion, and provision of services
are technological, and we already possess, or can
shortly have, solutions to them. We need only to
be willing to implement and pay for the solutions,
either locally or on a metropolitan basis. Problems such as the cost of education, crime, extension
of health and welfare services, and racial frictions
are basically economic or social in nature and, consequently, face other considerations. Solutions
may be as simple (though not easy) as locating the
necessary funds, even when we are willing to pay
the costs involved, or as complex as changing basic
attitudes and social values. All these problems
share in common an imperfect relationship between
costs and benefits.[13] What is required for their
solution is the intention to pay the costs necessary
to accomplish the task, whether they be governmental,
economic, or social. What is not required for all
of them, however, is metropolitan reorganization.

Only those which exist because of inadequate governmental structures, as noted above, merit such consideration.

Local governments have been unable to handle
many of the foregoing problems alone for at least
three important and interrelated reasons. Firstly,
many problems such as environmental pollution, mass
transit, and water and sewer service have facets
which extend beyond local boundaries. These "ex-
tended" problems, called spillovers, can be treated
adequately only on a collective basis. Secondly,
solutions to many of these problems are very costly,
generally beyond the means of any single government.
Lastly, no single unit of government can make the
necessary decisions for an entire metropolitan area.[14]
The metropolitan problem, according to Luther Gulick,
is then "millions of human beings who want to do
something effective to solve the rising difficulties
they are experiencing from the new pattern of urban
settlement, but who do not have the clear ideas, the
teamwork machinery, or the leadership with which to
proceed."[15] To put this another way, the metropolitan problem is the inability of government to make
the necessary decisions about area-wide development
as a consequence of the high degree of political
fragmentation in our metropolitan areas.

ALTERNATIVE APPROACHES TO REORGANIZING
GOVERNMENT IN METROPOLITAN AREAS

Over the years, a number of different proposals
have been made to bring order out of the chaos of
fragmentation of government in our metropolitan
areas. The hope is to achieve greater economy and
efficiency in operations and to coordinate area development. Typical of the approaches to metropolitan reorganization are those listed by the Advisory
Commission on Intergovernmental Relations.[16]

Extraterritorial Powers

Extraterritorial powers are those powers granted
by the state legislatures to permit a city to regulate

activities outside its territorial boundaries or to
assist it in providing services to the people living within them. These powers may include planning,
zoning, and subdivision regulations in unincorporated
fringe areas, the acquisition of water, and the disposal of sewage and refuse in other jurisdictions,
and the inspection of meat and dairy processing.
Application of them is limited, however, to unincorporated areas near the city. These powers do not
permit residents of the unincorporated areas to participate in decisions affecting them, nor do they
cope with other metropolitan problems such as transportation or pollution.

Intergovernmental Agreements

Joint exercise of powers and sales of service
are the most extensively used means to broaden the
geographic base for planning, administering, and
lowering costs of common functions. They permit
operation of an

> . . . activity jointly or cooperatively
> with one or more . . . governmental
> units, or by contracting for its per-
> formance by another governmental unit.
> The agreements may be permanent or tem-
> porary; pursuant to special act or gen-
> eral law; effective with or without
> voter approval; and may be formal or
> informal in character. . . . [They]
> may be for the provision of direct
> services to citizens of two or more
> jurisdictions, such as water supply
> or police protection; or they may be
> for governmental housekeeping activi-
> ties, such as joint purchasing or
> personnel administration activities.[17]

They are, however, not well suited to area-wide decisionmaking on matters transcending local interests and planning of area development. Under a
system of such agreements, decisions require unanimity rather than majority support and individual
purchasers of services do not participate in policy

decisions or administration at all. Consequently,
development plans do not include area-wide views and
interests. The best-known example of this arrange-
ment is the "Lakewood Plan" in Southern California
under which over 700 cities have contracted with Los
Angeles County for a wide variety of governmental
services.

Voluntary Metropolitan Councils of Governments

A Council of Governments (COG) is a voluntary
association of elected public officials representing
all or nearly all units of government in a single
metropolitan area. It is formed to achieve better
intermunicipal understanding, metropolitan consensus
on area needs, and a coordinated solution to common
problems. As such, it is an intergovernmental agreement "for joint conduct of activities in research,
planning, and deliberations on issues of area-wide
concern."[18] COGs do not have functional powers and
lack the authority to implement proposals, relying
almost entirely on persuasion of constituent governments to effectuate programs. The oldest organization of this type is the Supervisor's Inter-County
Committee of the Detroit metropolitan area which was
created in 1954.

The Urban County

This procedure involves the conferring of home
rule status on the county, which then provides a
wide range of municipal-like services while remaining an administrative subdivision of the state responsible for elections, law enforcement, and judi-
cial proceedings.

> This development may result from piece-
> meal transfer of functions from munici-
> palities or special districts; from
> the gradual enlargement of rural county
> responsibilities to encompass urban
> functions in unincorporated urban
> areas; or from State legislation

> simultaneously granting a number of
> functional powers to counties in
> metropolitan areas.[19]

Urbanizing a county is a frequently used and effective means to meet problems of metropolitan growth
in small and medium-sized metropolitan areas where
the county encompasses all or nearly all of the
metropolitan area. The approach is widely used in
Maryland, New York, and California. Perhaps the
most well-known example is Miami-Dade County,
Florida.

Transfer of Functions to State Government

This "involves the transfer and direct performance of an urban function by an executive agency
of the State Government in the metropolitan area."[20]
Operation of services is divided, with the state
agency handling metropolitan aspects and local governments handling internal aspects, e.g., the state
assumes responsibility for supplying water and major
trunk lines while leaving local distribution to the
communities. Transfers occur where (1) the state is
the only agency with the resources to perform them,
(2) they cannot be handled within the boundaries of
the metropolitan area, (3) minimum standards of performance can be met only at the state level, or
(4) when failure to perform them will adversely affect other parts of the state. The procedure is
most adaptable in small states or where metropolitan
areas constitute a major portion of the state and
its population. Its major weakness is the removal
of control of metropolitan matters from the area to
representatives of outside areas. Typical examples
of this are the New York State Water Supply Commission which supervises the distribution of water
among competing communities and the Minnesota Pollution Control Agency.

Metropolitan Special Districts:
Limited Purpose and Multi-Purpose

A limited purpose district is an independent
unit of government generally authorized by state law
and established without a referendum "to perform one
or a few urban functions throughout part or all of
a metropolitan area, including the central city."[21]
Most commonly it provides sewage disposal, water supply, parks, housing, airports, and port facilities.
Governing bodies are either appointed by the governor or concerned local councils, or they are elected.
They may also include ex-officio members drawn from
local councils. Operations are financed largely
through user charges. The use of special districts
has grown in recent years because (1) they "are free
from the constitutional and statutory limits on fiscal powers of general purpose local government,"[22]
(2) other means to deal with area-wide problems
were impossible, and (3) economy of scale and efficient operation substantially lowered costs. Major
shortcomings include (1) insulation from the normal
political process which creates problems of responsiveness to local and area needs and wishes,
(2) piecemeal approach to area-wide problems, and
(3) inadequate coordination of area development.
The Port of New York Authority is a classic example
of a metropolitan special district.

The multi-purpose district is an expansion of
the concept of the limited purpose district to
capitalize on its strengths while avoiding problems
of coordination of functions and fragmentation of
government. The district may be established by
state legislation with a wide range of functions,
or a limited district may be expanded, usually
through the initiative and approval of local councils or voters of the area. As a multi-purpose district approaches the breadth of a general purpose
government, it may be viewed as a threat to local
government and control and be voted down. The best-
known multi-purpose metropolitan district in the
United States is the Municipality of Metropolitan
Seattle, which provides sewage disposal and pollution

control. Under law, area communities may add other
functions to metropolitan Seattle, such as transportation, garbage disposal, water, parks, and comprehensive planning, but they have not as yet done so.

Annexation and Consolidation

These are two means by which municipal boundaries can be expanded and adjusted.

> Annexation is the absorption of terri-
> tory (usually unincorporated) by a
> city. . . . The result is a larger
> and not essentially different govern-
> mental unit. Consolidation is the
> joining together of two or more units
> of government of approximately equal
> stature to form a new unit of govern-
> ment.[23]

With the growth of suburbanization around the turn
of the century and the introduction of limitations
on the annexation of incorporated areas by the city,
the process of geographical expansion of our major
cities has sharply declined. Only in the South and
West, as in Atlanta, Oklahoma City, and Kansas City,
has annexation played an important role in controlling the development of urbanizing but unincorporated areas. Consolidation is a little used approach to reorganization, even among small units of
government where it is most appropriate. The decline in its use is due to the prohibition or limitation on special legislation, which previously imposed consolidation on communities.

City-County Separation

This action involves the separation of a major
city from the county in which it is located,

> . . . sometimes with simultaneous ex-
> pansion of its boundaries, and there-
> after exercises both city and county
> functions within its boundaries,

> although sometimes not all the county
> functions. Use of the method usually
> requires special constitutional provi-
> sions since the detached city-county
> usually does not conform to the general
> provisions setting up a uniform system
> of county government throughout the
> state.[24]

Except for the state of Virginia, there has been
very limited use of this approach. During the nineteenth century, however, many cities like Baltimore,
Denver, San Francisco, and St. Louis separated from
their counties. While it offers greater economy
and efficiency of operation of governmental processes
through elimination of duplication, rapid urbanization soon places the city-county under the territorial restrictions and problems of county borders
again and militates against an area-wide approach
to problems.

City-County Consolidation

This procedure expands on the urban-county approach, creating a more unified governmental structure for the area. It takes three forms

> . . . (1) the merger of a county and
> the cities within it into a single
> government. . .; (2) substantial
> merger of the county and the cities,
> but the retention of the county as a
> separate unit for some functions;
> (3) unification of some, but not all,
> of the municipal governments and the
> county governments. Sometimes the
> consolidation is broadened to include
> the territory of two or more counties
> and the county and municipal govern-
> ments within them, or to include
> other local governments. . . . [It]
> requires enabling legislation and
> sometimes also a local referendum,
> frequently with separate majority

approvals in the central city and
the remainder of the county.[25]

It offers a more unified and coordinated program of
services, effective control over development in a
larger area, economy of scale, and greater efficiency
of operation than the urban county. Its major short-
coming, like that of the urban county, is its inadequacy for major metropolitan areas that span more
than one county. The most significant recent consolidations are those of Nashville, Tennessee, with
Davidson County; Jacksonville, Florida, with Duval
County; and Indianapolis, Indiana, with Marion
County.

Federation (Borough Plan)

This approach involves the transfer of some
urban functions to a new level or extension of government, operating metropolitan-wide. Existing
units of government continue to operate local functions. The area-wide or metropolitan government encompasses the geographic limits of the units from
which it assumes functions. Smaller municipal units
are sometimes grouped or enlarged in territory to
form boroughs. Urban counties and multi-purpose
special districts in their more advanced states "re-
semble the federation as a form of governmental organization, since they provide a clear separation
of most, if not all, area-wide and local functions."[26]
Three major virtues of federation are these: (1) the
assignment of functions to the appropriate level or
extension of government to facilitate their optimum
handling with respect to "planning, decisions, and
scale of operation,"[27] (2) retention of local government with its greater immediacy and opportunity for
individual participation, and (3) effective area-
wide planning and coordination of approaches to common problems. Federations can be created whole or
in embryo form, with provision for increasing responsibilities and authority incrementally. To
date, there has been no true major metropolitan federation established in the United States, although
the Metropolitan Council of the Twin Cities closely

approaches it. Canada has two excellent examples in the Municipality of Metropolitan Toronto and the Metropolitan Corporation of Greater Winnipeg.

OBSTACLES TO METROPOLITAN REORGANIZATION

There are a number of serious obstacles which must be overcome before any successful reorganization of the metropolitan political structure can be achieved. All of them can be grouped into three interrelated categories. They are, as Scott Greer has noted, "(1) the underlying cultural norms of Americans concerning local government, (2) the resulting legal-constitutional structures, and (3) the political-governmental system built upon them."[28] These popular attitudes, political rules, and political systems have created and now encompass the universe of obstacles that the reorganizers of the metropolitan scene must face. Each one will vary in severity, of course, from area to area, but all must be considered. More specifically, the variety of obstacles to reorganization includes at least five factors: home rule, accountability, political bloc interests, popular suspicion of "big government," and legal-constitutional barriers.

Home Rule

Most attempts at metropolitan reorganization have foundered on this very issue. It involves a grant of power from the state to a municipality, enabling it to do a number of things for itself, without going to the legislature for approval each time it wishes to do something. At the same time, it prohibits or restricts the state from intervening in prescribed local matters, without prior approval of the municipality.

As noted earlier, of the more than one hundred referenda held on reorganization, scarcely a handful have been approved. In recent years, only the voters in Miami-Dade County, Nashville-Davidson County, Jacksonville-Duval County, and Indianapolis-Marion County

have supported the restructuring of local governments.[29] Yet, the requirement that a referendum be
held to permit voters to decide governmental reorganization is _not_ found in most state constitutions.
It would seem, therefore, that difficulties in sur-
mounting home rule are specious. In reality, the
difficulties are extremely hard to overcome--not because of constitutional considerations, but because
of political expediency.[30] Politicians are afraid
to cast votes or make decisions on such a volatile
issue as metropolitan reorganization and thereby
antagonize the public and lose its votes. Whichever
the electorate decides must be politically accepted
by the public official, even if he privately supported reorganization.

     The difficulties in achieving electoral ap-
proval for restructuring local government have led
to a variety of proposals to modify, even eliminate,
the provisions of home rule. Indeed, the Minnesota
legislature did eliminate the requirement of the
state constitution calling for a referendum on
special laws affecting local government to enable
the Twin Cities Metropolitan Council to be established. (For discussion of this, see Chapter 6,
pp. 141-45.) Other proposals have called for the
substitution of simple majorities rather than an
absolute majority of registered voters; the requirement for an overall majority of voters in the affected jurisdictions rather than a majority in each;
and the substitution of local council approval for
the referendum. The hope has been to simplify or
eliminate the need for unanimity of approval to
gain reform, which in our large metropolitan areas
is all but impossible. There is at least one community out of the hundreds in each area that can be
found to oppose almost any proposal. Nevertheless,
there is great need for local participation and accountability in all measures of metropolitan reorganization, both in terms of making policy decisions
and administering functions. It is up to the state
legislatures, then, as the key to metropolitan reorganization, to act.[31] Only the state can modify
home rule; only it possesses the legal power to

create effective mechanisms to resolve area-wide
problems.

Accountability

Related to the question of home rule is that of
political accountability. The special district, as
the device most frequently used to meet metropolitan
problems, has been the subject of great criticism on
this point. It is, in general, insulated from the
normal political process of elections; its functions
directly affect the activities of other local governments, but without their participation; and it
does not necessarily coordinate its policies and
projects with other area governments. The question,
then, in the minds of proponents, opponents, and
general public alike is: How can metropolitan government be made accountable? The answer commonly
given is simply to make it elective. But this does
not consider that the kind of reorganization proposed will also affect accountability. Voters in a
federated structure, for example, may have greater
strength because of the grouping (districting) inherent in the system than those usually found in a
consolidated approach. Pertinent to this is the
question of whether elections should be held at
large or based on districts; if the latter, districts
must be established on a "one-man one-vote" basis.

Even where the governing body of a metropolitan government is appointed, there can be a substantial measure of accountability. Governing bodies
may be appointed by elected local officials, or by
the governor from among elected local officials of
the area. Quite often when the Governor appoints
members of a governing body, he consults with local
officials and legislators before making his decision to ensure that local views and interests are
considered. Enabling legislation may require also
that all appointees be residents of the area and be
representative of districts, as in the Twin Cities
area.

An important aspect of accountability is the
problem of inadequate representation of urban and

metropolitan areas in state legislatures. In the
past, most state legislatures were dominated by
rural interests who were able to frustrate attempts
by urban legislators to obtain greater benefits for
urban areas. Because of the Supreme Court decision
in Baker v. Carr, both houses of the state legislature must now be organized according to population.
Consequently, urban interests may be in a position
now to push through the legislative reforms that
they wish, including metropolitan reorganization.
To do so, urban legislators must recognize that the
new center of political power will, generally, not
rest with the central cities, but rather with the
suburbs. This shift in power can mean the achieve-
ment of necessary urban reforms--central cities and
suburbs alike--or it can serve as the vehicle for a
heightened central city-suburban split. The important measure, however, to achieve metropolitan reorganization is the satisfactory and accurate reapportionment of our state deliberative bodies; we
now have the means to do so.

Political Blocs

An important element in the success of any proposed metropolitan reorganization is the role of
highly politicized interest groups, such as political parties and ethnic groups. Banfield and Grodzins
doubt that the integration of local governments can
be brought about in an area where a strong two-party
system or large minority groups exist.[32] Our metropolitan areas are increasingly being polarized politically, with Democrats controlling the central
cities and Republicans controlling the suburbs. It
is highly unlikely, they agree, that either party
would be willing to compromise or dilute its strength
by increasing the size of its constituencies through
metropolitan reorganization, and possibly lose power.

Such thinking is particularly true of Blacks
who only lately have acquired significant political
strength and who live largely within the central
city. They are not anxious to support any measure
which threatens to weaken the political power they
have worked so hard to obtain. Analyses of

referenda in several cities, including Cleveland,
St. Louis, and Tampa, support this argument.[33]

A federated structure might not have this dis-
advantage. In a federation there is no merging of
jurisdictions that could water down the power of a
political base. Both central cities and suburbs cooperate within the same structure to resolve common
problems. Further, it affords all power blocs an
opportunity and vehicle to obtain consideration and
benefits in all areas. They can bargain, compromise,
and logroll to whatever extent they deem advisable
to gain concessions from their metropolitan partners.

Closely related to the anxieties of political
blocs over metropolitan integration are the issues
of the urban-suburban split. In previous years,
suburban interests feared domination by the central
city. Today, with the suburbs accounting for the
major portion of metropolitan growth, this fear may
no longer be real. In its place is the spectre of
central city problems that the suburbs might have
to share in any metropolitan accommodation. And
this, few suburbs are willing to do.

Suspicion of Big Government

Another major hurdle to overcome before any
kind of metropolitan reorganization can be achieved
is the eradication or minimization of popular
anxieties over metropolitan--big--government. Past
attempts at reorganization have emphasized economy
of scale and efficiency of function to the exclusion
of the desires of the people for small, human scale,
and more responsive government. Many proponents of
reform have failed to realize that people living
under our politically fractionalized system may be
willing to pay the added costs of less efficient
government in order to preserve these long sought
and worked for values. Equally important, economies
of scale are not always present with increased size,
nor are the boundaries of service areas for different functions necessarily the same.[34] The limited
experience of people with metropolitan government,

i.e., metropolitan special districts and state agencies, has not been the best. Too often the public
and community officials have been frustrated by the
lack of responsiveness and seemingly arbitrary actions of these bodies to the point where they view
them as a threat to local government and their life
styles. Thus, metropolitan government, regardless
of form, is damned.

To overcome these public attitudes and achieve
reorganization, proponents of change must first educate the public on the need for metropolitan approaches to metropolitan problems and then establish a consensus on the kind of reorganization required to do the job. This must include means
within the proposed structure to safeguard or mini-
mally compromise those political and social considerations much valued in the area's communities.
Only in this way will the public support metropolitan reorganization, whether in a referendum or their
representatives' actions in the state legislature.

Legal-Constitutional Barriers

In some areas complete reorganization may prove
nearly impossible because of legal-constitutional
considerations. Metropolitan areas of New York,
Washington, Detroit, and Chicago manifest differences of great magnitude--(1) involvement of more
than one state or nation, (2) reluctance of states
to accept a reorganization that might subject a part
of its jurisdiction to another state, (3) the fears
of citizens in one state of domination by a jurisdiction over which they have only partial control.
And under such circumstances, organization of a
single metropolitan structure is unlikely for a
long time.[35] But even here, hope exists. Congress
can authorize interstate compacts; partial or subregional reorganization is both possible and advantageous even when interstate compacts are neither
feasible nor practical. (For a discussion of this
possibility, see Chapter 10 (pp. 236-37.)

THE PLANNER, THE POLITICIAN, AND
THE METROPOLITAN PROBLEM

As spillover of urban growth limits the effectiveness of government to plan and provide services,
the need for metropolitan approaches to planning,
controlling, and coordinating increases. As a result, the planner and politician are faced with a
tremendous challenge and opportunity to influence
the structure of the urban community and its future
metropolitan development. The most effective planning and coordination would be achieved through an
effective area-wide government. In fact, it is the
only means by which plans can be assured of transla-
tion into action--and that is the major problem confronting metropolitan planning.[36]

Metropolitan reorganization raises the question
of integrating planning with the political process
if community goals are to be accurately determined
and adequately achieved. With close integration,
we can effectively direct and control all aspects
of development, not just meet existing problems and
needs. Integration, however, must await not only
metropolitan reorganization, but also general understanding and acceptance. Gulick recognized this
when he noted that, in addition to the inadequacies
of service, the metropolitan problem involves
shortages or failures in determining area-wide development goals and an area-wide governmental mechanism to deal with problems.[37] The following case
study of the Metropolitan Council of the Twin Cities
Area will shed light on this interrelationship and
the role this can play in shaping metropolitan reorganization.

NOTES

1. John Fischer, "The Minnesota Experiment:
How to Make a Big City Fit to Live In," Harper's
Magazine, CCXXXVIII, 1427 (April, 1969), 12.

2. Daniel J. Elazar, "Urbanization and Federalism in the United States," in Robert A. Goldwin, ed.,
A Nation of Cities (Chicago: Public Affairs Administration, University of Chicago, 1966), pp. 7-8.

3. Bernard J. Frieden, Metropolitan America:
Challenge to Federalism (Washington, D.C.: Advisory
Commission on Intergovernmental Relations, 1966),
p. 19.

4. Ibid., p. 20.

5. Urban and Rural America: Policies for
Growth (Washington, D.C.: Advisory Commission on
Intergovernmental Relations, 1968), p. 175.

6. Ibid., p. 174.

7. Elazar, op. cit., pp. 5-7.

8. Edward C. Banfield and Morton Grodzins,
Government and Housing in Metropolitan Areas (New
York: McGraw-Hill Book Company, Inc.), pp. 32, 43;
Luther H. Gulick, The Metropolitan Problem and
American Ideas (New York: Alfred A. Knopf, Inc.,
1962), pp. 23-27; Elazar, op. cit., p. 10.

9. Ibid.

10. Banfield and Grodzins, op. cit., pp. 32-33;
Gulick, op. cit., pp. 125-26.

11. Banfield and Grodzins, op. cit., pp. 32, 156.

12. Ibid., pp. 32, 40, 41, 156; Performance of
Urban Functions: Local and Areawide (Washington,
D.C.: Advisory Commission on Intergovernmental Re-
lations, September, 1963), pp. 5, 6, 8.

13. James Q. Wilson, "The War on Cities," in
Goldwin, op. cit., p. 15.

14. Gulick, loc. cit.

15. Ibid., p. 163.

16. Alternative Approaches to Governmental Reorganization in Metropolitan Areas (Washington, D.C.: Advisory Commission on Intergovernmental Relations, June, 1962), pp. 20-80.

17. Ibid., p. 26.

18. Ibid., p. 23.

19. Ibid., p. 39.

20. Ibid., p. 46.

21. Ibid., p. 49.

22. Ibid., p. 50.

23. Ibid., p. 58.

24. Ibid., p. 68.

25. Ibid., pp. 71-72.

26. Ibid., p. 76.

27. Ibid., p. 79.

28. Scott Greer, Governing the Metropolis (New York: John Wiley and Sons, Inc., 1962), pp. 124-25.

29. For a discussion of eighteen referenda on governmental reorganization held between 1950 and 1961, see Factors Affecting Voter Reactions to Governmental Reorganization in Metropolitan Areas (Washington, D.C.: Advisory Commission on Intergovernmental Relations, May, 1962); Thomas P. Murphy, Metropolitics and the Urban County (Washington, D.C.: Washington National Press, 1970), pp. 232-39.

30. Victor Jones, discussion with Stanley Baldinger, September, 1969.

31.   Gulick, op. cit., p. 135.

32.   Banfield and Grodzins, op. cit., pp. 45-52, 156-57.

33.   John C. Bollens and Henry J. Schmandt, The Metropolis: Its People, Politics, and Economic Life, 2nd ed. (New York: Harper & Row, Publishers, Inc., 1970), pp. 382-83.

34.   Banfield and Grodzins, op. cit., pp. 34-36.

35.   Murphy, op. cit., pp. 15-16.

36.   Frieden, op. cit., p. 112; Banfield and Grodzins, op. cit., p. 166.

37.   Gulick, op. cit., pp. 121-23, 165.

CHAPTER **2** ENVIRONMENT FOR
CHANGE AND
INNOVATION
IN MINNESOTA

As do all other states and metropolitan areas,
Minnesota and the Twin Cities possess a unique combination of characteristics and attributes. In
other areas of this country, with but few limited
exceptions, the combinations have been insufficient
to overcome the social, economic, and political obstacles to metropolitan reform long sought. In
contrast, the combinations of factors in Minnesota
and the Twin Cities area have enabled the people
and their leaders to bring needed change and innovation to the planning and governmental process.
The changes here are significantly beyond experi-
ments anywhere else in the country. The following
chapters attempt to explore the most significant
factors contributing to this phenomenon and to describe the events which have led to metropolitan
government there. This chapter will focus on the
ethnic, social, and political factors which have
made the state and metropolitan area so fertile to
change and their leaders so responsive to needs.

GOVERNMENT AND POLITICS IN MINNESOTA

"Minnesota is the best governed state in America. It also is the most imaginative, farsighted,
and ambitious."[1] So spoke an anonymous Minnesotan
recently to John Fischer, Contributing Editor to
Harper's Magazine. After reviewing the recent development toward metropolitan government in the
Twin Cities area, he concluded "with a suspicion
that its local patriots might be speaking something

close to the literal truth."[2] Other observers of
the national and Minnesota scene have come to similar conclusions. Daniel Elazar has noted that a
common view prevailing among Minnesotans was that
their state was "more 'honest,' more 'community
minded,' more 'stable,' more 'homey,' . . . more
concerned with the individual than are the [other]
centers of the nation, and more 'vital' and 'progressive' than its immediate neighbors. . . ."[3] In
a more recent study of the "quality of life" in the
fifty states, John O. Wilson of Yale University,
using criteria established by the Commission of National Goals of former President Eisenhower, ranked
Minnesota highest in the nation with respect to
"individual equality" and fourth in the "democratic
process." He defines "individual equality" as the
state of concern "with the elimination of all discrimination on the basis of race, sex and religion";
its major objectives cover the elimination of discrimination "in the areas of justice, voting, office holding, access to education and employment,
home ownership, and community participation." The
"democratic process," he defines as " a goal relating to an informed and involved citizenry, an improved quality of public administration, and a
greater collaboration and sharing of power among
all levels of government."[4] Minnesota's composite
ranking was second of all fifty states.

     The evidence presented by these and other ob-
servers supports, in large part, the conclusion
taken independently by Fischer that Minnesota is
widely recognized as one of the best-governed states
in the union. It possesses one of the strongest
two-party systems[5] in which competition between
parties is often in terms of progress or liberal
policies that are "more responsive to the interests,
needs and/or desires of the 'have nots'" of its
citizenry.[6] The Republican party emphasizes the
more practical aspects of solutions to problems in
contrast to the Democratic-Farmer-Labor party's
more ideologic approach. At the same time, the
state is recognized as having one of the most honest
political systems in the nation, with a high degree

of citizen participation.[7] This has contributed to
the surprising number of political leaders who have
achieved national recognition for their capabilities and liberal views.

The state's voting registration procedures are
among the nation's simplest; election turnouts are
among the highest. For example, in the 1960 presi-
dential election, Minnesota had a turnout of 77.0
percent in comparison with Idaho, the highest, which
had 80.7 percent. Similarly, in gubernatorial and
senatorial elections, between 1952 and 1960, it
averaged 58.8 percent turnout in comparison with
Idaho, the highest, which had 64.6 percent.[8] The
tax system is considered to be one of the nation's
most progressive, with the total tax burden on citizens consistently among the highest of the states;
state revenues are derived mainly from income taxes
on individuals or corporations.[9] Minnesota ranks
second only to New York for states having the highest tax bracket on personal income, with 12 percent
in comparison with New York's 14 percent; it also
has one of the highest local revenues provided by
property taxes.[10] Since 1957, the state has also
had a sales tax of 3 percent.

Reasons for these phenomena are more difficult
to pin down. Their origins lie, apparently, in the
character of its settlers and the traditions they
handed down, as well as in the residue of Populist
sentiment still found among the people and institutions of the state. Although Minnesota has two
state-wide political parties, Republican and
Democratic-Farmer-Labor (DFL), the state legislature
and local councils are nonpartisan.[11] The two parties operate ostensibly only to name the governor
and representatives to the federal Congress. The
nonpartisan legislature and local councils, however, organize themselves into Liberal and Conservative caucuses and, frequently, align themselves
with the state political parties.[12] The "grass
roots" and nonpartisan nature of its legislature
and local councils is a carryover from the Populist
agrarian reform movement of the late nineteenth and

early twentieth centuries when organized politics and professional politicians were often suspected of being "partial" to private interests.[13] This Populist residue contributes to what Elazar calls the high moralistic attitudes of the state's original Yankee and Scandinavian settlers who shared similar attitudes related to the Puritan tradition.[14] As a consequence, Minnesota, along with other moralistic (Yankee) states, followed the early New England tradition of strong participation in state and local politics--heavy turnouts and the sense of public service in politics and other civic capacities.[15] Because of this, politics in a very real sense is a state-wide avocation with an extremely solid base of integrity and responsiveness and accessible political leaders. There is a strong acceptance of the private individual's participation in government being part of "the formal channels of political activity. . . ."[16] The moralistic tradition, together with the Populist, has helped shape a political system which is quite long on individual independence and comparatively short on machine politics and patronage.[17] Thus, the Minnesota politican benefits from a minimum of political indebtedness and vested interests, leaving him free to make decisions. For example, State Senator Karl Grittner (Liberal, St. Paul), a sponsor of the recently passed act making the Metropolitan Council responsible for metropolitan-wide sewage disposal and treatment, solicited the views of those St. Paulites opposed to the legislation. He found that they objected on the grounds that the metropolitan benefits to the central cities would not be commensurate with the costs they would have to bear. He considered this objection insufficient and continued his work to pass the bill, and without bitter reaction.[18] These diverse strains have combined, it appears, to produce an attitude of high respect for government and politics as a field of human endeavor and widespread public support and participation.

THE CHARACTER OF THE POPULATION

The population of the state is largely homogeneous, composed mostly of Northern and Western European peoples--Scandinavians, Germans, some Irish, and, as noted before, a base of Yankee stock.[19] The Yankee heritage has bequeathed qualities to Minnesota beyond those which have contributed to a high level of integrity and responsiveness of government. It has motivated the people to an unusually great support for education and social welfare, in which field the state is a national leader.[20] As of 1967, it ranked first among all states in the percentage of ninth graders who complete high school after entering (lowest dropout rate).[21] In addition, it has rated among those states lowest in the percentage of draftees rejected because of failure to pass military intelligence tests; between 1962 and 1967, it was lowest three times and less than 1 percent above the lowest ranked states during the other two years.[22] Further, 35 percent of all high school graduates go on to college or to vocational or trade and professional schools; the state is consistently among the top ten granting Ph.D. degrees.[23]

In matters of social welfare, the state is a national leader in initiating programs and providing services, often moving the country along with it.[24] A recent issue of Resident Physician cites a poll of 467 interns and residents on the best teaching hospitals (based on the best clinical and research facilities and most skilled senior staff) that indicates that Minnesota has two of the nation's top ten hospitals.[25] In addition, a "jury of experts" gathered by the Ladies' Home Journal stated that Minnesota possessed two of the nation's top ten hospital centers.[26] In his study of the states, Wilson ranks Minnesota first in the nation in programs and services with respect to "welfare assistance, vocational rehabilitation, and the provision of medical services in both the public and private sectors."[27] Along with this, Minnesota has been a leader both nationally and locally in advancing

civil rights, even during periods when there was
little national movement, such as much of the
Republican-Dixiecrat coalition of the Eisenhower
administration.[28] In this respect, the state fitted
the pattern of other states in 1960 having a strong
two-party system: a low percentage of Blacks (0.7
percent), most of whom are in Minneapolis and St.
Paul; a high percentage of foreign stock (25.3 percent); a high median income ($5,573); and a large
urban population (62.2 percent).[29] Its rate of increase for total personal income in 1967 was 8.9
percent, sixth in the nation, some 2.1 percent above
the national performance.[30] Its overall ranking for
economic growth was third in the nation.[31]

Independent studies have shown that these qualities apply specifically to the Twin Cities area as
well. Elazar points out that the population base
of the cities is essentially the same as that for
the entire state, with no "apparent cultural cleav-
age of importance. . . ."[32] This, he notes, contributes significantly to the greater community of
interest between the metropolitan area and the state
than in the other larger heterogeneous centers of
the nation, while still recognizing material urban-
rural differences.[33] The Twin Cities in 1967, in
proportion to their population, were seventh in the
nation in the number of high school and college
graduates and fourth in the number of persons with
five or more years of college studies.[34] Further,
in 1966, they were eighth in the total number of
scientific population.[35]

The Twin Cities also share honors with the
other urban centers of Minnesota where local con-
tribution to all welfare funds--federal, state, and
local--has been highest in the nation, e.g., the
local share was 35 percent in 1961.[36] One of the
top ten hospitals--the University of Minnesota Cen-
ter--is located in the Twin Cities and is recognized as a leading research and treatment center.

In his study of the "quality of life" in several states, Wilson notes that the rankings given

TABLE 1

Social and Economic Characteristics of Major U.S. Metropolitan Areas, 1967

Standard Metropolitan Statistical Area	Population in 1960	Rank	Area (square miles)	Pop. (square miles)	Pop. Change 1950-60 (percent)	Population Characteristics			
						Urban (percent)	Black (percent)	Foreign Stock (percent)	Ov 6 (per
New York	10,694,632	1	2,136	5,007	11.9	97.4	11.5	45.8	
Chicago	6,220,913	2	3,720	1,672	20.1	95.1	14.3	32.4	
Los Angeles-Long Beach	6,038,771	3	4,069	1,484	45.5	98.8	7.6	27.4	
Philadelphia	4,342,897	4	3,553	1,222	18.3	89.7	15.5	25.1	
Detroit	3,762,360	5	1,952	1,927	24.7	94.7	14.9	30.1	
San Francisco-Oakland	2,648,762	6	2,478	1,069	24.0	95.5	8.5	30.9	
Boston	2,595,481	7	986	2,632	7.5	93.9	3.0	41.8	]
Pittsburgh	2,405,435	8	3,049	789	8.7	81.8	6.7	28.8	
St. Louis	2,104,669	9	4,119	511	19.9	87.5	14.0	12.7	
Washington, D.C.	2,001,897	10	1,485	1,348	36.7	91.6	24.3	13.4	
Cleveland	1,909,483	11	1,519	1,257	24.6	94.0	13.6	31.8	
Baltimore	1,727,023	12	1,802	958	22.9	85.0	21.9	13.5	
Newark	1,689,420	13	701	2,410	15.0	95.7	13.3	36.2	
Minneapolis-St. Paul	1,482,030	14	2,107	703	28.8	94.3	1.4	25.0	
Houston	1,418,323	15	6,286	226	51.6	88.8	19.5	8.8	
Buffalo	1,306,957	16	1,591	821	20.0	85.1	6.3	32.5	
Cincinnati	1,268,479	17	2,150	590	24.0	82.1	10.3	9.4	
Milwaukee	1,232,731	18	1,028	1,199	25.7	94.5	5.1	27.8	
Paterson-Clifton-Passaic	1,186,873	19	427	2,780	35.5	99.1	3.6	43.0	
Seattle-Everett	1,107,213	20	4,229	262	31.1	84.3	2.6	26.8	
Kansas City	1,092,545	21	2,767	395	28.7	88.2	10.7	9.1	
Dallas	1,083,601	22	3,603	301	45.1	92.1	14.3	5.8	
San Diego	1,033,011	23	4,262	242	85.5	88.9	3.8	19.9	
Atlanta	1,017,188	24	1,727	589	39.9	82.3	22.8	3.2	
Miami	935,047	25	2,042	458	88.9	95.6	14.7	28.3	:
Denver	929,383	26	3,662	254	51.8	93.3	3.4	16.0	
Indianapolis	916,932	27	2,653	346	30.4	78.4	11.0	5.5	
New Orleans	907,123	28	1,975	459	27.3	94.6	30.6	7.9	
San Bernardino-Riverside-Ontario	809,782	30	27,295	30	79.3	77.8	3.7	20.3	
Anaheim-Santa Ana-Garden Grove	703,925	38	782	900	225.5	95.9	0.5	19.2	

ucation, 1960; ons Over 25 Yrs.		Employment, 1960		Income, 1959			Owner Occupied Housing (percent)
n Less than 5 Yrs.	Compl. High School	Mfg. (percent)	White Collar Jobs (percent)	Median (dollars)	Under $3,000 (percent)	Over $10,000 (percent)	
9.0	41.2	25.8	49.5	6,548	13.2	22.2	33.8
6.7	42.1	34.2	45.5	7,342	10.6	25.9	50.6
4.7	53.1	30.7	49.0	7,046	12.6	24.6	54.6
7.0	38.8	35.8	44.1	6,433	13.0	19.1	70.0
6.7	40.9	40.7	43.1	6,825	13.5	21.9	71.0
5.5	54.4	20.9	51.4	7,147	11.7	24.8	54.4
5.2	53.4	28.8	49.8	6,687	11.0	21.3	52.3
7.1	40.7	37.0	42.7	5,954	14.7	15.8	65.4
6.7	35.1	33.1	42.9	6,243	15.3	16.7	62.2
4.7	57.8	7.5	58.8	7,577	10.5	30.5	48.9
6.6	43.4	39.4	44.2	6,938	11.5	22.1	62.6
8.6	33.7	30.2	43.2	6,199	14.5	17.5	63.6
6.8	44.3	35.6	47.4	7,149	10.4	26.5	54.1
2.8	52.6	26.1	50.8	6,840	10.0	19.8	68.2
9.7	43.6	21.5	44.6	5,900	19.7	16.6	65.0
5.7	37.9	38.0	41.9	6,455	12.2	17.4	60.9
5.9	37.3	34.0	43.3	6,271	15.0	17.3	59.2
4.7	44.8	40.5	43.5	6,999	9.6	20.8	58.8
6.2	43.2	38.3	49.6	7,431	8.4	27.1	65.4
2.9	56.1	27.8	51.2	6,896	11.2	21.9	66.8
4.4	49.4	24.5	47.3	6,262	14.6	16.9	65.5
7.2	48.4	22.1	49.0	5,925	18.6	17.7	64.3
3.3	54.6	23.2	49.5	6,545	15.1	20.1	58.9
10.0	44.3	22.1	48.2	5,758	20.8	17.0	59.1
7.5	46.6	11.6	46.3	5,348	22.8	14.0	59.4
3.3	57.3	19.1	52.5	6,551	13.1	19.0	61.9
4.1	46.1	31.4	44.8	6,457	13.7	18.9	66.6
13.4	35.5	15.8	44.8	5,143	25.0	13.2	47.6
6.1	48.8	16.7	42.9	5,890	18.5	15.1	66.8
3.2	57.7	29.4	48.6	7,219	11.0	24.2	71.8

Source: U.S. Bureau of the Census, <u>County and City Data Book, 1967</u> (Washington, D.C.: U.S. ɔnment Printing Office, 1967), Tables 3 and 4 <u>passim</u>.

for measures of "individual equality" in which
Minnesota ranks highest nationally--third in "economic growth," tenth in "living conditions," and
first in "health and welfare"--reflect in particular urban considerations.[37] These include open
housing laws and "racially balanced schools," comparatively low unemployment, living conditions, development of markets, antipoverty programs, physical decay and urban renewal, recreation, refuse
disposal and pollution controls; and health, police,
and fire protection and welfare programs, respec-
tively, for the above measures.[38] In this connection, it must be noted that the Twin Cities area
has the smallest percentage of Blacks (1.4 percent)
and other nonwhites (0.5 percent, mostly Indian) of
SMSAs with over 1 million population; the national
average for nonwhites in these centers where there
is greater unemployment discrimination, and welfare
assistance, is 26 percent.[39] (See Table 1.) This
factor reinforces the number three ranking of the
area in home ownership (68.2 percent in 1959), the
number seven ranking in median income ($6,840 in
1959), and the number three ranking for persons
having incomes under $3,000 in 1960.[40] The small
percentage of minority groups was also a factor in
the general lack of opposition by such groups to
proposals for federation of the metropolitan area.
Even though dilution of political bloc power is not
a major concern in federation, their small number
precluded any significant "watering down" of political power. More important, however, was the significant lack of opposition from suburbs that might
be generated by sharing major social and economic
problems of central city Blacks and other nonwhites.
Such stresses are widely recognized as crucial in
formulating policies for and organizing the structure of metropolitan regions.[41] In this matter,
therefore, the Twin Cities metropolitan area has
been lucky indeed to avoid the problems involved in
central city-suburb cooperation created by large
scale racial and economic issues.

MINNEAPOLIS AND SAINT PAUL

The Twin Cities area is the center of one of
the largest, most agriculturally rich regions in
the entire world. It dominates an area extending
from the dairy country of Wisconsin on the east; to
the cattle and sheep country of the Dakotas and
Montana on the west; to the lake, recreation, and
minerals country of Minnesota and portions of
southern Canada to the north; to a great portion of
the grain belt of Iowa, Nebraska, the Dakotas, and
Wyoming to the south and west. The Twin Cities are
the principal industrial, commercial, cultural, and
service centers of a vast subcontinent. Originally
the major markets for agricultural produce, today
they constitute a national--even worldwide center--
for transport, manufacturing, and research and development, especially in the fields of electronics,
chemicals and plastics, food processing, and medicine. It possesses one of the nation's most dis-
tinguished universities, a symphony orchestra of
the first order, major museums, galleries and the-
atres, and a full range of major league sports.
Its richest resource is its people and the quality
of their efforts to achieve a better environment
for living.

The most distinctive characteristics of the
Twin Cities area is its "bicentrism" and the long-
standing, and oft times bitter, rivalry that, up to
a decade ago, prevented the area from acting and
being treated as a unity.[42] It is one of two metropolitan areas in the country with over 1 million
population that has more than a single major central city. (The other is San Francisco-Oakland.)
Indeed, this fact alone has supported the century-
long competition between the two cities for dominance of the region. For over three-quarters of a
century Minneapolis--the younger and more virile--
has increasingly set the pace and tone of development for the area; the resulting feelings of bit-
terness and inadequacy inflicted upon Saint Paul--
and worse, upon the whole metropolitan area outside
the city of Minneapolis[43]--have frequently generated

a failure of cooperation which has thwarted earlier
efforts to develop the metropolitan area as fully
as its regional potential might have permitted.
These centrifugal pressures, despite recent important moves toward cooperation,* have created very
significant differences that have led to a "pal-
pable separatism" characterized by a recent observer as follows: "Though the centers of the cities
were only about ten miles apart, in an important
sense they lay back to back, a position not conducive to intercourse."[44]

Although commonly known as the Twin Cities,
both locally and nationally, Minneapolis and Saint
Paul are not identical siblings in any sense of the
word. Only in the sense that the two developed
concurrently, in adjacent areas and to the same
general magnitude, may they be considered twins.
From their very beginnings both cities grew quite
differently: economically in terms of markets and
direction, ethnically by different groups with different social and cultural outlooks, and politically by leaders with divergent attitudes and traditions. Over the years, each city developed its own
separate central business districts with "major
hotels and convention facilities, separate financial institutions, separate airports and railroad
terminals, and even separate sports facilities.
Each central city has its suburbs that are oriented
primarily to itself in jobs, trade, and interest."[45]
Minneapolis tends to think of the entire upper Midwest as its "hinterland" while Saint Paul often
thinks of the differences between itself and Minneapolis. It is the last outpost of the East; Minneapolis the beginning of the West. These distinc-
tions, which at first glance appear to be superfi-
cial to an outside observer, are very real and of

---

*An example of recent cooperation is the suc-
cessful combined efforts to acquire major league
baseball, football, and hockey teams for the area,
utilizing a single, agreed upon metropolitan sports
center in suburban Bloomington.

vital importance to an understanding of "local adaption to metropolitan change, for they increase measurably both the need for and the difficulty of local adjustment."[46]

Minneapolis started its life between 1845 and 1855 as a grain mill; Saint Paul started in 1837 as a gin mill or trading post selling liquor to the Indians. From the 1840's, when Saint Paul established itself as the territorial capital, through the early post-Civil War period when it became the principal railhead of lines to the East and West and a major center for the lumber industry, the city grew rapidly to where it was a major midcontinental center. The city looked to the east for its development; the hugh Chicago-Milwaukee urban complex only some 400 miles to the east afforded a substantial market for its wares as well as finances for its growth. In contrast, Minneapolis was oriented toward the west, which, though of unlimited space, was but sparsely populated.[47] Distribution industries catering to this huge, virgin land, however, found Minneapolis to be a more convenient and expeditious place in which to locate. Here, they could build transit, processing, and storage facilities more readily without contending with the congested and more limited urban area to the east--Saint Paul. With the development of the western areas of the United States toward the end of the nineteenth century, Minneapolis came to surpass Saint Paul in size and economic importance.[48] Its new dominance was reinforced by a much more active and progressive leadership than its more conservatively oriented sister city.[49]

Both cities grew rapidly between 1880 and 1910, Minneapolis reaching 301,000 and Saint Paul, 214,744. By the time of the Depression their growth had slowed considerably, and leveled off following World War II. In 1950, Minneapolis had a population of 521,718; Saint Paul, 311,349.[50] By 1960, Minneapolis had experienced a substantial loss of population characteristic of many of America's major cities, falling to some 483,500. Saint

Paul filled in the interstices of its development,
growing fractionally to 313,000. This radical decline in growth was due largely to their inability
to expand physically, both cities being almost completely surrounded by suburban development dating
back to the turn of the century. In contrast, the
suburban and exurban areas were undergoing one of
the nation's greatest development booms. Whereas
in 1950, 72 percent of the population lived in the
central cities, only 53 percent remained in 1960.[51]
The 1970 census will undoubtedly show that less
than one-half of an estimated population of 1.9
million live in the central cities of Minneapolis
and Saint Paul.[52] A major characteristic of this
suburban development has been the extreme degree of
fragmentation taking place--the extensive incorporation of cities, villages, and townships.

ORGANIZATION OF LOCAL GOVERNMENT

Minneapolis possesses a weak mayor-council
form of government with the mayor having "less formal power than in any large city in America."[53]
Its current structure, based on a collection of
state laws, provides for nonpartisan elections every two years for the mayor, a comptroller, a treasurer, thirteen aldermen, and thirty-three other
officials covering an independent school board,
library board, park board, board of estimate, and
municipal judges. The mayor is able to appoint
only a chief of police, a director of civil defense,
and his own secretary. He or his representative
also sits on the above mentioned boards. He does
not submit a budget for the city; the extent of his
power through nonformal means is in direct proportion to his ability to demand strong political
backing by aldermen and personal leadership in the
community, as was the case with Hubert Horatio
Humphrey when he was mayor from 1945-1948. The
council chooses the city attorney, clerk, assessor,
and engineer.[54] Attempts to reform the city's
structure have been repeatedly turned down by the
voters.[55]

Saint Paul has had a modified commission form
of city government since 1912, the last in any major American city. As is the case with a city commission, each of the seven commissioners serves in
the dual capacity of legislator and chief depart-
mental administrator, the assignments to departments being made by the mayor. The six comission-
ers and mayor are elected at large every two years
on a nonpartisan basis and serve together as the
city council. The mayor, while a weak executive,
has powers greater than his colleague in Minneapolis. As noted above, in Saint Paul, he assigns the
commissioners to their respective departments after
each election (but cannot remove or effectively
control them), appoints the city planning board,
presides at council meetings with voting and veto
powers (the latter of which can be overridden by a
two-thirds majority or five votes), and appoints
members of local dependent boards, e.g., the Park
Board. The council passes upon ordinances, licenses, and contracts; confirms appointments, and
elects a corporation counsel and city clerk.[56] In
contrast to Minneapolis, the council is weak; it
does not determine or control the city's budget.
It is in this respect that the classic commission
form is modified. In addition to the mayor and commissioners, there is an independently elected at-
large comptroller who prepares the budget, based
upon recommendations of the commissioners, and pre-
sents it to the council for its approval.[57] He im-
poses economies on expenditures from which the
council has limited power to increase--a maximum of
3 percent for the entire budget or 10 percent for
any one fund. As such, he is also the chief audi-
tor and accountant for the city and presides over
the city's widely respected and venerable (1914)
Civil Service Bureau. Other elected officials include members of an independent school board and
local judges.[58]

The seven counties of the legally defined metropolitan area (five in the Bureau of the Census
SMSA) are essentially administrative agencies of
the state, responsible for providing a variety of

state services and functions, including: the enforcement of the state civil and criminal codes;
supervision of state elections in the county; collection of state and local taxes and equalization
of assessment; recording and registering titles,
deeds, etc.; supervision of common school districts,
construction and maintenance of county highways;
and welfare services.[59] With the exception of
Ramsey County (the seat of which is Saint Paul),
each county is governed by a nonpartisan, elected,
five-member board of commissioners which adminis-
ters the major county functions. Ramsey County
elects a seven-member county board whose chairman
is the Saint Paul mayor. Other elected officials
include the sheriffs, county attorneys, coroners,
judges, court commissioners, treasurers, and regis-
trars of deeds and surveyors, none of whom are directly controlled by the boards or their members.

Politically, as units of local government, the
counties have been considered weak, lacking many of
the functions and powers exercised by counties in
other states.[60] They have the authority to perform
a variety of other functions, such as land use
planning (except in Hennepin and Ramsey Counties),
zoning in unincorporated county areas, and the provision of library and hospital services, but have
not fully utilized them. At the same time they
have been slow or reluctant to push for additional
powers to help meet new or growing needs, such as
sewage disposal, housing, and coordinating intermunicipal plans, programs, and policies. Minnesota
has a home rule provision for counties in its constitution, but there has been little thought to using the county as a metropolitan building block.
The metropolitan counties are simply too small to
do the job, even if given a full range of municipal
powers. To do so would require substantial consolidation of all the area's seven counties as well as
the exercise of home rule powers. This is an even
more radical solution than the Metropolitan Council,
as originally proposed, and probably would have
been more than is necessary. Such a solution might
threaten other local governments even more than a

simple federated approach. However, in recognition
of the problems that counties and municipalities
outside the Twin Cities area have in providing major
services and establishing area-wide development
policies, the state legislature may have taken the
first step during its 1969 session to reorganize
the structure of county government. It has set up
eleven state planning regions, exclusive of the
seven-county Twin Cities metropolitan area.[61]
These eleven planning regions, each composed of several counties and patterned somewhat after the Twin
Cities Metropolitan Council and regional COGs, will
prepare comprehensive development plans encompass-
ing the counties within their jurisdictions and coordinate local and county development programs and
federal programs operative within the counties.[62]
(There has been some recent [1969] discussion of
consolidating Saint Paul and Ramsey County, the
smallest county in the state and of which the city
has almost 75 percent of the population and half of
the land area.)[63]

Other major units of local government include
villages, towns, and school and other special districts. Villages are one of two categories of government which may be incorporated; the other is
home rule charter cities. Villages, under the
Minnesota Village Code, may be one of three kinds:
(1) Standard Plan or weak mayor-council form of
government, usually with five elected council members composed of a mayor, a clerk, and three trustees; (2) Optional Plan A or a modified weak mayor-
council structure which provides for an elected
mayor and four trustees who appoint a clerk, treasurer and assessor; and (3) Optional Plan B or
council-manager plan.[64] Towns or townships (unincorporated settlements) in Minnesota, unlike their
counterparts in New England, were based largely
upon six-mile square surveyors' divisions. They
are administered by a three-man Board of Supervi-
sors, who are elected for three-year overlapping
terms and responsible for all town affairs, subject
to the decision of all voting citizens at the annual
town meeting. To meet increasing problems of

urbanization in the 1950's, the legislature provided for a modified town--the urban town. It follows the regular (rural) town form, but has additional powers similar to that of villages. It is
defined as "any town with plotted area and 1,200 or
more people or any town with plotted area within
twenty miles of the city halls of Minneapolis and
St. Paul."[65] But with increased size, direct de-
mocracy becomes difficult and towns have increasingly incorporated into representative villages.

In addition to villages and towns, legislation
permits settlements with a population of 1,000 or
more to incorporate as cities, all of which (outside the central cities) have either the weak mayor-
council or council-manager forms of government.
(While there were five area-wide special districts,
there were fourteen others [total of nineteen]
which cover more than one governmental subdivision.)
At the time the 1967 legislature considered and
passed legislation establishing the Metropolitan
Council, there were also operative four area-wide
special purpose districts operating under state
authorization (the Metropolitan Airports Commission
[MAC], the Minneapolis-St. Paul Sanitary District
[MSSD], the Metropolitan Mosquito Control District,
and the Metropolitan Planning Commission [MPC]), one
area-wide agency operating under the state's Joint
Powers Act (the Metropolitan Transit Commission
[MTC]), and some seventy-seven school districts.
(Cities are incorporated under either Minnesota
Statutes, Chapter 411; a special law of the legislature with respect to one category of city; or
home rule charter.) Concluding this categorization
of local government are one borough (similar to a
village) and one federal reservation.

As with state politics, political activities
are carried on at the local level formally in a
nonpartisan fashion. The political parties, however, actively recruit and endorse candidates. Local councils, as does the legislature, organize
themselves into Liberal and Independent or Conservative caucuses. For the most part, the Liberals

are Democratic-Farmer-Labor (DFL), and Independents
or Conservatives are members of or affiliated with
the Republican party. Within the Twin Cities community, the principal stronghold of the DFL is
Saint Paul, which has had a Conservative or Republican mayor only three times since the late 1930's.
The Independent (anti-DFL or nonpartisan) or Conservative (Republican) source of power is found in
the suburban rings of communities. Minneapolis,
in contrast, has frequently shifted from Liberal
(DFL) to Conservative (Republican), with the Independent being a decisive swing element, as witnessed
in the June, 1969, mayoralty contest in which an
Independent won.[66]

FRAGMENTATION OF THE LOCAL
POLITICAL SCENE

Minnesota and the Twin Cities metropolitan
area in particular constitute one of the most highly fragmented systems of government in the entire
nation. According to the 1967 Census of Government,
Minnesota ranks fourth among all states with a total of 4,185 units of government, but ranks twentieth among the states by population.[67] The state's
record with respect to elected units of government
--county, municipal, and township--shows fragmentation to be even more extensive. Minnesota ranks
second in the nation with 2,754 units. Only Illi-
nois, with 2,790 units, surpassed the state, and it
has three times the population. Minnesota ranked
only slightly better with respect to the number of
independent school districts. With 1,282 districts,
it ranks fifth, but shows a sharp decline in number
since 1962 when it ranked third. Between then and
1967, the state reduced its number of districts by
45.3 percent, a loss of 1,061 districts. This was
in addition to a reduction of 6,227 districts, or
60 percent, between 1962 and 1952.[68] The reduction was deliberately done by the state through
legislation requiring those school districts not
having classified schools to combine with those
having classified elementary and secondary schools.

It was in no small way, too, part of a concerted
effort to work toward the reduction in the proliferation of governments and the problems this has
created in the provision of services.

In the decade and a half following World War
II, increasing urbanization of the state, especially in the seven-county Twin Cities metropolitan
area, saw an extreme increase in the amount of incorporation, much of it completely irrational.
The legislature established the special Commission
on Municipal Annexation and Consolidation in 1957
to study the myriad of problems arising from recent
incorporations, to study the state laws concerning
incorporation, annexation, and consolidation, and
to recommend changes in them to provide for more
orderly growth.[69] In its report to the 1959 legislature, it found the present laws inadequate and

> . . . sometimes ineffectual to govern
> or administer orderly growth in the
> metropolitan area or in Minnesota's
> other growing cities. . . . We find
> paradoxical results from the opera-
> tion of present statutes including
> the Village of Orono which consists
> of four separate and distinct parts,
> the main part of which completely
> surrounds the Village of Long Lake;
> White Bear Township which has nine
> separate and detached parts, all of
> which except for one side of one part
> are surrounded by incorporated munic-
> ipalities; and other configurations
> which do not lend themselves to effi-
> cient, economical municipal services
> or effective government.[70]

It then recommended the establishment of a Minnesota Municipal Commission to supervise all incorporation, annexation, and boundary change procedures,
"to recodify and revise" existing law, and to continue the study of problems arising from increased
urbanization with the view toward promoting more

orderly growth and needed services.[71] The 1959
legislature, in response, established the Municipal
Commission, as recommended by the prior commission,
and an interim Commission on Municipal Laws to study
further the state's laws on consolidation and annexation. It was to include in these studies the

> . . . problems created by the co-
> existence of separate governmental
> subdivisions and special districts
> within the metropolitan and rural
> areas, . . . the problems which re-
> sult from the increasing multiplica-
> tion of local units of government
> within the metropolitan area and in
> the fringe areas surrounding our other
> cities and villages as their popula-
> tion extends past existing bounda-
> ries, . . . and the coordination of
> municipal services. . . .[72]

The following years saw the legislature provide a
series of significant grants of power to the Municipal Commission to help it promote more rational
incorporation of communities, including the limited
elimination of referenda for incorporation or consolidation of a municipality within a township, the
power to alter boundaries, and the power to initiate consolidations and annexations.[73]

Only with respect to the special districts
does Minnesota show up well in comparison with
other states. The special district has never found
particular favor as a means of providing local or
intermunicipal functions. For the most part, it is
considered to be too insulated from the political
process and electorate to meet satisfactorily the
increasing problems of governmental services.[74]
Minnesota ranked thirty-fifth among the fifty
states in 1967 with 148 special purpose districts.
The lowest sixteen states collectively had but 6.1
percent of the national total of 21,265. Thus,
while there are states with larger populations,
i.e., Michigan, Wisconsin, and Virginia, which have

fewer special districts, Minnesota's reliance on
this mechanism has been markedly cautious for a major state with significant urban problems. Indeed,
this caution may well be one major reason that the
Twin Cities Metropolitan Council has been established with the form and powers it has. The Council has separate, but dependent, administrative
(operating) boards exercising special functions
under it, e.g., sewage disposal, parks and open
space, as well as a complete veto over plans and
projects of independent special districts and the
right to membership on them.

From this brief discussion of the fragmentation of government in Minnesota, one can only con-
clude that the state possesses a disproportionately
large number of governmental units as a whole, and
of standard units of general elected local govern-
ments--counties, cities, villages, and townships--
in particular. This superabundance of governments
and resulting problems has been especially acute
in the Twin Cities area. Between 1945 and 1960,
the seven-county area experienced the creation of
fifty-one municipal governments, twenty-two of
which contained less than 1,000 persons; one had
only forty-three residents.[75] This extreme fragmentation complicated earlier attempts to resolve
metropolitan and intermunicipal problems and has
made local officials and legislators more fully
aware of the difficulties to be overcome in their
attempt to give order and improved service to the
Twin Cities area growth.

The Twin Cities metropolitan area in the Spring
of 1967 had an aggregate of 304 units of government
in its seven-county area. This included 7 counties,
77 school districts, 19 special districts, and 199
cities, villages, and townships.

To show how the Twin Cities area compares with
other major metropolitan centers of the nation, it
will be necessary to use data from the Bureau of
the Census SMSAs, which define the Twin Cities SMSA
as having five counties rather than seven counties

TABLE 2

Fragmentation of Government in the Twin Cities, 1967

County	School Districts[a]	Townships	Villages[a]	Cities	Other[b]	Total
Anoka	7	7	9	5	0	28
Carver	16	11	10	2	0	39
Dakota	11	17	15	3	0	46
Hennepin	25	3	34	10	1	73
Ramsey	5	1	13	2	0	21
Scott	8	13	4	3	1	29
Washington	5	16	20	1	0	42
Metropolitan Area	77	68	105	26	2	278
					Counties	7
					Special Districts[c]	19
					Total Governmental Units	304

[a]School districts and villages in more than one area county are shown only in the county in which most of the population resides.

[b]One borough (Belle Plaine) and one federal reservation (Fort Snelling).

[c]Includes only special districts covering two or more governmental subdivisions.

Source: 1965-1966 Biennial Report (St. Paul: Twin Cities Metropolitan Planning Commission, March, 1967), p. 23.

TABLE 3

Fragmentation of Government in Major U.S. Metropolitan Areas, 1967

Standard Metropolitan Statistical Area	Pop. 1967 (1000s)	Total No. of Local Govts.	Rank	No. of General Govts.[a]	Rank	Special District	Rank
New York	11,556	551	4	175	5	184	5
Los Angeles-Long Beach	6,857	233	14	77	17	61	14
Chicago	6,771	1,113	1	369	1	417	1
Philadelphia	4,774	876	2	346	2	328	2
Detroit	4,114	242	12	136	10	9	27
Boston	3,250[b]	146	23	78	16	62	13
San Francisco-Oakland	3,009	312	6	60	20	162	7
Washington, D.C.	2,704	84	26	66	18	18	24
Pittsburgh	2,386	704	3	312	3	263	3
St. Louis	2,311	474	5	221	4	145	8
Cleveland	2,050	207	17	137	9	13	26
Baltimore	1,990	27	30	19	28	8	28
Newark	1,889	207	17	85	14	49	17
Houston	1,788	214	16	59	21	107	10
Minneapolis-St. Paul	1,636	220	15	161	8	17	25
Dallas	1,405	183	20	84	15	38	19
Cincinnati	1,361	266	11	162	7	30	20
Milwaukee	1,342	174	21	93	13	5	30
Paterson-Clifton-Passaic	1,341	200	19	98	12	24	22
Buffalo	1,332	145	24	65	19	39	18
Atlanta	1,289	884	26	48	23	27	21
Seattle-Everett	1,262	268	10	49	22	183	6
Anaheim-Santa Ana-Garden Grove	1,231	111	25	25	27	53	16
Kansas City	1,214	272	9	123	11	57	15
San Diego	1,198	164	22	15	30	98	11
Miami	1,114	36	29	28	26	7	29
Denver	1,090	296	7	36	24	214	4
San Bernardino-Riverside-Ontario	1,086	234	13	29	25	136	9
New Orleans	1,059	41	28	17	29	20	23
Indianapolis	1,042	282	8	167	6	70	12

School District	Rank	Land Area (square miles)	Rank	Pop. (square miles)	Rank	General Govt. (square miles)	Rank	Pop. (general govt.)	Rank
192	3	2,149	18	5,363.4	1	12.3	24	66,034	4
95	7	4,060	7	1,688.9	7	52.7	10	89,052	2
327	1	3,714	8	1,823.1	6	10.1	27	18,350	19
202	2	3,553	10	1,343.6	11	10.3	26	13,798	24
97	6	1,965	22	2,093.6	5	14.5	20	30,250	14
6	26	987	27	3,292.9	2	12.8	23	41,666	8
90	9	2,486	14	1,371.3	9	41.4	11	50,150	6
-	29	2,347	15	1,152.1	12	35.6	13	40,908	9
129	4	3,051	12	782.0	16	9.8	28	7,647	29
108	5	4,119	6	561.0	20	18.6	17	10,457	25
57	16	1,519	25	1,349.5	10	11.1	25	14,964	22
-	29	2,255	16	882.4	14	119.7	3	104,737	1
73	13	698	29	2,706.3	4	8.2	29	22,224	17
48	18	6,258	2	285.7	28	106.1	5	30,305	12
42	20	2,111	19	774.9	17	13.1	22	10,162	26
61	15	4,467	3	314.5	25	53.2	9	16,726	20
74	12	2,154	17	636.4	19	13.3	21	8,401	28
76	11	1,458	26	920.0	13	15.7	19	14,430	23
88	10	427	30	3,140.5	3	4.9	30	15,239	21
41	21	1,587	24	839.3	15	24.1	15	20,492	18
9	25	1,723	23	751.5	18	35.9	12	26,854	15
36	22	4,234	5	298.0	26	86.4	7	25,959	16
33	23	782	28	1,575.4	8	31.3	14	49,240	7
92	8	2,760	13	439.8	23	22.4	16	9,870	27
51	17	4,255	4	281.0	29	283.7	2	79,867	3
1	28	2,054	20	542.3	21	73.4	8	39,786	10
19	24	3,665	9	297.6	27	101.8	6	30,278	13
69	14	27,295	1	39.8	30	934.3	1	37,448	11
4	27	2,026	21	522.7	22	119.2	4	62,294	5
45	19	3,082	11	338.0	24	18.5	18	6,240	30

[a]Includes county, municipal, and town governments.

[b]Metropolitan State Economic Area.

Sources: U.S. Bureau of the Census, Provisional Estimates of the Population of 100 Large Metropolitan Areas, July 1, 1967, Series P-25, No. 411 (Washington, D.C.: U.S. Government Printing Office, December 5, 1968), Table 3, p. 13; U.S. Bureau of the Census, Census of Governments, 1967, Vol. I, Governmental Organization (Washington, D.C.: U.S. Government Printing Office, 1968), Table 19.

as prescribed by state law. A brief overview will
show that the Twin Cities area follows closely the
pattern of political fragmentation achieved by the
state. Among the thirty SMSA's with over 1 million
population in 1967, the Twin Cities ranked fifteenth,
with some 1.64 million persons.[76] (For exact figures on this and the discussion following, see
Table 3.) Where the state ranked second in the nation in the number of elected units of general gov-
ernment--counties, cities, villages, and townships
--the Twin Cities lagged only a short way behind,
ranking eight with 161 units. This extreme fragmentation is made even more significant when one
realizes that five of the seven metropolitan areas
having more units are larger by as much as three or
more times and can therefore, be expected to have
more units. Nine centers--Los Angeles, Detroit,
Boston, San Francisco-Oakland, Washington, Cleveland,
Baltimore, Newark, and Houston--are larger but have
fewer governments. This degree of fragmentation
shows up markedly again when population per elected
government is compared with the other metropolitan
areas. The area ranks twenty-sixth of thirty in
the amount of population with only 10,162 persons
per governmental unit. Only four cities have smaller populations per government. Its ranking for total governmental units conforms to its population
ranking--fifteenth. Recent efforts to reduce school
districts has had its effect; the metropolitan area,
with forty-two school districts, ranks twentieth
and special districts, with seventeen, rank twenty-
fifth. In terms of the amount of land per unit of
elected government, the Twin Cities SMSA ranks
twenty-second in the nation with 13.1 square miles
per unit. The area ranks seventeenth in population
per square mile, not far behind its simple population ranking. The fragmentation of government,
therefore, is greatest and most problematic precisely in the same category that plagues the state
--the proliferation of elected general government
units that most acutely reflect intermunicipal and
metropolitan cooperation and functioning, especially
in large areas with low densities.

NOTES

1. John Fischer, "The Minnesota Experiment: How to Make a Big City Fit to Live In," _Harper's Magazine_, CCXXXVIII, 1427 (April, 1969), 12.

2. _Ibid_.

3. Daniel J. Elazar, _American Federalism: A View From the States_ (New York: Thomas Y. Crowell Company, 1966), p. 20.

4. John O. Wilson, "Regional Differences in Social Welfare" (Kansas City: Midwest Research Institute, 1967), pp. 8-11. (Mimeographed.)

5. Elazar, _op. cit._, p. 122.

6. Richard E. Dawson and James A. Robinson, "The Politics of Welfare," in Herbert Jacobs and Kenneth N. Vines, eds., _Politics in the American States: A Comparative Analysis_ (Boston: Little, Brown and Company, 1965), p. 405.

7. Herbert Jacobs, "State Political Systems," in Jacobs and Vines, eds., _op. cit._, p. 15; Wilson, _op. cit._, pp. 8-9.

8. Lester W. Milbrath, "Political Participation in the States," in Jacobs and Vines, eds., _op. cit._, pp. 38-40.

9. Clara Penniman, "The Politics of Taxation," in Jacobs and Vines, eds., _op. cit._, pp. 305-12; Advisory Commission on Intergovernmental Relations, _State and Local Finance: Significant Features, 1956-1966_ (Washington, D.C.: U.S. Government Printing Office, 1968), pp. 10-11.

10. "Financing Our Urban Needs," _Nation's Cities_, March, 1969, pp. 35, 38.

11. G. Theodore Mitau, _Politics in Minnesota_ (Minneapolis: University of Minnesota Press, 1960),

pp. 3, 4, 10, 42, 57-59; Austin Ranney, "Parties in
State Politics," in Jacobs and Vines, eds., op.
cit., p. 64.

12. Mitau, loc. cit. and pp. 66-71.

13. Mitau, op. cit., p. 7.

14. Elazar, op. cit., pp. 96-100.

15. Ibid., pp. 120-23.

16. Ibid., p. 122; Mitau, op. cit., pp. 81,
100-01.

17. Mitau, op. cit., pp. 4, 18-19, 27, 29,
52-53; Jacobs and Vines, eds., op. cit., p. 15.

18. Karl Grittner, Interview, April 23, 1969.
(Interviews cited are with Stanley Baldinger, unless stated otherwise.)

19. Elazar, op. cit., p. 100.

20. Robert H. Salisbury, "State Politics and
Education," in Jacobs and Vines, eds., op. cit.,
pp. 354-56; Dawson and Robinson, in Jacobs and
Vines, eds., op. cit., pp. 382-87; Elazar, op. cit.,
pp. 190, 193.

21. The "Quality of Life" Dimension in Minne-
sota's Growth (St. Paul: Minnesota Department of
Economic Development, December, 1967), p. 5.
(Mimeographed.)

22. Ibid.

23. Ibid.

24. Elazar, op. cit., pp. 82-83.

25. Resident Physician as cited by Phyllis
Wright, M.D., with David R. Zimmerman, "Medicine
Today," Ladies' Home Journal, LXXXVI, 5 (May,
1969), 46.

26. Ibid.; Ladies' Home Journal, February, 1967, as cited by Minnesota Department of Economic Development, op. cit., p. 4.

27. Wilson, op. cit., p. 8.

28. Elazar, op. cit., p. 208.

29. Ranney, in Jacobs and Vines, eds., op. cit., p. 69; Bureau of the Census, U.S. Census of Population: 1960. Detailed Characteristics. Minnesota. Final Report. (Washington, D.C.: U.S. Government Printing Office, 1962), Table 25, p. 25-340; Table 95, p. 25-332; Table 96, p. 25-333; and Table 139, p. 25-522.

30. The "Quality of Life" Dimension in Minnesota's Growth, op. cit., p. 3, from Business Week Magazine, August, 1967.

31. Wilson, op. cit., p. 11.

32. Elazar, op. cit., p. 119.

33. Ibid., pp. 181-82.

34. Proposed Rosemount Site (Upper Midwest Research and Development Council, September, 1965), p. 55.

35. National Register of Scientific and Technical Personnel, p. 54.

36. Dawson and Robinson, op. cit., pp. 380-82.

37. Wilson, loc. cit.

38. Ibid., pp. 6, 8, 22.

39. U.S. Bureau of the Census, County and City Data Book, Tables 3 and 4, pp. 432-573 passim; and U.S. Department of Labor, Bureau of Labor Statistics, and U.S. Department of Commerce, Bureau of Census, Social and Economic Conditions of Negroes

in the United States, BLS Report No. 332, Current
Population Records, Series P. 23-45 (Washington,
D.C.: U.S. Government Printing Office, 1967), p.
11; "Negroes' Urban Concentration: Strengths and
Weaknesses," Minneapolis Tribune, September 19,
1966; see also footnote 29.

40. U.S. Department of Commerce, Bureau of
Census, loc. cit.

41. Henry Cohen, in Derek Senior, ed., The
Regional City (Chicago: Aldine Publishing Company,
1966), p. 61.

42. Charles Whiting, Interview, April, 1969.

43. "Metropolitan Co-operation Plea Cheered,"
Minneapolis Star, July 4, 1961; Charles A. Backstrom,
"Minneapolis-St. Paul," in Robert H. Connery, ed.,
Politics of Mental Health (New York: Columbia Uni-
versity Press, 1968), pp. 410-12.

44. Backstrom, in Connery, ed., op. cit.,
p. 410.

45. Ibid.

46. Roscoe C. Martin, Metropolis in Transition: Local Government Adaptation to Metropolitan
Growth (Washington, D.C.: U.S. Government Printing
Office for the Housing and Home Finance Agency,
1963), pp. 51-52.

47. Martha Coleman Bray, "Minneapolis," XV,
p. 556; and "Saint Paul," XIX, p. 852, Encyclopaedia
Britannica, 1964 ed.

48. Alan A. Altshuler, A Report on Politics
in St. Paul and A Report on Politics in Minneapolis,
copyrighted by Edward C. Banfield (Cambridge:
Joint Center for Urban Studies of Massachusetts
Institute of Technology and Harvard University,
1959), pp. I-1; Backstrom, in Connery, ed., op.
cit., p. 410.

49. Backstrom, in Connery, ed., _op. cit._,
pp. 407-66 _passim_.

50. Altshuler, _loc. cit._

51. Backstrom, in Connery, ed., _op. cit._,
p. 408.

52. Preliminary 1970 census figures, subject
to change, show a seven-county metropolitan population of 1,865,312 with a central cities population
of 740,663; and a suburban population of 1,124,649;
that is, only 39.7 percent of the total population
now lives in Minneapolis and Saint Paul proper.
"Minnesota Population Shown To Be 3,770,241 in Preliminary 1970 Census Counts," _U.S. Department of
Commerce News_, Release No. CB70-88, June 30, 1970
(Washington, D.C.: U.S. Department of Commerce,
1970), pp. 1-4. (Mimeographed.)

53. Backstrom, in Connery, ed., _op. cit._, p.
411.

54. Altshuler, _A Report on Politics in Min-
neapolis_, _op. cit._, pp. II-3.

55. Backstrom, in Connery, ed., _loc. cit._

56. Altshuler, _Report on Politics in St.
Paul_, _op. cit._, pp. II-3.

57. Backstrom, in Connery, ed., _op. cit._,
p. 412.

58. Altshuler, _op. cit._, pp. I-3.

59. F. Robert Edman, _Background Cases Prepared for the Sub-committee on State Departments_
(St. Paul: January, 1967), pp. 9-10. (Mimeographed.); Backstrom, in Connery, ed., _op. cit._,
pp. 413, 442; Robert A. Barrett, _Metropolitan Inter-
County Council: Organization Study_ (St. Paul:
Metropolitan Inter-County Council, March, 1967),
p. 7.

60.   Barrett, op. cit., pp. 8-9.

61.   F. Robert Edman, Interview, June, 1969;
and Wilfred "Andy" Anderson, Executive Secretary of
the Metropolitan Inter-County Council, Interview,
June, 1969. Both agreed that the inadequacies of
county government and the too small populations of
many counties (some as few as 20,000 persons) were
stimuli to the legislation and likely first steps
to county reorganization.

62.   1969 Minnesota Sessions Law, Chapter 1122.

63.   James Dalglish, St. Paul Commissioner of
Finance, Interview, June 20, 1969.

64.   Minnesota Statutes Annotated, Chapter 412
et al.; The Joint Program, Governmental Responsibilities and Resources, Part D (Draft, p. 20 IIIJ)
(St. Paul: Twin Cities Metropolitan Planning Commission, January, 1967), pp. 4-5. (Mimeographed.)

65.   Minnesota Statutes Annotated, 368.01, as
quoted in The Joint Program, Social Studies Paper
No. 19: Characteristics of Local Government Structure (St. Paul: Twin Cities Metropolitan Planning
Commission, June, 1964), p. 5.

66.   Backstrom, in Connery, ed., op. cit.,
pp. 440-46; Altshuler, Report on Politics in Saint
Paul, pp. II-3, and Report on Politics in Minneapolis, pp. II-3.

67.   U.S. Bureau of the Census, 1967 Census of
Government, Vol. I, Governmental Organization
(Washington, D.C.: U.S. Government Printing Office,
1968), pp. 1-15, and Tables 4 and 19 passim, pp.
375, 376. All data, except where otherwise noted,
are from this census.

68.   The Joint Program, Social Studies Paper
No. 10G1 (Draft), Governmental Units: A Comparative
Study of the Twin Cities and Other Metropolitan
Areas in 1962 (St. Paul: Twin Cities Metropolitan

Planning Commission, August, 1965), p. 5. (Mimeographed.)

69.   1957 Minnesota Sessions Law, Chapter 833.

70.   Report of the Commission on Municipal Annexation and Consolidation (St. Paul: State of
Minnesota, 1959), p. 6.

71.   Ibid.

72.   Report of the Commission on Municipal
Laws (St. Paul: State of Minnesota, 1961), p. 12.

73.   1969 Minnesota Sessions Law, Chapter 1142.

74.   James Hetland, Jr., Chairman of the Metro-
politan Council, Interview, April, 1969; Reynold
Boezi, Program Coordinator of the Metropolitan
Council, Interview, June, 1969.

75.   Report of the Commission on Municipal
Laws, op. cit., p. 14.

76.   U.S. Bureau of the Census, Current Population Reports: Population Estimates, Series P.
25-411 (Washington, D.C.: U.S. Government Printing
Office, December 5, 1968), p. 13.

CHAPTER **3** EARLY EFFORTS TOWARD
METROPOLITAN PLANNING

Formal city planning came to the Twin Cities
following World War I as part of the great explo-
sion in the nation's planning activities. Minneapolis established a planning commission in 1919 that
played a prominent role in the city's development
until the 1930's. The economic crisis of the Great
Depression brought the commission's role into a
sharp decline that did not revive until stimulated
by the Federal Housing Act of 1949.[1] Saint Paul
established a planning board in 1920, which, in contrast to its sister city, had relatively minor impact on the city's subsequent development. It assumed more importance in the 1950's as a result of
federal stimulation to urban redevelopment.[2] Metropolitan planning in the Twin Cities also received
its first impetus during the 1920's. Area-wide
pressures, which had first become apparent shortly
after the turn of the century, began to create popular sentiment for a more comprehensive and realistic
approach to planning. The two cities which had
started life some eleven miles apart had grown together and now shared many common problems.

THE EMERGENCE OF METROPOLITAN
PLANNING IN THE TWIN CITIES

In 1925, a group of publicly interested citizens, under the leadership of Robert Jones, a Professor of Architecture at the University of Minnesota, sought to emulate the experience of New York
(and the Regional Plan Association) and organize a
voluntary metropolitan planning association, the
first such effort known for the area.[3] By 1928,

the group had progressed sufficiently to establish
an "informal" Metropolitan District Planning Commission to formulate plans for both cities and "certain
surrounding territory. . . ."[4] Specifically, it proposed "to study plans and advise in matters of common and of intercommunity interest . . ., such as
the establishment of arterial highways, interurban
transit, boulevards, bridges, parks, recreational
agencies, zoning, conservation of lakes, water supply, sewerage, garbage disposal, a grand round drive,
and other elements of regional planning."[5] Inter-
estingly, the area proposed to be covered is identical to that over which the Twin Cities Metropolitan
Council is now responsible and for which the previous Twin Cities Metropolitan Planning Commission was
also responsible. Unfortunately, the first effort
soon died because it was unable to gain any significant official or popular support and, therefore, was
unable to finance its work.[6] With the coming of the
Depression, further efforts toward comprehensive and
metropolitan planning fell into abeyance, not to re-
appear for a quarter century.

A second major undertaking in metropolitan
planning occurred during the same period, one that
was more successful and that had, and still has,
significant bearing on the development of the Metropolitan Council. In 1927, following reports of the
Minnesota Board of Health that there was increasingly serious pollution of the Mississippi River, which
both cities were using as a sanitary sewer, the
state legislature created the Metropolitan Drainage
Commission to study the problem and recommend solutions on sewage disposal.[7] In 1929 and again in
1931, the commission recommended establishment of a
metropolitan sanitary district, but it failed to
achieve legislative enactment. Principal obstacles
to passage were lack of agreement on financing,
method of treatment, and the inclusion of South
Saint Paul (one of the nation's largest meat-packing
centers) in the district.[8] Finally in 1933, the
legislature enacted a law which permitted the State
Board of Health to call into existence the
Minneapolis-Saint Paul Sanitary District (MSSD).[9]

It resolved the financing problems by excluding
South Saint Paul and its problems. Construction of
the MSSD began almost immediately and was completed
in mid-1938. Between 1938 and 1970, the MSSD func-
tioned along the lines of the proposals of the Metropolitan Drainage Commission, constructing and operating interceptor sewers and a single treatment
plant. At the time of its acquisition by the Twin
Cities Metropolitan Council on January 1, 1970, it
serviced some forty-five suburban communities on a
contract basis.[10]

   Again in 1943, the state legislature intervened
in a metropolitan controversy over where to build
the area's major airport.[11] Both Minneapolis and
Saint Paul had eagerly sought the facility, each
having built competing airports just prior to World
War II. The legislature recognized that there was
opportunity then for only one major facility and
enacted legislation establishing the Metropolitan
Airports Commission (MAC), a public corporation, to
take control of both cities' airports and to develop the major facility for the area.[12]

POST WORLD WAR II DEVELOPMENTS
IN THE TWIN CITIES

   The Twin Cities area experienced, as did other
major metropolitan areas in the country, extensive
growth following World War II, particularly in the
suburbs. The 1960 census showed the two central
cities with a combined population of 833,000 and
the suburbs with 353,000, or a total metropolitan
population of 1.19 million.[13] By the mid-1950's,
the two cities had completed most of their growth,
and expansion in the area was predominantly in the
suburbs, particularly the second and third tiers of
communities.[14] In March, 1953, as a measure of increasing concern over the problems of metropolitan
growth, the League of Minnesota Municipalities (LMM)
sponsored a Twin Cities Regional Planning Conference at the University of Minnesota to discuss common problems and approaches to their solution.[15]

The conference was attended by over one hundred governmental officials and concerned private individuals, about half of whom came from suburban communities. Executive Secretary of the LMM at the time was Clarence C. Ludwig, who was also a Professor of Political Science at the University of Minnesota and Director of the University's Municipal Reference Bureau.[16] He came later to be recognized as "the father of the metropolitan planning idea in the Twin Cities area."[17] Ludwig successfully persuaded the conference to continue its interest in metropolitan planning for the area by endorsing draft legislation introduced in the 1953 legislature to create a mechanism for such an activity.[18] The legislative proposal failed in passage, but it stimulated Ludwig to greater effort. He appointed an advisory body of public officials and private citizens from the two central cities and suburbs to study the efforts of other metropolitan areas in resolving their problems and to prepare proposals to be submitted to the legislature in 1955. The LMM's legislative conference of municipal officials endorsed these activities in 1954, recognizing the need for the legislature to authorize a metropolitan planning agency.[19]

On the eve of the 1955 legislative session, the LMM met again in conference to discuss draft legislation, to plan efforts to push its bills in the legislature, and to gain public support. Some sixty people from state and local government, central cities and suburbs--legislators, professors, private citizens--attended the December, 1954, conference and supported the League's efforts.[20] Initially, the League's efforts appeared to command wide public support.[21] Newspapers in both central cities and suburbs were in favor of a metropolitan planning commission; Ludwig and C. David Loeks, Planning Director for Saint Paul and Chairman of the LMM's Planning Committee, actively lobbied for a metropolitan approach to resolving the area's environmental problems.[22] Their biggest opposition appeared to rest with those who felt that a metropolitan approach to planning would erode the

principles of local self-government and home rule.[23]
Elmer L. Andersen, Conservative (later Governor),
sponsored the LMM's bill in the Senate, as he had
in 1953, and succeeded in getting favorable action.[24]
The proposal, however, was not voted upon by the
House of Representatives.[25] This was directly attributable to opposition from the central cities,
particularly Minneapolis, which believed that it
would be required to pay a disproportionate share
of the costs of the commission while being under-
represented on it.[26] Efforts to reach some kind of
compromise failed.

Despite some moments of indecision among the
supporters of metropolitan planning for the area,
Ludwig and Loeks renewed their efforts. The LMM's
legislative conference met in June, 1956, and re-
affirmed its support of metropolitan planning and
endorsed Loeks's proposal for a Twin Cities metropolitan planning bill. Further efforts were made
to gain the support of central cities and suburban
councils that was essential to any successful legislative enactment.[27] In the following months, local
council after council, including those in Minneapolis and Saint Paul, adopted resolutions in favor
of the concept of metropolitan planning.[28] Later
that year, in September, Governor Orville Freeman,
a long time personal friend of Ludwig, joined the
LMM in sponsoring yet a third conference on community and metropolitan planning.[29] The Governor gave
his full backing to a metropolitan planning commission. This, together with the continued vigorous
support of Senator Andersen, demonstrated the nonpartisan character of the movement that was pro-
gressively increasing its influence in the Twin
Cities community.

A fourth and final LMM conference was held at
the university in December, 1956, in anticipation
of the pending 1957 session of the legislature.[30]
As with the conference held exactly two years earlier, emphasis was on the measures to be taken to
secure passage of the proposals for a metropolitan
planning commission. The merits of metropolitan

planning had already been accepted.[31]   Once again,
Senator Andersen sponsored and pushed the legisla-
tion successfully through the Senate.   This time
the proposal quickly moved through the House and
was passed without a single negative vote.   Governor
Freeman signed the legislation establishing the Twin
Cities Metropolitan Planning Commission (MPC) on
April 17, 1957.[32]

THE TWIN CITIES METROPOLITAN
PLANNING COMMISSION

The legislation called for the MPC to "make
plans for the physical, social and economic development of the metropolitan area with the general purpose of guiding and accomplishing coordinated and
harmonious development of the area. . . ."[33]   Further, it was to "promote the cooperation of the
planning commissions of governmental units within
its Metropolitan Area, the coordination of the plans
of such units, and the coordination of such plans
adopted by the Commission."[34]   These two basic responsibilities were to be exercised within the five
counties of Anoka, Dakota, Hennepin, Ramsey, and
Washington, which included an aggregate of some 320
units of local government--cities, villages, townships, school districts, special districts, and one
federal reservation, as well as the seven counties[35]--
and over 1.35 million persons.[36]   To finance its
activities, the MPC possessed the power to levy a
0.10 mill rate on real property in addition to ac-
cepting gifts and grants from private and public
entities, including the federal government.[37]   Membership on the MPC, as determined by the legislation, was to be composed of twenty-seven representatives as follows:

> -4 members from Minneapolis and Saint
>   Paul together; one being each mayor
>   or his representative, the other two
>   representing each city council;
> -5 members from the counties, one from
>   each;

-7 members from the incorporated
suburbs, one for each 50,000 of
population;
-2 members representing all townships;
-2 members from two special districts
(corporations), one from each;
-7 members appointed by the Governor
to represent the citizenry of the
area with at least three from the
central cities and no more than
four from any one political party.[38]

Members were initially to serve varied and staggered
terms, after which they would serve overlapping five-
year terms.[39]

    The law establishing the MPC also provided for
the addition of contiguous counties to the metropolitan planning area upon application from the concerned county boards and the concurrence of the Commission.[40] In September, 1958, Carver County joined
the MPC and in April, 1959, Scott County adhered,
thus creating a metropolitan planning area totaling
2,981 square miles[41] (the same amount that exists
presently under the Metropolitan Council), of which
over 500 square miles were urban or urbanizing.[42]
At the same time, MPC membership was increased to
twenty-nine. The 1960 census showed the greatest
increase in suburban population in contrast to the
decline of the central cities.[43] (Minneapolis lost
close to 39,000 while Saint Paul gained just over
2,000 in population.)[44] This shift in population
balance threatened to destroy the "mix" that the
proponents of the 1957 legislation had worked out
to gain the support of the central cities. Consequently, the MPC in 1961 requested amendment of the
formula for incorporated suburban representation to
eliminate the provision of one member for each
50,000 of suburban population and to fix its permanent representation at the earlier figure of seven.
The legislature acceded to the request, putting
membership at thirty of which twenty came from
suburbs.[45]

WORK OF THE MPC

The MPC began its work on June 19, 1957, at which time Ludwig was named Acting Chairman and Loeks its first Planning Director.[46] It spent much of the following year completing its organization, acquiring staff, and initiating programs of research. It then started the first of three phases of its operation--research, the gathering of data on the "physical, social and economic development . . . of the area."[47] The research was done effectively and the findings distributed widely to government, business, industry, the general public, etc. The other two phases--formulation and implementation of plans for the metropolitan area--were continuous programs in which the MPC hoped to play a vital role.[48]

Under its basic charges of preparing plans for the orderly development of the area and coordinating plans and programs of governmental units within the metropolitan area, the MPC assumed four additional subordinate responsibilities.[49] It would conduct research upon which to base its plans and recommendations, prepare plans based upon this research, assist local government units within the area with their planning activities, and coordinate these plans and activities.[50] With respect to this responsibility, the MPC had no positive or implementing review powers. Its power was solely advisory, and then only when a local government requested MPC review; the question of whether or not a particular local plan had a metropolitan impact was left to the local unit to decide. MPC plans for an area, similarly, were to be accepted in the area on a voluntary basis.[51] The MPC possessed no initiatory or sanctional powers on metropolitan or intermunicipal matters. Its success would depend upon an effective program of community and public relations.[52]

During this first phase of operations--from 1958 through 1961--the MPC prepared seventeen reports and bulletins on major issues and on general background of the Twin Cities. The focus of the process during this period was upon education of

the Twin Cities community--both official and private.[53] Publications included detailed discussions
of the problems of metropolitan growth (The Challenge
of Metropolitan Growth) directed toward governing
bodies of the area, population studies (Metropolitan
Population Study: Part I and Part II), land use
(Metropolitan Land Study), area economics and finance (Metropolitan Economic Study), water (Metropolitan Water Study: Part I and Part II), sewerage
(Metropolitan Sewerage Study), transportation (Metropolitan Transportation Study: Part I and Part II
and Street and Highway Standards), parks and open
space (Metropolitan Parks), and miscellaneous ma-
terials for local planning districts of the metropolitan area. In addition, Director Loeks visited
eighteen major metropolitan centers in the country
to look first hand at their planning activities,
and the MPC assumed joint leadership in two major
area-wide projects.[54] The first involved chairing
a 1961 conference sponsored by Governor Andersen to
discuss planning problems of the area;[55] the second
involved a contract with the University of Minnesota
and the Upper Midwest Research and Development Council (UMRDC) to prepare a three-year study of the development of the urban portion of the Ninth Federal
District. This second project, like the Loeks
visit to eighteen cities, was financed by a grant
from the Ford Foundation.[56]

The MPC during this period was also drawn into
the growing controversy over provision of sewage
service that arose from the discovery in 1959 of
major contamination of ground water in the area.
(For details, see Chapter 4, pp. 77-79.) It noted
the need for a metropolitan mechanism to control
the problem and the urgency to prepare a comprehensive metropolitan plan to guide the area's development before time and opportunities ran out.[57] Because of its limited powers, it was unable to do
more than draw attention to these urgent matters.

In sum, the MPC during this initial phase of
its operation was largely research and community
relations oriented. In a very real sense it "was

still substantially an agency on the outside, looking in."[58] It possessed no significant enforcement
or review powers. And aside from routine reports
on its finances to the legislature, it was not
obliged to report on its work or progress to any
local or state body until 1965, when legislation
passed which increased its mill rate levy and con-
curred in federal legislation requiring metropolitan review for transportation planning proposals.[59]
It then began to submit biennial reports to the
legislature, outlining its activities during the
preceding two years.

PHASE II OF THE MPC:
THE JOINT PROGRAM, 1962-1967

In mid-1961, at the instance of the U.S.
Bureau of Public Roads (BPR), and the Housing and
Home Finance Agency (HHFA), the MPC undertook joint
responsibility with the Minnesota State Highway Department and other area planning and governmental
bodies for one of the nation's major land use-
transportation studies.[60] The study was one of a
series of large computerized pilot projects financed
throughout the nation largely by the two federal
agencies as part of an agreement to resolve the growing conflict between urban planners and highway engineers over their respective programs. The two
agencies had finally recognized that the development
of transportation facilities was "inextricably" interrelated with that of future land uses in urban
areas and that decisions on metropolitan development
should be worked out through special studies on a
cooperative, comprehensive, and continuous basis.[61]
In the future--after June 30, 1965--federal highway
funds might be withheld from any area of 50,000 or
more where such planning was not undertaken.

The study--later to be called the Joint Program--
was formally started in April, 1962, after nine
months were spent working out a detailed three-year
work program with the BPR and the HHFA.[62] A budget
of 1.8 million dollars was established, with the

federal government contributing two-thirds of the
total costs. In addition to the MPC, the Joint Program group included the Minnesota Highway Department
and the county engineering agencies of the seven area
counties and of the two central cities. The counties and cities were included as they were intimately involved with the actual construction and maintenance of the area's highway system.[63] The MPC
played the major role in developing the land use
portion of the study, receiving the HHFA grant.
The State Highway Department played the primary
role in developing the transportation element of
the plan. It was the recipient of federal highway
funds and the agency, under federal legislation,
responsible for planning and building the state's
portion of the federal interstate highway system.
The 1962 Federal Aid Highway Act and BPR regulations did not eliminate these responsibilities;
they only changed the context in which they were to
be carried out.[64]

With this study, the MPC seized the opportunity to become an effective force in the development
of the area and the Joint Program soon began to
dominate its planning efforts.[65] During the ensuing years, the Joint Program assembled data on the
prospective growth model and published a series of
findings and alternative proposals in the form of
reports to the community. Beginning in 1963 and
1964, the Joint Program began to shift its focus
from the traditional forms of plan preparation to
the selection of "basic policies for metropolitan
growth," with the goal of producing a metropolitan
"development guide."[66] It soon became apparent
that the original goal of mid-1965 for completing
the program could not be met, and the schedule was
revised in early 1965. The new target date was to
be early 1967, before the end of the 1967 legislative session.[67] The budget was increased by
$375,000, with the federal government again con-
tributing two-thirds of the total.

The Joint Program expanded its community relations elements for the guide and prepared and

published a series of four principal reports--<u>Meeting the Challenge of Metropolitan Growth</u>; <u>4,000,000 by 2000: Preliminary Proposals for Guiding Change</u>; <u>Goals for Development of the Twin Cities Metropolitan Area</u>; and <u>Selecting Policies for Metropolitan Growth</u>. The Joint Program collectively covered "alternative patterns for future development" by testing models through a computer, and then the reports explained and presented them to the community. The presentation was accomplished through two groups--the Elected Officials Review Committee composed of 300 area mayors and officials and the Technical Advisory Committee composed of civic, business, and development leaders.[68] These reports achieved a widely respected place, not only in the Twin Cities community, but throughout the nation.[69] This second phase of operations--plan preparations-- ended in late summer, 1967, with the termination of the MPC and the creation of the Twin Cities Metropolitan Council, and on the eve of the publication of the Twin Cities Metropolitan Development Guide in April, 1968. In closing its work, the MPC never got into the third phase of its proposed program-- plan implementation and a continuing planning process--but it had contributed materially to the developments in the area which led directly to the creation of the Metropolitan Council.

NOTES

1. Alan A. Altshuler, <u>The City Planning Process: A Political Analysis</u> (Ithaca: Cornell University Press, 1965), pp. 12, 200.

2. <u>Ibid</u>., pp. 12, 40.

3. Roscoe C. Martin, <u>Metropolis in Transition: Local Government Adaptation to Metropolitan Growth</u> (Washington, D.C.: U.S. Government Printing Office for Housing and Home Finance Agency, 1963), p. 52.

4. <u>Ibid</u>.

5. Ibid.

6. Ibid.

7. Report on Water Supply and Sewage Disposal
in the Minneapolis-St. Paul Metropolitan Area
(Saint Paul: State Board of Health, 1961), p. 4;
M. Barry Peterson, A Brief History of Sanitary Sewage Disposal in the Twin Cities (St. Paul: Metropolitan Council, 1967), p. 1. (Mimeographed.)

8. Ibid.

9. "1961 Minnesota Statutes," Sections 445.01-
445.21.

10. Peterson, op. cit., p. 2.

11. Martin, op. cit., p. 53.

12. "1961 Minnesota Statutes," Sections 360.101-
360.144.

13. Metropolitan Population Study: Part Two,
Numbers and Distribution (Saint Paul: Twin Cities
Metropolitan Planning Commission, 1961), pp. 15-16,
22-24, 53.

14. Ibid., pp. 6-8.

15. Martin, op. cit., p. 54. The ensuing history through 1962 has been drawn largely from Chapter V, "Planning: The Twin Cities Metropolitan
Planning Commission," pp. 51-62.

16. Ibid., p. 53.

17. Ibid.; Annual Report, 1959 (Saint Paul:
Twin Cities Metropolitan Planning Commission, 1959),
p. 3.

18. Martin, op. cit., p. 54.

19. Ibid.

20. _Ibid_.

21. _Ibid_., pp. 54-55.

22. C. David Loeks, Interview, February, 1969. (Interviews cited are with Stanley Baldinger, unless stated otherwise.)

23. Martin, _op. cit._, p. 55.

24. Elmer L. Andersen, Interview, April, 1969; Martin, _op. cit._, p. 55.

25. _Ibid_.

26. _Ibid_.

27. _Ibid_.; Loeks, _loc. cit._

28. Martin, _op. cit._, p. 55.

29. _Ibid_.

30. _Ibid_., pp. 55-56.

31. _Ibid_., p. 56.

32. "1957 Minnesota Laws," Chapter 468.

33. _Ibid_.

34. _Ibid_.

35. _Annual Report, 1958_ (Saint Paul: Twin Cities Metropolitan Planning Commission, 1958), p. 2.

36. _Metropolitan Population Study, Part II: Numbers and Distribution_ (Saint Paul: Twin Cities Metropolitan Planning Commission, 1961), Appendix B, p. 53.

37. "1957 Minnesota Laws," Chapter 468.

38. Ibid.

39. Ibid.

40. Ibid.

41. Annual Report, 1959, Twin Cities Metropolitan Planning Commission, loc. cit., p. 3.

42. Martin, op. cit., p. 57.

43. Metropolitan Population Study, Part II (St. Paul: Twin Cities Metropolitan Planning Commission, 1961), pp. 5, 6.

44. Ibid., p. 20.

45. Martin, op. cit., p. 56.

46. Ibid.

47. Metropolitan Policy and Metropolitan Development (Minneapolis: Citizens League, 1968), p. 29, hereafter cited as Met. Pol. and Met. Dev.

48. Ibid.

49. See pp. 63-64, this Chapter.

50. Met. Pol. and Met. Dev., loc. cit.; Martin, op. cit., p. 58.

51. Martin, loc. cit.

52. Ibid.

53. Loeks, loc. cit.

54. Martin, loc. cit.

55. Andersen, loc. cit.

56. Martin, op. cit., pp. 58-59.

57. _Annual Report, 1960_ (Saint Paul: Twin Cities Metropolitan Planning Commission, 1960), p. 3.

58. _Met. Pol. and Met. Dev._, _loc. cit._

59. Reynold Boezi, Interview, March, 1969.

60. _1965-1966 Biennial Report to the Minnesota Legislature_ (Saint Paul: Twin Cities Metropolitan Planning Commission, 1967), p. 7; Martin, _op. cit._, p. 59; _Met. Pol. and Met. Dev._, _op. cit._, p. 2.

61. Federal Aid Highway Act, 1962 (P.L. 87-866, 76 _Stat._, 1145).

62. _1965-1966 Biennial Report to the Minnesota Legislature_, _loc. cit._; Martin, _loc. cit._; _Met. Pol. and Met. Dev._, _op. cit._, p. 20.

63. _Met. Pol. and Met. Dev._, _op. cit._, p. 37.

64. Federal Aid Highway Act, _loc. cit._

65. _Met. Pol. and Met. Dev._, _op. cit._, p. 20.

66. _Ibid._, p. 30.

67. _1965-1966 Biennial Report to the Minnesota Legislature_, _loc. cit._; _Met. Pol. and Met. Dev._, _loc. cit._

68. _Ibid._

69. _Ibid._, pp. 7-8; Paul D. Spreiregen, _Urban Design: Architecture of Towns and Cities_ (New York: McGraw-Hill Book Company, 1965), p. 169.

PART II

TAMING THE METROPOLIS

CHAPTER **4** DEVELOPMENTS
LEADING TOWARD
METROPOLITAN
REORGANIZATION

OCCASION FOR CHANGE: A CRISIS IN SEWAGE

By the end of the 1950's, the Twin Cities metropolitan area had experienced a rate of growth almost unparalleled in its history--28.7 percent between 1950 and 1960.[1] This rate was tenth among
all major metropolitan areas in the country. Minneapolis and Saint Paul had reached virtual maximum
growth, but the suburbs were exploding at a rate
more than double the national average. Suburban
expansion for the nation during this period amounted
to 47.7 percent. The Twin Cities suburbs, in contrast, increased at the phenomenal rate of 115 percent,[2] fragmenting the local political structure
into "the largest number of governmental subdivisions in any American metropolis. . . ."[3] This
fragmentation of the metropolitan geography, much
of it irrational and gerrymandered, created a crisis
in municipal services which had a direct bearing on
the development of the movement toward metropolitan
government in the Twin Cities.[4]

In September, 1959, Governor Orville L. Freeman called an emergency meeting of Twin Cities'
area mayors and public officials to discuss a recent survey by the State Department of Health of
water wells in suburban communities that showed
serious contamination of ground water. Some 47.5
percent of all wells in thirty-nine suburban communities, involving 63,000 water supplies and serving

77

over 250,000 persons, showed signs of contamination
from elevated concentrations of sewage chamicals--
nitrates and detergents--based on a standard of one
part per million of nitrate nitrogen. Using a
standard of ten parts per million, over 24 percent
were contaminated. In only one community were
wells free of contamination; in five, all wells
were affected. The survey had been undertaken at
the request of a local health officer and a home-
owner in a suburban Hennepin County community when
well water was suspected of causing illness in the
family. In much of the metropolitan area, ground
water is obtainable at depths of from twenty to
one hundred feet. At the same time, the soil of
the area is particularly "favorable to subsurface
disposal of sewage."[5] The state lacked any means
to control residential development, and even though
local governments possessed limited authority to do
so, they exercised this authority with some hesi-
tance. Tract developers, taking advantage of this
situation, built thousands of homes without "provision of permanent facilities for water supply
and sewage disposal."[6] As a result, by 1960, some
400,000 persons in the Twin Cities area were living in such areas; one-quarter million of them
were "drawing water from the same soil formations"
that sewage was being discharged into.[7] The State
Department of Health had noted the possibility of
such recirculation as early as 1950.[8]

The resultant discussion became widespread
throughout the metropolitan community. Dozens of
meetings were held at which numerous suggestions
were broached. The situation became more difficult
when the Federal Housing Authority announced that
it would no longer process loans for homes in suburban communities which could not guarantee the
creation of a central water system within one year.
Almost immediately pressures were created in and
outside of the legislature to establish new sewer
districts in addition to the central cities'
Minneapolis-Saint Paul Sanitary District (MSSD).
Some communities pressed for ties to MSSD for

service on a contractual basis. Efforts were made
in the state legislature to expand the MSSD into a
truly metropolitan sanitary district. Proposals
were made to create a combined water and sewage
special district.

The MPC during this period had undertaken a
metropolitan water study, calling for a state, metropolitan, and locally coordinated program of research, policy formulation, and development of service.[9] It recommended both a state agency to col-
laborate with local governments on service and to
prepare a plan for the area's future water and
sewage needs. Pending legislation to establish
these agencies, the MPC study called upon municipalities to undertake immediate programs to build
new or expand existing local water and sewage systems that could be tied later into a metropolitan
system. A subsequent MPC study noted the close
interrelationship between water supply and sewage.
disposal as parts of the total problem of "water
resource management" and the need to plan the
area's future.[10] These recommendations closely
paralleled in concept the proposal of Joseph Robbie,
Executive Secretary of the Commission on Municipal
Laws (CML), that came to be known as the Robbie report and the center of a full-fledged metropolitan
controversy.[11]

THE ROBBIE REPORT

In April, 1960, Joseph Robbie officially proposed to the CML that it recommend a single multi-
purpose agency to handle the water and sewer problems of the metropolitan area. Testimony of the
State Department of Health, the State Department of
Conservation, the MPC, and the MSSD agreed that a
metropolitan-wide sewage disposal district should
be created. Most of the suburban communities
agreed. The major problem was tying water and
sewer services together, especially deciding whether or not they should be incorporated into an expanded MSSD that had been widely criticized for its

reluctance and inability to service suburban needs
because of a contract system requiring agreements
between second, third, and even fourth parties.[12]
Because of the complexities that these considerations raised, the CML concluded that it propose to
the 1961 legislature the establishment of a solely
"metropolitan Sanitary district" and further study
of state-wide and metropolitan water resources policy. It also gave consideration to creating a governmental mechanism that could assume a variety of
other metropolitan functions, such as transit and
air pollution control, where the area's governments
and legislature agreed. At the time that Robbie
was retained as the CML's Executive Director in
September, 1959 (he was also the Executive Secretary
of the antecedent Commission on Municipal Annexation
and Consolidation), he noted the possible need for
such a multi-purpose agency and proceeded during
the following years to promote the idea.

Robbie's proposal, as contained in the afore-
mentioned memorandum of April, 1960, generated
widespread and heated debate.[13] Many of the area's
officials expressed deep concern at the spectre of
a possible metropolitan government and a resulting
loss of local identify and local consent.[14] To
assuage these fears, Robbie together with the League
of Minnesota Municipalities (LMM) prepared a statement of principles that called for a public service
corporation operated jointly by the area's governments. There would be no loss of local autonomy
and only sewage service would be involved in the
enabling legislation. Augmentation of service
would be through legislation and agreement of a
majority of the area's governments, including both
central cities.

While this proposal satisfied some officials,
others feared that such a complex mechanism would
jeopardize legislative chances for a metropolitan
sanitary district. Many central cities officials
believed that a multi-purpose district would work
against their constituents in favor of the suburbs.
Minneapolis and Saint Paul, they believed, would

foot most of the bill of any expanded system because they already possessed their own--one already
paid for. In turn, suburban interests opposed the
lack of provision for suburban consent and the
greater power to be given to Minneapolis and Saint
Paul. And there was no guarantee that functions
other than sewer and water would not eventually be
joined to the district, with a resultant erosion of
local services and control.[15] Despite denials that
the multi-purpose district would be the vanguard of
metropolitan government--it would be in fact an al-
ternative--few in the area's central cities or suburbs were satisfied with the plan. As one news-
paper put it, "I think it is the beginning of the
end."[16] This comment was indicative of the opposition, even hostility, that Robbie's proposal stimulated in the metropolitan community.[17]

Discussion continued throughout 1960 and 1961.
Efforts to reach a compromise over mutually satisfactory central cities-suburban representation and
costs were made, but failed. Failure carried over
into the legislature where a move to establish a
limited metropolitan sewer district came to naught.
This was due also, in part, to negative feelings
personally aroused by Robbie's forceful presentation of his idea as well as to the fear of its being an opening wedge to metropolitan government.[18]
These hostile feelings were to remain a significant
and negative force for another three years, before
a radical change in public opinion overtook the
community.

In October, 1961, as a result of the failure
of passage of the metropolitan sewer district legislation and the ill feelings generated by the
Robbie proposal, newly elected Governor Elmer L.
Andersen called a conference on metropolitan problems as the first step in preparing a new program
for the 1963 session of the legislature. The conference would lay the groundwork for key area problems, recommend on policy matters, and serve to
educate the public, local officials, and legislators to accept metropolitan approaches as valid

solutions to the area's problems.[19]   The theme of
the conference, "Intergovernmental Relations, A
Basis for Effective Governmental Patterns in Urban
Areas," emphasized the use of traditional lines of
area governments as fully as possible to meet problems of urban growth.   Discussions centered on local as well as metropolitan problems and the means
by which they could be effectively met.   Devices
such as voluntary cooperation and coordination,
metropolitan federation, combined services, contractual services, special single and multi-purpose
districting, etc., were discussed.   It soon became
clear that the participants--state and local officials and leading private persons and organizations
interested in good government--preferred a metropolitan federation approach to area-wide problems.
It would give local units of government a measure
of participation in metropolitan functions and in
those local operations which they could do adequately.   The conference concluded that it was up
to the legislature to create such a metropolitan
mechanism, based upon ideas of the area's representatives.[20]   However, interest lagged and a
nineteen-member coordinating committee that the
Governor appointed in December, 1961, to continue
the conference's work of preparing recommendations
to the 1963 legislature, failed to function.[21]

The metropolitan discussion lay largely quies-
cent during the next two and one-half years.   Because of the ever-increasing problems of local administration and costs generated by rapid growth in
the Twin Cities and other state metropolitan areas,
the legislature created committees and subcommit-
tees on metropolitan affairs.   And the still critical problems of sewage and water confronted the
area, particularly its growing suburban component.
As the 1961 legislature failed to act on these
metropolitan problems, the suburban communities increased their efforts to resolve them locally by
contracting for service with the MSSD or building
their own sewer systems, e.g., communities, mostly
in Anoka County, organized the North Suburban Sanitary Sewer District (NSSSD).   Those communities

fortuitously located directly on the Mississippi or
Minnesota Rivers could build their own systems
without serious restrictions, regardless of the impact elsewhere in the area. In contrast, most of
the suburban communities were separated from major
water courses by as much as several miles and a
number of other political subdivisions. There was
no place to put sewage even if they wanted to dispose of it into their own system. It, therefore,
became increasingly necessary for them to rely upon
service from the MSSD. This increased reliance on
contract servicing led to an unusual dichotomy--a
further split in central cities-suburban relations
while generating a call for metropolitan federation
government.

RESURGENCE OF THE METROPOLITAN DISCUSSION

The only viable means by which forty-five suburban municipalities could solve their sewage disposal problem was to contract the services of the
MSSD. Many of these contracts, rather than being
negotiated with central cities officials, were especially arranged on a subcontracting basis through
other contracting municipalities. Typical of the
arrangements (and instrumental in generating a renewed metropolitan discussion) was the one involving the city of Minneapolis and a second tier suburb, New Hope.[22]

New Hope is a relatively new, incorporated
village of some 3,300 acres to the west of Minneapolis. It began a separate existence as a township
in 1936 and was incorporated in 1953. The 1960
census recorded a population of 3,552; it has an
estimated population today of over 20,000. While
the community is principally Republican (as is the
Mayor), it has been a "professionally planned,"
mainly residential suburb since 1955. Planning is
largely imposed upon it by physical and financial
considerations. The entire village sits on virtually solid clay soil and is consequently incapable of
supporting private (home) sewage systems, e.g.,

septic tanks. It was essential, therefore, to provide public service to meet the pressures of rapid
growth. In 1954, the village sought to tie into
the MSSD system and that required separate contracts
with the city of Minneapolis and neighboring Golden
Valley, which lay between Minneapolis and New Hope.
It was successful in negotiating a contract with
Golden Valley to use the latter's facilities to
move sewage to the MSSD, but failed to get service
when Minneapolis refused its permission. According
to Minneapolis, New Hope's growth would not require
MSSD connection until 1970. Repeated appeals to
Minneapolis for a change failed. The village then
appealed to the State Board of Health for its in-
tercession and received the strong recommendation
for either immediate tie into MSSD or its own system and plant which would discharge effluent sewage
into streams (many of which were in parks) coursing
through Minneapolis and intervening communities.
Finally, Minneapolis, in 1956, acceded to the village's request to tie into the MSSD system. However, instead of resolving the problem over sewage
service, the agreement caused renewed conflict between New Hope and Minneapolis.

In negotiating the contract, Minneapolis insisted upon rates which New Hope considered exces-
sively profitable to the central cities. In 1962,
to strengthen the village's negotiating position,
Mayor Honsey helped organize the Suburban Sanitary
Sewer Commission (SSSC) with other suburbs suffering
the same rate "exploitation." At the same time, he
successfully appealed to the legislature to prohibit
any municipality from taking a profit on the sale of
its service to another municipality. The SSSC then
authorized a consultant to study new sewer charges
and verify SSSC figures should lower rates be challenged in court. After several meetings, Minneapolis agreed to reduce rates to suburban contractees
by an average of 60 percent. While this represented
a victory for New Hope and the other suburbs, the
experience left a "bad taste in their mouths" because of heightened central city-suburban hostili-
ties and the continued lack of a comprehensive approach to the area's service problems.[23]

In 1962, Honsey was elected President of the
Hennepin County League of Municipalities and proceeded to make a politically active organization of
it. For several years, the suburban communities
had become increasingly dissatisfied with the service received from the county long dominated by
Minneapolis. (Four out of five commissioners were
from Minneapolis although the population was about
evenly divided between it and the rest of the county.) Over the years a variety of proposals had
been broached--city-county separation, metropolitan
federation, etc.--but nothing was done until the
controversies of the Robbie report and sewage service contracting overtook the metropolitan area.
With his election, Honsey established a "rural area
development committee" to study the problems of
urbanization and service to the outer reaches of
the county. The committee was headed by D. L.
Gehrman, a former resident of Toronto. Discussions
were also initiated with the Ramsey County League
of Municipalities over mutual problems. The Executive Director of the Ramsey County League, Mickey
Kastner, had coincidentally also come from the
Toronto area and had experience with its metropolitan government.

Over the next two years, Honsey, together with
Gehrman, studied Hennepin County's problems and
discussed area-wide issues with Kastner. During
this period Honsey became convinced that a metropolitan, rather than a simple county-wide approach,
was essential if the area's problems were to be
truly resolved. There was an ever greater need to
provide some kind of rational direction to its
rampant growth. From his discussions with Gehrman
and Kastner, Honsey acquired an increasing interest
in the Toronto experience and officially proposed
that a delegation from the Hennepin County League
go there and study it. On May 14, 1964, the Hennepin County League endorsed the proposal and appointed Honsey and its Executive Director, Vernon E.
Bergstrom (this league's first such staff person),
to go to Toronto and report back their findings.[24]
The two visited Toronto for one week--June 23-30,

1964--and discussed metropolitan government, local
attitudes, distribution of local and metropolitan
functions, public opinions and reactions, and many
other common problems with public officials, community leaders, operating departments, and even the
general public. They issued a report on their reactions to metropolitan Toronto on September 2,
1964.

The Honsey-Bergstrom report commented favorably
on the Toronto experience, described its origins and
history, and strongly recommended the study of a
metropolitan approach to a whole range of area-wide
issues--from traditional planning, through municipal-
metropolitan services, to "health and welfare facilities and programs."[25] It did not recommend adoption of the Toronto system. The report received
considerable coverage in the Minneapolis, Saint
Paul, and suburban press. Honsey and Bergstrom
were quickly invited to talk before various citizen
groups, Leagues of Women Voters, the Citizens League,
the Ramsey County League of Municipalities, committees of the state legislature, and various other
local groups and public bodies. Within a matter of
months, metropolitan government had become an "in"
topic and the metropolitan discussion was revived.

While Honsey and the Hennepin County League of
Municipalities were instrumental in stimulating the
discussion of metropolitan government for the Twin
Cities area, they were not alone. In April, 1964,
Mayors Arthur Naftalin of Minneapolis and George
Vavoulis of Saint Paul had come out strongly for a
"multi-city mechanism . . . achieved . . . with
state authorization."[26] Naftalin, since coming
into office in 1961, had called for greater cooperative efforts to resolve the metropolitan area's
problems. The proposal fitted into a pattern that
many local officials had considered favorably at
Governor Andersen's conference--a "council of governments" type of mechanism with representation
from area legislators and officials that would have
only those powers called for by the legislature.
At the time that the Hennepin County League endorsed

Honsey's proposal to study metropolitan Toronto,
Mayor Kenneth Wolfe of nearby Saint Louis Park
(also an activist in the Hennepin County League)
proposed an "openended" metropolitan federation of
the seven area counties to handle service functions.[27] Other community and professional groups
were showing more concern over local and intermunicipal problems, much of it arising out of the
ground water contamination-sewage service controversy and the Robbie report of 1960-1962. As noted
before, the MPC had continued its educational activities, calling for a metropolitan response to
the area's problems. The Citizens League increased
its studies of the area's problems with a view toward providing more efficient government. The business community was beginning to realize that good
and efficient government was becoming increasingly
important to expanding commercial development, not
only in the Twin Cities, but also throughout the
upper midwest region. But it was the activities of
the Hennepin County League of Municipalities that
served as the catalyst to the renewed metropolitan
discussions in 1964; the other contributors, as
well as this league, built the consensus which
brought about metropolitan government a short three
years later.

NOTES

1. Metropolitan Population Study: Part II
(Saint Paul: Twin Cities Metropolitan Planning
Commission, February, 1961), p. 5.

2. Ibid., p. 12.

3. Report of the Commission on Municipal Annexation and Consolidation (Saint Paul: State of
Minnesota, 1959), p. 9.

4. Report of the Commission on Municipal Laws
(Saint Paul: State of Minnesota, 1961), pp. 6-8,
23-33. Except where otherwise noted, the following
discussion is based on this source.

5. Frank L. Woodward et al., "Experiences with Ground Water Contamination in Unsewered Areas in Minnesota," American Journal of Public Health, LI, 8 (August, 1961), 1130-1136.

6. Report on Water Supply and Sewage Disposal in the Minneapolis-Saint Paul Metropolitan Area (Saint Paul: Minnesota Department of Health, December, 1961), p. 5.

7. Ibid., p. 4.

8. Woodward, op. cit., p. 1131.

9. Metropolitan Water Study: Parts I and II (Saint Paul: Twin Cities Metropolitan Planning Commission, February and July, 1960), passim.

10. Metropolitan Sewerage Study (Saint Paul: Twin Cities Metropolitan Planning Commission, August, 1960), p. 3.

11. Report of the Commission on Municipal Law, pp. 30 and 33-37.

12. Reynold Boezi, Interview, April, 1969; Milton Honsey, Mayor of New Hope, Interview, April, 1969. (Interviews cited are with Stanley Baldinger, unless stated otherwise.) For a discussion of relations between the MSSD and Twin Cities suburbs, see pp. 83-87.

13. Report of the Commission on Municipal Laws, pp. 32-33, Appendix K.

14. Honsey, loc. cit.

15. "Mr. Robbie's Toughest Selling Job," Golden Valley Suburban Press, June 30, 1960.

16. "Newsmen Voice Protest Against Robbie 'Metro' Service Plan," Columbia Heights Record, quoted by Betty Wilson, June 30, 1960.

17.   Ted Kolderie, "Agreement Has Almost Been Reached," _Minneapolis Star_, October 27, 1965.

18.   Editorial, "The Metropolitan Monster," _Fridley News_, June 23, 1960.

19.   Elmer L. Andersen, Interview, April, 1969.

20.   Kolderie, _loc. cit_.

21.   _Ibid_.; Anderson, _loc. cit_.

22.   Honsey, _loc. cit_.

23.   _Ibid_.

24.   Milton C. Honsey and Vernon E. Bergstrom, _Report on the Study of the Municipality of Metropolitan Toronto_ (Minneapolis: Hennepin County League of Municipalities, September 2, 1964), p. 1. (Mimeographed.)

25.   _Ibid_., p. 36.

26.   Kolderie, _loc. cit_.

27.   Carol Honsa, "Federation Suggested," _Minneapolis Star_, May 1, 1964.

CHAPTER **5** CREATING A CONSENSUS:

THE YEARS 1965-1967

AN INFORMAL COALITION

The community-wide discourse generated by the
sewage controversy, the Toronto experience, and problems of metropolitan planning of the early 1960's
was conspicuous in its lack of centralized leadership or strategy. It was not university or elitist
led; it was not foundation inspired or financed; it
was not a concerted and disciplined movement for
more efficient or less costly government; it was not
even a deliberate educational process intended to
sway officialdom and public to the need for metropolitan government.[1] It was, rather, the vocaliza-
tion of a widespread reaction to metropolitan problems that had precise, immediate, and visible im-
pacts locally. The events and issues of the late
1950's and early 1960's apparently had created a
favorable attitude toward metropolitan solutions to
the area's problems. Dissatisfaction over existing
and proposed limited solutions was current. Various
groups and individuals, which can be described best
as an informal coalition, participating in the discussions, transformed these general feelings into a
precise statement of desires representing virtually
all elements of the metropolitan community.[2] A
"sense of urgency" prevailed among the groups for-
malizing the consensus--something had to be done,
not merely to correct existing problems, but to
keep comparable difficulties from arising in the
future.[3]

Leadership in defining the issues and formaliz-
ing the consensus was diffused throughout the metropolitan community. It was most pronounced, however,
among suburban officials and the Citizens League
(initially of Minneapolis, then of Hennepin County,
and finally just "The Citizens League" of the entire
area), a "good government" group. But there were
many other groups involved--political parties, business groups, the MPC, newspapers, politicians,
Leagues of Municipalities, Leagues of Women Voters,
etc.--and each one had its own ideas. Whatever collective strategy may have existed was limited.
Knowledge that state action was a prerequisite to
success of any proposal and that the legislature,
dominated by rural and outstate interests, would be
unresponsive to metropolitan needs in the absence
of a concerted show of strength and a clear metropolitan consensus, forced the protagonists into a
remarkable degree of unity.[4] There was already a
surprising agreement by the end of 1965 on the nature of the area's problems, the kind of legislation
required to solve them, and the need for a metropolitan approach.[5] There remained only the need to define the issues and demands precisely, to organize
their strengths, and to convince the legislature of
essential action. Experience with the sewer bills
between 1959 and 1965 demonstrated the need for this
approach. The consensus was to be the vehicle that
gave the sense of urgency to the metropolitan demands and created a momentum that forced the legislature to act the very first time it faced the issue
of metropolitan government.[6] The legislature could
modify the demands of the metropolitan citizenry,
but could not deny them.

The legislature recognized the heightened interest in the Twin Cities for area reorganization
with a series of visits to other major metropolitan
areas. During 1966, committees of both houses visited the following places: (1) San Francisco and
Los Angeles to study their approaches to the maze
of metropolitan problems afflicting them; (2) Toronto
and Winnipeg, Canada, to see first hand the operations of the metropolitan governments there; and

(3) Washington, D.C., to discuss state-federal relations and grant programs to states and localities with federal officials.

The effort to bring metropolitan government to the Twin Cities area was conspicuous as well by a general lack of opposition, at least effective opposition. Indeed, this may have been a major factor underlying the lack of a centralized leadership or strategy for the metropolitan drive. There simply was no need for such an effort. What little opposition that did exist--Bloomington and some of the outer-ring suburbs, county governments, and certain suburban press--was late in appearing, was badly fragmented, and was characterized by an obvious parochialism and inadequate, if any, alternative proposals.[7] At most, they reinforced outstate opposition or reservations to metropolitan government for the Twin Cities area. Basically, outstate opposition and reservations lay in the fact that the Twin Cities area constituted one-half of the state's population and two-thirds of its wealth and economic development. They feared that the Twin Cities "tail" might wag the state "dog." Further, the Conservatives in the Senate represented the traditional philosophy of the legislature: The state was supreme, the seat of sovereignty, and the legislature was the principal means by which its power could be exercised. For practical reasons such powers can be and are delegated to local units of government and state bodies as agents of the state.[8]

MEMBERS OF THE COALITION

The Citizens League

According to the mast head in its reports and publications, the Citizens League

> is a nonpartisan, independent educational organization of 3,600 members, founded in 1952, and dedicated to the improvement of local government in

> the Twin Cities area. . . . Member-
> ship is open to the public. The
> League's annual budget is financed
> by annual dues . . . and contributions
> from more than 600 businesses, founda-
> tions and other organizations.[9]

It has a full-time professional staff. The group
is highly respected for its purpose, quality of
work, and the participation of its membership,
which is drawn from a wide range of professions,
local officials, trades, business, industry, labor,
and similar segments of the Twin Cities community.
They represent the same high quality and sense of
involvement, perhaps even more, that characterizes
the general population. As noted in the preceding
section, the League originally focused its efforts
on Minneapolis and then Hennepin County before becoming a metropolitan-wide organization. It is
considered the single most influential organization
in crystallizing a metropolitan-wide public opinion
favorably disposed toward metropolitan solutions to
metropolitan problems and in defining issues. This
would be true, if for no other reason than it most
accurately reflected a cross section of the metropolitan community at the leadership level.

Beginning in 1963, the League began to study a
series of issues confronting the metropolitan area,
including sewage, solid waste disposal, transit,
annexation and incorporation, and comprehensive
planning. With the rise of the "metropolitan discussion" following the sewage controversy and
Toronto trip of the Hennepin County League of Municipalities, the Citizens League increasingly became
concerned with problems of metropolitan growth and
how it could be best accomplished. In May, 1965,
the League proposed that the 1965 legislature undertake a study of the area's metropolitan and intermunicipal problems and needs and prepare recommendations to the 1967 legislature on their resolution,
utilizing alternative governmental structures and a
strengthened planning function to meet them.[10]
While there was no legislative follow-up, it did

contribute substantially to the discussion and to
pointing up problems of directing the area's growth.

During the spring of 1966, the League noted
that a principal issue to face the 1967 legislature
would be an increased demand for a coordinated approach to solving the metropolitan area's problems.
In June, it organized a Metropolitan Affairs Committee to study the area's problems and "develop recommendations for the 1967 Legislature."[11] Between
mid-June and November, 1966, it held twenty-four
public meetings at which area leaders in business,
labor, local and state government, education, politics, the professions, the mass media, and community
affairs experts in pertinent fields were heard and
questioned.[12] At the same time, it reviewed and
considered league reports on a variety of issues,
such as those listed at the beginning of this paragraph, and reports of the MPC and the Committee for
Economic Development. A summary of the minutes of
the meeting was published in November, 1966, and
distributed to "governmental, civic, business and
labor leaders of the Twin Cities area. . . ."[13]

The summary listed seventeen area-wide problems
which the various speakers and groups considered important: sewage disposal, public transportation,
highways, parks and open space, area planning, tax
assessments, inequitable distribution of business
and industrial properties, metropolitan zoo, refuse
disposal, area zoning, water supply, air pollution,
police, annexation and incorporation, Dutch elm
disease, libraries, and debt financing.[14] It also
noted the shortcomings of existing metropolitan
structures (single purpose metropolitan districts),
the need for a more effective structure to make decisions affecting future metropolitan growth, the
need for an adequate metropolitan agency to deal
with the federal government, and major points of
agreement and disagreement on metropolitan proposals.[15] There was complete agreement that the
Twin Cities metropolitan area was but one economic
and social unit and its area-wide problems should
be resolved on a metropolitan basis; that legislative

action was necessary to create a metropolitan organization; and that it should be directed by a "broadly representative policy board." It should take responsibility for metropolitan planning, review local requests for federal funds, constitute the vehicle of a "metropolitan consensus," and, apparently, review budgets, and coordinate activities of metropolitan functions as well as exercise "policy control" over major metropolitan function decisions. There was also substantial agreement on geographical coverage (five to eight counties) and representation according to population. Disagreement existed on whether members should be elected or appointed, or represent local public officials or the citizenry at large, and whether it should have operating powers or not.[16] There was insufficient information to determine metropolitan attitudes on taxation and local consent (home rule). Some one hundred written responses were received from community leaders and they "were unanimous in urging some form of metropolitan government."[17]

The Board of Directors of the League approved the committee's findings in February, 1967, and called for a directly elected, nonhome rule metropolitan agency exercising "only those powers and responsibilities specifically granted by the Legislature. . . ."[18] Representation would be from senatorial districts in the seven-county area, totaling twenty-nine to thirty-one members depending on the apportionment of four districts partially in the area. Members would serve staggered four-year terms and function on a part-time basis. It would not replace any existing unit of local government or exercise any "major new powers at the metropolitan level," but, rather, coordinate existing ones.[19] The Board of Directors did not set priorities on the assumption of specific functions. These findings focused the attention of both the legislature and Twin Cities community on the issues to be confronted and closely paralleled the work of other groups and individuals working toward metropolitan solutions. (For a comparison with other proposals, see Table 4.)

TABLE 4

The Consensus: Summary of Proposals for a Metropolitan Council

Group[a]	Seven County Coverage	General Purpose Government	State Agency	Direc Elect Counc
1. Citizens League	Yes	Yes	No	Yes
2. Metro Section of the LMM	Yes	Yes	No	Yes
3. Hennepin County League	Yes	Yes	No	Yes
4. Ramsey County League	Yes	Yes	No	No, local appt'
5. Governor	Yes	Yes	No	Yes
6. Chambers of Commerce	Yes	Yes	No	Yes
7. St. Thomas Conference	Yes	Yes	No	Yes
8. Political Parties	Yes	Yes	**	**
9. Metropolitan Planning Commission	Yes	Yes	No	Yes
10. Frenzel-Odgahl Bills	Yes	Yes	No	Yes
11. Ashbach-Newcome Bills	Yes	Yes	Yes	No, Gover appoi

[a]DFL--Yes on direct elections and equal population districts, no on a state agency; Republicans--equivocal.

qual ulation tricts	Full-Time Executive	Minimum Operating Functions	Open Federal Multi-Purpose	Coordinate Special Districts	Modify Local Consent	Review Federal Grants
Yes	Yes	Yes	Yes	Yes	Yes	-
Yes	Yes	Yes	Yes	Yes	Yes	-
Yes	Yes	Yes	Yes	Yes	Yes	-
Yes	Yes	Yes	Yes	Yes	Yes	-
Yes	Yes	Yes	Yes	Yes	Yes	-
Yes	-	Yes	Yes	Yes	Yes	-
Yes	No comments	Yes, not specif.	Yes	No comment	Yes	-
**	-	Yes	Yes	Yes	-	-
Yes	-	Yes	Yes	Yes	Yes	-
Yes	Yes	Yes	Yes	Yes	-	Yes
No, at- rge	Yes	No	No	Yes	-	Yes

97

The Metropolitan Section of the LMM

The Metropolitan Section served as the "semi-official" voice of local government officials by defining and achieving an internal consensus and representing it to the legislature.[20] The LMM, through its Metropolitan Affairs Committee, had long been interested and active in resolving the various metropolitan problems of the state, not just those of the Twin Cities, although these were admittedly the most critical. It had been instrumental, as noted in Chapter 3, under Ludwig, in bringing about the MPC. Between 1953 and 1957, it had arranged or participated in more than a half dozen conferences on metropolitan problems. With the establishment of the MPC and the start of its work, the LMM's Committee on Metropolitan Affairs fell into inaction. Pressures from growth within the Twin Cities area, however, were increasing. By 1964, concern about them among area officials had risen to the point where demands were being heard for an organization that would vocalize their collective interests and prepare legislation.[21]

In response to these demands, the LMM reactivated its Metropolitan Affairs Committee to determine how the area's municipalities could best organize to deal with their problems. Impetus to do this came from the Hennepin County League of Municipalities (under the presidency of Honsey), which found it could not resolve the problems alone. Municipal officials soon realized that metropolitan pressures required a new organization which was certain to come about. The only question was whether it should be within or without the LMM. The existing committee structure, while helpful in the past, was not adequate to improve and protect municipal interests in the Twin Cities area. Demands were for an organization devoted exclusively to the Twin Cities area as well as for adequate staffing and financing. However, to have set up a new and separate body would have bled the LMM of its "primary resources."[22] The LMM, rather than fight the move for a Twin Cities-wide organization, amended its constitution in June, 1966, to provide for a new, semiautonomous Metropolitan Section devoted exclusively to the area's municipalities and their problems. The Metropolitan Section was formally organized in September, 1966, with membership from municipalities representing about 80 percent of the area's population, and immediately set to work preparing for the 1967 session of the legislature.

By February, 1967, the Metropolitan Section had worked out a general six-point proposal which it was presenting to the legislature. It was developed after four months of both extensive and intensive discussion among local officials, particularly in the four more urbanized counties of Hennepin, Ramsey, Anoka, and Dakota. Because of differences in approach, attitudes, and needs, the final program represented a compromise legislative proposal and, therefore, was less detailed and comprehensive than that advocated by other groups. Yet, the program testified to the remarkable degree of concurrence that had grown over the years among Twin Cities officialdom for it closely paralleled the proposals of such reformers as the Citizens League.

In its testimony before the 1967 legislature, the Metropolitan Section noted that the opinion of area officials, not too many years before, had been sharply divided between those looking toward some form of metropolitan consolidation and those who considered area-wide coordination almost "subversive."[23] Since then, opinions had significantly changed to a middle approach. It noted that

> . . . while mayors and councilmen, as
> a group, are conservative in their
> orientation and although they are
> very jealous of the prerogatives of
> local government, there is a general
> recognition and acceptance of the
> need for some type of governmental
> structure encompassing the seven-
> county metropolitan area. The pur-
> pose of such a unit . . . is not to

rationalize the structure of local
government or to perform services
which have traditionally been provided
at the municipal level, but rather to
assume responsibilities and render
services which are not, in a histori-
cal sense, municipal functions and
which municipalities, either individually, or collectively, are not capable
of performing.[24]

As the result, and despite its being a "compromise"
program, the six points proposed were sufficiently
clear for all to understand: (1) a single multi-
purpose, open-ended district to perform and coordinate service functions while preventing the "proliferation of single purpose districts"; (2) minimum initial functions to provide for planning, sanitary sewage, and transit, with possible control
over storm water, air pollution, solid waste disposal, mosquitos, preservation of open space, and
the coordination of airport operations and civil
defense; (3) a governing body to consist of thirty
members based on population and representing state
senatorial districts; (4) terms of office for governing board members to be four years, concurrent
and "by direct election"; (5) members to be part-
time officials; and (6) a full-time chairman chosen
by the board to serve as its executive. As the
area's population was almost evenly divided between
the central cities and their suburbs, chances of
domination by either was considered minimal. The
Metropolitan Section also considered the area's
problems to be in need of such immediate action
that it proposed the possible appointment of an interim board pending action of an elected one in
1968.[25] (For comparison with other council proposals, see Table 4.)

Underlying all these proposals was the belief
that policy planning was an integral part of a
proper decisionmaking process if the metropolitan
structure was to be successful.[26] It was both to
plan and to do--at least to insure that its

proposals came about. The area had gone through
ten frustrating years of planning in the abstract
and of even more with operations of single purpose
districts not necessarily responsive to the area's
collective interests and needs. There should now
be no distinction between the planning and service
functions; they were parts of the same proces. The
power to "do" was necessary; local officials fully
realized that complete voluntary cooperation and
subordination of local self-interest were impossible.[27]

County Leagues of Municipalities
and Local Officials

Related closely to the activities of the Metropolitan Section of the League of Minnesota Municipalities was that of the area's county Leagues of
Municipalities and local officials working separately. Only four of the area's counties--Hennepin,
Ramsey, Anoka, and Dakota--have local leagues. The
other three--Washington, Carver, and Scott--are the
least urbanized and developed; local officials, if
affiliated, are members of the state league's Metropolitan Section. At the beginning of the metropolitan discussion, the county leagues projected, as
might be expected, a more provincial attitude toward
solution of their problems.[28] As the discussion
generated and their own involvement in deliberations
increased, they realized that there existed a great
community of interests and agreement in approach to
resolving their problems.

By the time the legislature considered the
various proposals for a metropolitan council, the
local leagues had achieved independent positions
nearly identical in substance to that of the Metropolitan Section and other groups. (An indication
of the closeness of interests and cooperation between the county leagues and the Metropolitan Section is that the Ramsey and Anoka County Leagues of
Municipalities maintain their offices adjacent to
those of the Metropolitan Section at the University
of Minnesota in Minneapolis and Hennepin County,

but consider it "neutral" ground.)   The proposals
of the Hennepin County League were almost identical
to those of the Metropolitan Section, calling for a
seven-county, multi-purpose operating and coordinating body, with membership based on population and
directly elected by the people.[29]   (For details, see
Table 4.)   The proposals of the Ramsey County League,
again, closely paralleled those of the other leagues,
differing only in one significant area.   It proposed
that members of the Metropolitan Council be appointed
by a caucus of local councils of city, village, or
township boards; members would represent senatorial
districts and be based on population.[30]   Appointment
by local officials was defended on the grounds that
it gave small communities a more effective voice
than would elections.   In addition to the powers
shown in Table 4, it proposed that the Council be
empowered to establish uniform tax assessment
throughout the metropolitan area and to study the
area's problems with respect to water resources and
conservation, health inspection and control, special
police communications and investigations, and public records.[31]   The Anoka and Dakota County Leagues
did not exist in 1967; their officials worked
through the Metropolitan Section of the LMM.

In general, local officials worked through
their county leagues and the Metropolitan Section
of the LMM.   A few individuals also worked separately.   Men like Honsey, Mayor of New Hope, Wolfe,
Mayor of St. Louis Park, and Stanley Olson, Mayor
of Richfield, came up with specific proposals.
Honsey advocated an appointed federation of municipalities as a state agency possessing substantially
the same powers as those proposed by the groups discussed above.[32]   Wolfe proposed an open-ended federation.   Olson sought to achieve a COG type arrange-
ment, but later joined his efforts to the LMM's
Metropolitan Section.[33]   Each later came to support
an open-ended multi-purpose, operating, and directly
elected metropolitan federation unit of government.[34]

Central city Mayors Naftalin of Minneapolis
and Thomas Byrne of Saint Paul went through a

similar metamorphosis. As noted earlier, both had
proposed a COG structure, but they came to support
the stronger proposals for an elected metropolitan
government with operating powers.[35] Indeed, Naftalin's ideas on a strong metropolitan government,
including control over education, law enforcement,
welfare, land use controls, total financing arrangements, and eventual metropolitan consolidation for
the area had long been a disquieting irritant to
the whole "informal coalition," frightening those
wanting an effective but more limited structure.[36]
Byrne's ideas (and those of his predecessor Vavoulis)
were more modest, tending to agree with the position
of his Minneapolis and suburban colleagues. This
may have been in part because of a sensitivity to
the fears of its suburbs to Saint Paul's domination
and because Saint Paul is a slower, more conservative city than Minneapolis.[37] In any event, both
central cities and suburban officials strongly endorsed the concept of a metropolitan government,
popularly elected, and operating specific service
functions. This position was to be even more
strongly supported in February, 1967, and after,
when Senator Gordon Rosenmeier proposed an appointive state agency with only coordinating and policy
planning powers as an alternative to the metropolitan consensus. (For a fuller discussion, see Chapter 7. County officials' views are discussed below
in this Chapter, pp. 120-24.)

Political Parties

     The two parties strongly endorsed the concept
of a multi-purpose metropolitan body with effective
powers to insure implementation and coordination of
plans and responsible to the area's electorate. It
would perform only those functions essentially metropolitan in nature, leaving traditional local
functions to municipalities, townships, and counties. (For details of each party's proposals, see
Table 4.) The 1966 Republican platform, noting
that the most critical problems needing metropolitan solution--sewage disposal, mass transit, regional parks and open space, tax revenues, and

planning--centered in the seven-county Twin Cities
area and called for "an open end or multiple purpose
metropolitan district or governmental unit. . . ."[38]
It noted, too, that the area constituted almost one-
half of the state's population and two-thirds of its
economic wealth. The metropolitan body, therefore,
should be structured to insure that it would not adversely affect the continued vitality of local government or threaten to become more important ·than
the state government. It should operate under the
ultimate control of the legislature "through a delegation of power by appropriate legislation" and be
subject in some degree to coordination with the
state's executive in the administration of programs.[39] Members of the metropolitan body would be
either directly elected, composed of legislators
themselves, or appointed by the legislature directly or through delegation.[40]

These hedged proposals were obviously the
product of considerable compromise between the
area's proponents for effective metropolitan government, a great many of whom (possibly the majority) were local officials and outstate interests.
The platform proposal was written largely by James
Hetland, Jr., Chairman of the Republican Advisory
Committee on Intergovernmental Relations. Hetland,
it should be noted, until June, 1969, was also a
member of the Board of Directors of the Citizens
League, one of its past presidents and, more important, a vigorous advocate of a strong, operating,
and popularly elected metropolitan council.[41] Two
years later, 1968, the Republicans came out for
effective administrative controls over metropolitan
service functions, e.g., sewers and sewage treatment.[42] The change was brought about, evidently,
by an even stronger metropolitan consensus and the
happy results of the Metropolitan Council's work
since its establishment in 1967 as well as by a
heightened realization of the need for "positive,
decision making powers" if the Council was to continue successfully.[43]

The DFL, in contrast, was more precise in its
proposals, calling for the

establishment of a multipurpose district for the Twin Cities metropolitan
area, to be granted specified powers
and functions which are metropolitan
in scope and cannot be effective or
economically provided by each individual municipality. All powers that
are not specifically assigned to the
multipurpose district should be retained by the local units of government. . . . The policy-making body
of the metropolitan district should
be popularly elected from evenly apportioned districts. Among those
functions which are metropolitan in
character and whose management may be
delegated to the multipurpose district are mass transportation, air and
water pollution, sanitary sewage disposal, regional planning, equalization
of tax assessments, pure water supply,
recreation and parks, and all those
functions now managed by single-
purpose metropolitan districts.[44]

As noted early in this study, the DFL is the syn-
thesis of radical, liberal, and other Democratic
elements of the state, with the locus of its power
in the central cities area and in academic institutions. Consequently, its metropolitan proposals
should be expected to reflect more precisely the
metropolitan consensus and avoid a Twin Cities-
outstate compromise. The surprising thing is the
closeness of approach of both parties, despite the
considerable compromise reflected in the Republican
proposals. It should be noted also that both Republicans and DFLers of the area worked with and
contributed to the positions of the groups described
above--the Citizens League, the Metropolitan Section
of the LMM, county Leagues of Municipalities, and
individual efforts. In turn, the parties reflected
the sentiment of the consensus.

It must be remembered that 1966, besides being the year in which a metropolitan consensus

crystallized, was also an election year and, as
such, the party platforms represented the views and
interests of the parties' supporters. For the Republicans, metropolitan proposals were a critical
balance between the Twin Cities and outstate partisans; for the DFL, they were the presentation of
members' views in its stronghold of the Twin Cities
area. The nominal leaders of the parties--Karl F.
Rolvaag, DFL incumbent, and Harold LeVander, Repub-
lican--were engaged in a heated contest for the gov-
ernorship. Rolvaag, as early as February, 1966,
called for a new multi-purpose metropolitan agency
to handle a variety of functions, including sewage
disposal, transit, air and water pollution, and
zoning.[45] Members would be elected local and county
officials. He maintained that voluntary intergovernmental cooperation, stronger county government, municipal annexation, single purpose districts, and
similar proposals were inadequate; a new, more comprehensive and effective structure was necessary to
resolve the area's problems.[46] As the campaign progressed, his position and that of the 1966 DFL party
platform grew closer and coincided, calling for a
directly elected, open-ended, multi-purpose, operating, and coordinating metropolitan council.

Republican candidate LeVander, shortly before
the election, proposed the creation of "an agency
with policy and decisional powers to coordinate,
plan and perform certain limited functions. . . ."[47]
He noted, as did the Republican platform, the overwhelming role that the Twin Cities area played in
the state and the fact that in the ensuing thirty-
five years the area would more than double in size.
The Twin Cities area, consequently, needed

> a new agency of local government capa-
> ble of . . . dealing with the broad
> problems which transcend the existing
> political boundaries of our munici-
> palities and counties . . . [and]
> which can provide order and coordina-
> tion to . . . development. . . . We
> must have a local unit of government

> which is <u>representative</u> of and <u>re-
> sponsible</u> to the people who are
> affected by its decisions.[48]

He then went on to echo the party's platform, proposing a policymaking body for the seven-county
area, with sufficient authority and funds to conduct research and plan and carry out its policies.
Members would be elected or legislatively appointed.
There was no need to incorporate special purpose
functions into the agency as long as "ultimate coordination" of their functions rested with it.   The
agency would "be subject to the ultimate control by
the State Legislature. . . ."[49]   While he earnestly
believed in strong local government, "the state
must also have a voice . . . through the legislature [and] through its delegated agency, the Metropolitan Council. . . ."[50]

      Governor LeVander, in his inaugural address of
January 4, 1967, came forth with a significantly
stronger metropolitan council. He recommended a
metropolitan council for the seven-county area to
"coordinate the functions of the present single purpose districts" and have "operating authority over
most of these services: (1) sewage disposal,
(2) planning parks and open space, (3) transit system, (4) maintaining a central data center, (5) air
and water pollution, (6) planning, [and] (7) approval of federal aid applications from local communities."[51] Representation on the council would
be responsible to the metropolitan community, yet
function under legislative authority. Members
would be either directly elected by district or appointed by each district's legislators.[52]   (For a
comparison with other council proposals, see Table
4.) During the course of legislative battle over
the kind of metropolitan council to be created--
elective and operating as proposed in the Ogdahl-
Frenzel Bill or appointive and coordinating as proposed in the Ashbach-Newcome Bill--the Governor reluctantly stated his position as closer to the
former.[53] He preferred to have had an elective and
operating council, but realized that the probable

choice (quite rightly) was really between an elective, nonoperating council and an appointed, functioning body. He was convinced that the latter was
preferable.[54] Appointment, however, should reflect
area interests to keep the council local in character. Despite his sympathy for the local advocates
of an elected, operating council, he deliberately
refrained from actively participating in the legislative battle--an action characteristic of the traditional role played by the governor where the
legislature is the locus of power.[55]

The Twin Cities Business Community

Local business leaders played a vital role in
coalescing the consensus favorable to metropolitan
government and presenting it in unmistakable terms
to the 1967 legislature. For a decade they had become increasingly involved in local and area-wide
activities, ranging from the acquisition of major
league sports to the improving of urban life and
governmental reform--all with the view toward improving the area's economic position relative to
that of other major midwestern centers. The area
possesses a strong "homegrown" economic base--
Honeywell, General Mills, Pillsbury, Archer-Daniels-
Midland, Gamble-Skogmo, Land O'Lakes Creameries,
Bemis, Control Data Corp., the Dayton Corp., 3M,
Hoerner-Waldorf, Northwest Orient Airlines, Burling-
ton-Northern, Minneapolis Grain Exchange, Hamm Brew-
ing Co., West Publishing Company, Farmers Union
Central Exchange, Economics Laboratories, Mutual
Service Insurance Co., U.S. Bedding, Minneapolis-
Moline--a base which stresses development within
the area rather than elsewhere.[56] In addition,
such companies as UNIVAC (Division of Sperry Rand),
Whirlpool Corp., Toni, Rayette-Fabergé, Weyerhauser
Co., Montgomery Ward and Co., Sears Roebuck, Swift
and Co., Armour, and the Prudential Insurance Company of America, etc., maintain operational or regional headquarters in the area and are involved in
improving the area's economic vitality.

The area's Chambers of Commerce put forward a nearly united front to the 1967 legislature in support of a seven-county, thirty-one man, popularly elected, operating and coordinating service district responsible for metropolitan planning, sewage disposal and treatment, transit, mosquito control, and an area zoo.[57] (For details, see Table 4.) The service district would be the product of the legislature and ultimately responsible to it; only those functions authorized by the legislature would be performed. It would be neither a state agency nor a "home rule" government, but a responsible area-wide unit of government which would direct the area's growth without compromising local government.[58] The need was for a governmental structure to help the metropolitan community plan and make rational decisions on public investments to insure the best possible development of the area. A leading Minneapolis businessman and Chamber member, Dennis W. Dunne (Vice President of a major banking corporation and subsequently a member of the Metropolitan Council), claimed just one month before the legislature was to meet that "The time has come to merge the planning function of the MPC with a meaningful, decisionmaking operating unit of government."[59]

Enthusiasm for such an enterprise in the business community did not emerge quickly nor without substantial effort. During the spring and summer of 1965, three ranking officials in the Minneapolis Chamber of Commerce--Dunne, Chairman of the Legislative Committee; Russell Laxson, President, and Lloyd Brandt, Manager of the Legislative Department--became concerned that the Chamber was not adequately participating in the metropolitan discussion taking place.[60] Dunne, after looking at the local governmental scene, believed the Chamber had a significant role to play in the developments which were taking place. He, with Laxson and Brandt, was able to persuade the main body of the Chamber to accept greater involvement in metropolitan affairs. The idea of a multi-purpose service district was enticing; it could be an "end run" to

meet the area's needs, bypassing unresponsive special purpose districts and avoiding metropolitan
consolidation or "government."[61]

It was apparent, however, that the job of involving the business community of the entire area
could not be done by the Minneapolis Chamber alone.
This was brought home most effectively during September, 1965, when the Chamber of Minneapolis and
the Chamber of Saint Paul each undertook trips to
New York, seeking major investment in their respective cities. Until the last minute, the respective
trips were unknown to the other Chamber and the
duplicate receptions in the East proved a discour-
aging element in obtaining the desired investment.
This fiasco was to be the last of the failures in
communication between the two because it proved the
need for cooperation.[62] In December, 1965, Dunne
requested that Laxson call John Hay, Executive Director of the Saint Paul Chamber, to solicit his help
in organizing the business community. Hay's response was quick and enthusiastic. After seven
weeks of work, the two Chambers called a joint meeting with the suburban Chambers and with another commercial group, the Upper Midwest Research and Development Council (UMRDC). As a result of this
meeting, a fifteen-member Urban Study and Action
Committee was organized with Dunne as Chairman and
Ron Pratt of Saint Paul as Secretary. Membership
was divided equally three ways--five from Minneapolis, five from Saint Paul, and five from suburban
Chambers representing some twenty groups. The
group met through the spring and summer of 1966,
developing an eight-point recommendation in September, 1966, for consideration by each area Chamber.[63]

Initial reaction to the study group's recommendations was mixed. Over the fall and winter months,
the Chambers from both central cities and five major
suburban groups--Brooklyn Center, Fridley, Saint
Louis Park, South Saint Paul, and West Saint Paul--
endorsed the recommendations in toto or in concept.
These seven Chambers represented almost 6,000 of
the 8,200 members of all area Chambers, or 73 percent

of the total.[64] The only major holdout was that of
Bloomington, an act characteristic of that city's
opposition to the whole metropolitan discussion.
In general, the Bloomington Chamber remained aloof
from the deliberations of the Urban Study and Action Committee and formally opposed its recommendations before the legislature. Yet, several of
Bloomington's (and the area's) major concerns independently endorsed the eight-point recommendation.[65]

    With close to three-quarters of the area Cham-
bers' membership endorsing the proposal for an
elected metropolitan, multi-purpose operating district, Dunne organized a group to prepare a draft
bill for the legislature. The group included
Brandt, Tom Anding for the Upper Midwest Research
and Development Council, Ted Kolderie of the Minneapolis Star, Verne Johnson and Hetland of the Citizens League, William Frenzel, Conservative Representative from Golden Valley, Clayton LeFevere
(attorney for the group and, later, Council member),
and Dunne. The end product was the Frenzel Bill
for a metropolitan agency for the Twin Cities area.
Working at the same time on a separate bill was
Senator Harmon Ogdahl, also a member of the Minneapolis Chamber. These two bills were almost identical and were later combined and submitted to the
legislature. (See Chapter 7.)

    Despite the apparent overwhelming support of
the business community for a metropolitan approach
to resolving the area's growth problems, it was
felt necessary to demonstrate even greater support
and effort, particularly among top level business
and industrial leaders. The Chamber of Commerce
group obtained the cooperation of the UMRDC to
garner their support. The UMRDC is a nonprofit
corporation, organized in 1959 by a number of business and industrial leaders in the Ninth Federal
Reserve District who were concerned with the district's lagging development.[66] It is "financed by
money from the Ford Foundation, business firms,
private foundations, Hill Family Foundation and
individuals."[67] Its major function, as its name

implies, is "promoting the community welfare and economic growth of the Ninth Federal Reserve District . . . [through a] district-wide research program. . . ."[68] Groups throughout the district have relied increasingly upon the UMRDC for help in resolving problems of economic development, local government, trade promotion, processing of information, education, and similar programs.

The UMRDC's response to the invitation of the Chamber of Commerce was to undertake the Twin Cities Metropolitan Seminar on Governmental Structure, held on November 10, 1966, at St. Thomas College in Saint Paul. The Seminar was held at the height of the metropolitan discussion and included virtually every major business, industrial, and labor leader in the metropolitan area, several of whom subsequently testified in behalf of a metropolitan council before the legislature. Included among those active at the Seminar were Donald Dayton, Board Chairman of Dayton's Incorporated; Philip Nason, President of the First National Bank of Saint Paul; and Earl Ewald, President of Northern States Power Company--the area's most important business representatives. Also attending were area public officials, state legislators, community leaders, and members of the MPC. This was the first time that the highest echelon of the business community had met with government and community leaders to express their views on resolving the area's problems.[69]

In anticipation of the Seminar, the UMRDC had prepared a thirty-three page background paper entitled "Governing the Twin Cities Area."[70] It covered in a comprehensive fashion the nature of the metropolitan problem, the area's pattern of government, issues of and alternatives to metropolitan reorganization, the federal role, the Twin Cities' problems and proposals to resolve them, and current approaches to meeting metropolitan problems. The Seminar itself was devoted to a series of panel discussions on sewage disposal, environmental pollution, transportation, parks and open space, special districts and metropolitan reorganization, metropolitan planning, and business involvement in

community development in Pittsburgh, San Francisco,
Detroit, Cleveland, and Kansas City.[71] Toward the
end of the session, a questionnaire was distributed
to the participants to ascertain their views on the
issues discussed. At the closing dinner, Dayton
reported that almost 75 percent believed that a new
unit of government--one having "more than just a cooperative effort" among local government officials--
was necessary to resolve the area's problems.[72] The
participants further agreed that (1) the metropolitan area was one urban community, (2) the new governmental unit should be empowered to act, not just
to advise, (3) the unit should be responsible to
the local electorate, (4) local units of government
should not be able to block efforts of the new unit,
(5) the 1967 session of the legislature should act
"urgently" to get metropolitan reform started, and
(6) continued active participation in these efforts
by business leaders was necessary.[73] (For details
and comparison with other proposals, see Table 4.)

These initial efforts of the UMRDC demonstrated
to its Board of Directors the continuing need for a
"strategy of growth" in which the business community
should participate.[74] Public decisions on development had a profound effect on their commercial interests; the location of highways, sewage and water
service, zoning, etc., would determine in large
part the location of their investments. The business community was interested in maximizing economic growth and improving the area's competitive
position with respect to other centers and the national market. The discussions at the Seminar and
those which followed showed the need to anticipate
such growth and its pressures. Consequently, planning should be an integral part of policy formation
and decisionmaking. And a governmental mechanism
to achieve this was essential--even more important
than providing economically efficient service.[75]
The conclusions, made known to the legislature during the course of its deliberations on the Metropolitan Council, continued to be of major concern
to the UMRDC and the cause for another appeal to
the 1969 session of the legislature.[76]

The Metropolitan Planning Commission

Perhaps the most significant or central participant in the metropolitan discussion and "informal
coalition" was the MPC. As noted in Chapter 3, the
MPC had neither completed the programs it had undertaken nor formalized arrangements by which they
might be adopted or implemented. But its work--and
the quality of the work--was vital to crystallizing
the metropolitan consensus.[77]

First and foremost of the contributions of the
MPC was its role in "educating" the Twin Cities
area community. From the outset in 1957, it had
sought to identify and describe the area's metropolitan problems and to point the way toward their
solutions. The reports, bulletins, newsletters,
meetings, and talks came to be widely accepted in
the community and were, as the area's Citizens
League noted in 1968, "largely, . . . perhaps primarily," responsible for "the basic change in the
attitude of the community which occurred between
1957 and 1967." The community had not been "particularly receptive either to the concept of metropolitan planning, or even to the existence of specifically 'metropolitan' problems at the start."[78]

A second major contribution--one which was related to the foregoing educational activities, but
which had a greater impact on the character of the
council, i.e., its planning focus, was the MPC's
emphasis on "the process of development." Rather
than concentrating its efforts on the conventional
preparation of plans, the Joint Program chose to
raise the issue of governmental powers and organi-
zation--the means by which implementation of plans
could be achieved and growth directed.[79] The Citizens League has noted that:

> The Joint Program dealt not so much
> in specific proposals about <u>what</u>
> . . . that is, what roads or transit
> lines or commercial centers or parks
> . . . were to be built, as in

> proposals for <u>the way in which deci-</u>
> <u>sions were to be made</u> about the loca-
> tion of these major facilities. The
> thrust of the effort was to under-
> stand the process of development, and
> to bring the key elements of the pro-
> cess under public control. . . .
> This was part of a conscious decision
> to concentrate . . . on implementation,
> rather than newer and more sophisticated
> research techniques.[80]

The development guide (which came out in April,
1968) reinforced this approach; its entire first
section is devoted to the role of government and
how it can be utilized to determine goals, policies,
and financing of programs.[81] Earlier, Planning
Director Loeks, in appraising the Commission's approach to its plans, stated:

> In the task of guiding development,
> we note weaknesses in two areas--in
> research technique and in the making
> of development decisions. The Joint
> Program set out to balance efforts to
> improve the way in which development
> decisions are made . . .; it was our
> belief that research techniques need
> to be more sophisticated than our
> ability to make decisions based on re-
> search. . . . Our crude research pro-
> cedures were perfection itself com-
> pared to existing procedures for
> making organized metropolitan-wide
> development decisions.[82]

Traditional map type plans were rejected as not indicative of how development would be achieved and
were, therefore, much more subject to being ignored
by public officials. The major thrust of the effort was to prepare sets of alternative policies
evolved from specific goals for the development of
the area, a process which led logically to programs
to be put into effect.[83] This thinking along policy

lines not only served as a precedent for the community in consideration of metropolitan problems,
but also molded, or conditioned, the manner in
which subsequent consideration was given to proposals for a metropolitan council. In a very real
sense, the MPC not only educated the community to
think of metropolitan solutions to many of its problems, but also caused the community to think of the
manner in which these solutions could be achieved.
It introduced policy planning as an integral part
of the governmental process. It would seem only
natural, therefore, that a metropolitan council,
both when under consideration in the community and
when finally realized, would be conceived primarily
as a policy planning body with sufficient powers to
insure implementation of its plans and programs.

Another--third--way in which the MPC contributed to the establishment of the Council was through
a series of proposals on metropolitan governmental
organizations. Beginning in December, 1964, the
MPC initiated a discussion of the role of government in establishing development policies at the
metropolitan level, based upon the ten ways in
which local governments could "operate or cooperate
to help meet the challenge of metropolitan growth"
according to the U.S. Advisory Commission on Intergovernmental Relations (ACIR).[84] The ensuing year
saw extensive discussion of governmental goals, particularly with respect to the "authority and capability" of government to deal with metropolitan
problems, intermunicipal actions, and the redistri-
bution of taxes.[85] This led directly, in 1966 and
1967, to the heightened area-wide discussion of
metropolitan reorganization involving four alternative proposals: (1) a county-level intercounty
council with substantial "home rule" powers, (2) a
municipal-level federation to assume control over
functional area-wide services and transportation,
e.g., metropolitan Toronto, (3) a multi-purpose
district, with elected representation and powers to
assume new responsibilities as needs dictated,
(4) a system of separate single purpose districts.
In addition, two interim measures were proposed for

consideration: an interim commission of the legislature to study various metropolitan government proposals and the formation of a voluntary metropolitan council of governments to work up legislative
recommendations for solutions to area-wide problems.[86]

In January, 1967, to serve as a basis for the
anticipated legislative discussion of metropolitan
government, the MPC prepared a position paper which
called for its own replacement with a metropolitan
body similar to a multi-purpose district, but with
representation elected rather than appointed. It
would be responsible for highways, transit, sanitary sewage, open space, airports, development controls, and comprehensive planning and programming.[87]
It should have "power of taxation, bonding, special
assessment, eminent domain, and development."[88]
(For details and a comparison with other proposals,
see Table 4.) These proposals, along with those developed by other parties and groups in the Twin
Cities area, did indeed serve as the basis for the
legislature's discussion of a metropolitan council
for the area and were, in part, responsible for its
creation.

Finally, the MPC contributed greatly to the
consensus which called for a metropolitan unit of
government through the reaction of the community
to MPC activities. In good part, these reactions
were negative, critical of the failure of the MPC
to produce plans that were or could be implemented.[89]
The MPC was considered too large and unwieldy,
either unresponsive or unable to adopt a metropolitan position on a given issue, unable to influence
area-wide development significantly, etc. Its only
real power was that of persuasion which produced
little immediate effect (though subsequent developments showed that its educational impact, as discussed above, was enormous.)[90] Its supporters
noted that its staff was capable and highly re-
garded, though inadequate in size to meet its legislative obligations to plan and coordinate. Federal
funds could be used only for designated programs.

Local referral of plans was not mandatory and there
was no formal relationship to the legislative process at the state, local, or metropolitan level, despite official area-wide representation on the MPC
itself. It had no significant powers, save to make
plans, and it was not responsible, or responsive,
to any level of government with which it could effectively work to achieve concrete results.[91] The
reaction of both supporters and critics was in
large measure the same: Both saw the need to increase the powers of the MPC, or better still, to
create a new, more powerful body capable of developing and implementing plans while being responsive
to community needs and wishes.

Area Newspapers

The metropolitan consensus, of course, would
have had great trouble in materializing, or at
least in generating to the point it did, had it not
been for the area's newspapers. Although the local
press--both of the central cities and of the sub-
urbs--did not initiate or lead portions of the "discussion," their presentation of it and participation in exploring area-wide problems was essential
to its success. The press recognized that such
stories as the Robbie report and the sewer controversy were not simply routine items, but issues of
vital concern to a growing element of the public.[92]
They put the discussion of these issues before the
public and its leaders, giving extensive and thor-
ough coverage to events, activities, and diverse
views. They discussed and analyzed in detail the
various proposals and their ramifications on the
community.

Editorially, the central cities' press supported an area-wide metropolitan mechanism, responsible to the people (preferably through direct
elections) with effective power to plan, control,
and coordinate a variety of service functions.[93]
Initially, this support was somewhat vague; it
acknowledged the need to do something, but avoided
being specific on recommendations. As the character

of the consensus became clearer, so did the views
of the Minneapolis and Saint Paul papers. For example, the Saint Paul papers originally were less
committed to an elected council than were the Minneapolis papers, but came to support direct elections
by 1967.[94] It may be that the central cities' press
went through this change after learning that there
were surprisingly few people who would be antago-
nized by a strong metropolitan approach and that a
greater metropolitan area--one community--could
help increase circulation. In providing coverage,
both the Minneapolis and the Saint Paul papers assigned specific staff and editorial writers as well
as reporters. Chief among them were Ted Kolderie
for the Minneapolis Star editorial pages, Peter
Ackerberg for the Minneapolis Star, and Peter Vanderpoel for the two Saint Paul papers--the Pioneer
Press and Dispatch. Scarcely a day went by, particularly during the legislative sessions and times
of heated community discussion on critical issues,
without the appearance of an editorial or a byline
article.

    The suburban press supplemented and comple-
mented that of the central cities. In contrast to
the latter, which were the area's principal vehicles
for dissemination of the metropolitan discussion,
suburban papers presented issues and views of particular concern to their respective communities,
often catering to more parochial local interests.
This is not to say that they were generally of one
mind. For the most part, the papers of the inner,
intermediate distance, and older suburbs favored a
metropolitan approach to resolving the area's problems, reflecting the tenor of public and official
opinion in their communities.[95] The papers of the
outer and rural communities were largely opposed.
Most significant among the suburban press were a
chain of twenty-two newspapers serving forty to
forty-five communities--the Sun newspapers of John
Tilton. (See pp. 120-24.) While not categorically
opposed to a metropolitan mechanism, they were
against an elected and operating body. They did
recognize the need for a more effective planning

and coordinating body than the MPC. Within two
years Mr. Tilton and his papers underwent a metamorphosis. (See Chapter 8.)

Area Leagues of Women Voters

One last major participant in the metropolitan
discussion was the area's Leagues of Women Voters.
Neither the Minneapolis or Saint Paul group was involved as a partisan, but each individually and cooperatively worked to develop an informed public,
holding meetings and preparing publications on the
issues involved and approaches to metropolitan
solutions.[96]

OPPOSITION TO A METROPOLITAN COUNCIL

Opposition to the widespread efforts to create
a new metropolitan mechanism with operating powers
and direct responsibility to the people through
elections was conspicuous in its meagerness and
frailty. Only three elements appeared during the
years of the metropolitan discussion between 1964
and 1967: (1) Bloomington and many outer-ring
suburbs; (2) county officials; and (3) the suburban
Sun newspapers of John Tilton. Bloomington and
outer-ring suburbs demonstrated ambivalence and
parochialism at the same time, recognizing the need
for some measure to resolve area-wide service problems while opposing anything that might infringe on
their capacity to develop.[97] The counties equally
recognized that the pressures of growth in the area
required attention and they volunteered to do the
job, but too late. They feared a new unit of government would be the first step toward their dissolution or reorganization.[98] The Sun papers por-
trayed the typical suburban attitude of fear of
"big," i.e., metropolitan, government and the need
for a "new" approach to the area's problems. Government must be kept small to be responsive and the
only real need was for more effective planning and
coordination, preferably through existing mechanisms.[99] Indeed, the recognition by all that

area-wide problems existed and something should be
done to resolve them, coupled with the almost complete lack of advocates for metropolitan consolidation or assumption of purely local functions, may
be the reasons for the weakness of the opposition
and the lateness of its appearance.

Bloomington and Outer-Ring Suburbs

Bloomington is an intermediate-ring suburb and
the fourth largest city in the state. It is among
the wealthiest and most rapidly developing communities in the upper Midwest, principally because of
its fortuitous location. It is located adjacent to
the Minneapolis-Saint Paul International Airport,
one of the busiest in the nation; it is crossed by
two interstate highways, I 494 and I 35 W; it has
ready access to the Minnesota River which enables
it to provide adequate sewer service if necessary.
It has, moreover, extensive, commercially desirable
and buildable acreage in possibly the area's most
central and convenient location. Between 1950 and
1960, when it grew from 9,000 to over 50,000, it
successfully met, though with extreme cost and difficulty, the demands of great growth--sewers, water,
local roads, etc. It went into considerable debt,
split shifts at school, levied high taxes, and com-
promised on development standards.[100] Consequently,
by the mid-1960's, when it turned the corner of
financial success, it assumed the typical attitude
of the "rich" looking at its "poor" neighbors; it
had "made it" by itself--so could the others.

When the issue of metropolitan reorganization
appeared, the city felt that such an eventuality
could threaten its present favorable economic position; it would have to "subsidize" the costs of development elsewhere.[101] Nowhere was this truer
than in connection with the effort to create an
area-wide sewer and treatment system. Bloomington
had paid the high costs of tying into the MSSD to
avoid the problem of polluting its ground water;
it was now (1965-1967) in a position to provide its
own system if that were necessary. It needed only

to provide a treatment plant (the necessary local
sewers were already in) and it could count on the
financial assistance of at least two adjacent, outlying suburbs (Burnsville and Egan Township, both
on the Minnesota River). To participate in a metropolitan system would mean greater costs; to have
such a system as an operating subdivision of a metropolitan government would threaten it even more.
As noted in the preceding paragraph, it recognized
that area-wide problems existed, but felt that they
could be met through state "coordinated single-
purpose districts."[102] When faced with the reality
that there was going to be some kind of metropolitan mechanism passed by the 1967 legislature, it
reluctantly endorsed the concept put forward by
Senator Rosenmeier and Representative Albertson for
an appointed state agency to coordinate area single
purpose districts.[103] It still believed that no
new governmental unit was needed and that the
Ogdahl-Frenzel Bill--the consensus approach--was
the first step in creating a "monolithic metropolitan structure."[104] The views of Bloomington were
characteristic of the outlying suburbs opposed to a
metropolitan council.[105]

County Officials

It was not until late 1965 that the area's
county officials became concerned over the drift of
events which generally excluded county governments
from consideration in metropolitan government.[106]
They then hurriedly initiated action to create a
Metropolitan Inter-County Council (MICC), a voluntary, cooperative body of eight counties (the seven
metropolitan counties plus Wright County, the members of District Ten of the Association of Minnesota Counties) as a COG to press for grants of metropolitan powers. The MICC formally came into being in late 1966, on the eve of the 1967 session of
the legislature. Until then, counties had shown
little or no interest in assuming metropolitan responsibilities and apparently did so to avoid the
creation of a "metropolitan government or [have]
the state legislature and federal government . . .

step in."[107] Anoka County Commissioner Albert
Kordiak was to echo this when he said that metropolitan government would impose a new level of government over the counties and possibly deprive them
of certain powers.[108] As a consequence of these
parochial attitudes, the efforts of the MICC had
little impact on the legislature. As Robert Janes,
first MICC Chairman, put it, they were "too little,
too late."[109] He further stated that the counties
would not fight a metropolitan council in the future, but cooperate with it.[110] Hopefully, they
could share with the council or implement certain
of its administrative functions, such as solid
waste disposal and parks and open space.[111] This
appears to be one way to insure that the counties
will continue their governmental existence. The
choice for the counties now appears either to be
positive and cooperate with the council and state,
or possibly be reorganized or eliminated as an effective unit of local government in the metropolitan area.

Suburban Sun Newspapers

John Tilton and his suburban Sun newspapers
were the third element in the opposition to the consensus metropolitan council. He did not oppose the
need to meet the area's problems arising from its
rapid growth; he was fully aware of the problems of
sewer service, transit, solid waste disposal, coordination of special proposed district operations,
and the need to plan for the future. But he differed profoundly on the nature of the proposed
mechanism and the kind of powers it should have.
He believed that it need not be elected or operating.[112] He feared such a body would eventually
reduce local government to a meaningless level; it
would be the first step in creating a remote, unresponsive and huge monolithic structure. Efficiency
and less costly government were not sufficient reasons to accept metropolitan government.

The primary purpose of being for the suburb,
he believed, was the "local" nature of its structure.

It was a level of government to which a citizen
could relate and on which he could have an effect.
This, in fact, was the reason that so many were
leaving central cities for the suburbs.[113] With
this philosophy, he vigorously opposed a consensus
metropolitan council. Instead, he supported the
Rosenmeier-Albertson approach of an appointed state
planning and coordinating body to fulfill the need
to direct and control the area's growth.[114] He accepted budget control over special districts to insure necessary coordination. He was opposed to
granting the council taxing authority as this would
require its members to be elected. Tilton's views
were highly respected and well considered, but in
the final analysis they were not enough to prevent
the Twin Cities community from getting something
more than the Rosenmeier-Albertson proposal, though
less than that of the consensus.

The opposition to a metropolitan council was
too late in coming to be effective. It was not until the consensus jelled that it appeared and then
for reasons not completely acceptable to the community or legislature. Too often it appeared that
opposition was based on parochial interests of pro-
tecting a favorable financial base or a continued,
though possibly inadequate, role for existing local
governments. It may be that the meager nature of
the opposition was due to two factors of the metropolitan discussion: (1) Everyone agreed something
needed to be done, and (2) there was no push for a
comprehensive, home rule, metropolitan government--
consolidation.

NOTES

1. Ted Kolderie, Executive Director of the
Citizens League; Reynold Boezi, Metropolitan Council Staff; Interviews with Stanley Baldinger, April,
1969. (Interviews cited are with Stanley Baldinger,
unless otherwise stated.)

2. Kolderie, loc. cit.; and "Agreement Has Almost Been Reached," Minneapolis Star, October 27, 1965.

3. Verne Johnson, former Executive Director, Citizens League, Interview, April, 1969.

4. Ibid.

5. Kolderie, "Agreement Has Almost Been Reached," loc. cit.; Johnson, loc. cit.

6. Johnson, loc. cit.

7. Raymond Olsen, former City Manager of Bloomington; Reynold Boezi; Wilfred "Andy" Anderson, Executive Secretary of MICC; John Tilton, former publisher of the Sun suburban newspapers; and others, Interviews, April and June, 1969.

8. Gordon Rosenmeier, Interview, April, 1969.

9. A Metropolitan Council for the Twin Cities Area (Minneapolis: Citizens League, February, 1967), inside front cover.

10. The Future Role of the Metropolitan Planning Commission (Minneapolis: Citizens League, May, 1965), passim.

11. Summary of Comments and Proposals on Areawide Governmental Problems of the Twin Cities Metropolitan Area (Minneapolis: Citizens League, November, 1966), p. 1.

12. Ibid., pp. 1-2.

13. A Metropolitan Council for the Twin Cities Area, op. cit., pp. 3-6.

14. Summary of Comments and Proposals on Areawide Governmental Problems of the Twin Cities Metropolitan Area, op. cit., pp. 3-6.

15. Ibid., pp. 6-11.

16. Ibid., pp. 11-19.

17. A Metropolitan Council for the Twin Cities Area, op. cit., p. 14.

18. Ibid., pp. 16, 21.

19. Ibid., p. 16.

20. Kolderie, Kenneth Wolfe, Johnson, and Boezi, Interviews, April, 1969.

21. Dean Lund, Executive Secretary, Metropolitan Section, League of Minnesota Municipalities, Interview, April, 1969. Discussions on the origins and program of the Metropolitan Section is based on this interview.

22. Ibid.

23. Stan Olson, Report of Government Structure Committee (Minneapolis: Metropolitan Section, League of Minnesota Municipalities, February 3, 1967), p. 1. (Mimeographed.); Presentation of the Metropolitan Section of the League of Minnesota Municipalities Before the House Committee on Metropolitan and Urban Affairs (Minneapolis, February 13, 1967), p. 1.

24. Ibid.

25. Ibid., pp. 1-2.

26. Lund, loc. cit.

27. Ibid.

28. Ibid.

29. Peter Ackerberg, "Counties 'Fishing' for Share of Metro Government Duties," Minneapolis Star, January 9, 1967.

30. Peter Vanderpoel, "Ramsey League Urges Creation of Metro Unit," Saint Paul Pioneer Press, February 23, 1967; Report of Metropolitan Government Study Committee (St. Paul: Ramsey County League of Municipalities, January 4, 1967), p. 13. (Mimeographed.)

31. Ibid.

32. Milton Honsey, News Release, October 27, 1965.

33. David Beckwith, "Richfield Pushes for 7-County Task Force," Minneapolis Star, September 16, 1965; "Olson Group May Join Metro Group," St. Louis Post Dispatch, February 3, 1966.

34. Peter Vanderpoel, "Agency Foes Fear Metro Rule by State," Saint Paul Pioneer Press, February 28, 1967; Peter Ackerberg, "Ogdahl Reports Metro Council Compromise," Minneapolis Star, March 24, 1967.

35. Ackerberg, loc. cit.

36. Betty Wilson, "Naftalin Urges Strong Metro Council Government," Bloomington Sun, October 7, 1968; John E. Tilton, ". . . and a Vote Against It," Minneapolis Star, March 14, 1967 (reprinted from the Minnetonka Herald, March, 1967).

37. James Dalglish, Interview, June, 1969.

38. Report to Platform Committee (Minneapolis: Republican Advisory Committee on Intergovernmental Relations, 1966), p. 5. (Mimeographed.)

39. Ibid.

40. Ibid., p. 6.

41. James Hetland, Jr., Interview, April, 1969.

42. _Report of the Republican State Task Force on Metropolitan Affairs_ (April 16, 1968), p. 1.

43. _Ibid._

44. _Excerpts from 1966 DFL Platform_ (Minneapolis: Citizens League, September 6, 1966), p. 2. (Mimeographed.)

45. Frank Wright, "Rolvaag Asks Metropolitan Control Unit," _Minneapolis Tribune_, February 6, 1966.

46. _Ibid._

47. Harold LeVander, _This Is Where I Stand_ (Minneapolis: LeVander for Governor Volunteer Committee, October 20, 1966), p. 3.

48. _Ibid._, pp. 4-5.

49. _Ibid._, p. 6.

50. _Ibid._, p. 7.

51. Harold LeVander, _Inaugural Address_ (St. Paul: State of Minnesota, January 4, 1967), pp. 10-11.

52. _Ibid._, p. 11.

53. Peter Vanderpoel, "LeVander Backs Metro Council," _Saint Paul Pioneer Press_, March 22, 1967.

54. David Durenberger, Executive Secretary to Governor LeVander, Interview, April, 1969.

55. Peter Vanderpoel, "LeVander Backs Metro Council," _op. cit._

56. "Business at Work in the Twin Cities," _Fortune_, LXXVI, 2 (August, 1967), 123-24, 128.

57. Recommendations of the Urban Study and Action Committee for the Formation of a Multi-Purpose 7-County Metropolitan District (Minneapolis: Urban Study and Action Committee, September, 1966), pp. 1-2. (Mimeographed.)

58. Dennis W. Dunne, This Matter Is of Great Importance to You and to This Metropolitan Area (Minneapolis: Chamber of Commerce, January 25, 1967), p. 3. (Mimeographed.)

59. Editorial by Dennis W. Dunne, "A Challenge for the 1967 Legislature," Greater Minneapolis (Minneapolis: Chamber of Commerce, December, 1966), p. 7.

60. Dennis W. Dunne, Interview, June, 1969.

61. Ibid.

62. Lloyd Brandt, Interview, June, 1969.

63. Recommendations of the Urban Study and Action Committee for the Formation of a Multi-Purpose 7-County Metropolitan District, loc. cit.

64. Brandt, loc. cit.

65. Ibid.; Dunne, loc. cit.

66. Upper Midwest Research and Development Council Report, 1967 (Minneapolis, 1967), p. 2.

67. Ibid.

68. Ibid., inside front cover.

69. Thomas L. Anding, Interview, April, 1969; Boezi, Interview, March-April, 1969; Dunne, loc. cit.

70. Ted Kolderie, Governing the Twin Cities Area (Minneapolis: Upper Midwest Research and Development Council, 1969).

71. Anding, loc. cit.; Agenda of the Twin Cities Seminar (Minneapolis: Upper Midwest Council for Research and Development, 1966).

72. Peter Vanderpoel, "Businessmen Urge Area Government," Saint Paul Pioneer Press, November 11, 1966.

73. Ibid.; Jim Shoop, "New Government Unit Needed--Parley," Minneapolis Star, November 11, 1966.

74. Anding, loc. cit.

75. Ibid.

76. Resolution of the Board of Directors (Minneapolis: Upper Midwest Research and Development Council, April 18, 1969), pp. 1-2.

77. Lund, loc. cit.; Metropolitan Policy and Metropolitan Development (Minneapolis: Citizens League, 1968), p. 22.

78. Ibid., p. 29.

79. Ibid., pp. 20-22.

80. Ibid.

81. The Joint Program, Twin Cities Area Metropolitan Guide (St. Paul: Twin Cities Metropolitan Planning Commission, 1968), pp. 3-18.

82. C. David Loeks, as quoted in Metropolitan Policy and Metropolitan Development, loc. cit.

83. Metropolitan Policy and Metropolitan Development, loc. cit.

84. The Joint Program, 4,000,000 by 2000: Preliminary Proposals for Guiding Change (St. Paul: Twin Cities Metropolitan Planning Commission, 1964), pp. 49-50.

85. The Joint Program, Goals for Development of the Twin Cities Metropolitan Area (St. Paul: Twin Cities Metropolitan Planning Commission, 1965), pp. 44-46.

86. The Joint Program, Government-Taxation: Alternatives Paper 7 (St. Paul: Twin Cities Metropolitan Planning Commission, April, 1966), passim.

87. Position Paper on Legislation for Metropolitan Government (St. Paul: Twin Cities Metropolitan Planning Commission, January, 1967), passim.

88. Ibid., p. 2.

89. Metropolitan Policy and Metropolitan Development, op. cit., pp. 19-23, 29-30; Alan J. Wilensky, "The Twin Cities Metropolitan Council: A Case Study in the Politics of Metropolitan Cooperation" (unpublished senior thesis, Princeton University, Princeton, N.J., 1969), p. 55; Once Over Lightly (Minneapolis: League of Women Voters, February, 1965), pp. 1-2. (Mimeographed.)

90. Ibid., p. 2.

91. Ibid.

92. John Finnegan, editor, Saint Paul Pioneer Press, Interview, April 1969. Finnegan was also chairman of the MPC in 1964-1965.

93. Ibid.; Editorial, "The Metropolitan Council in 1969," Minneapolis Tribune, June 22, 1968, and "Two Cheers for the Metropolitan Council, Minneapolis Tribune, May 22, 1967, are typical.

94. Finnegan, loc. cit.

95. Charles C. Whiting, Public Information Officer of the Metropolitan Council, Interview, March, 1969. A perusal of the Council's clippings files confirmed this.

96. Two examples: <u>Minnesota's Twin Cities Metropolitan Area</u> (Minneapolis: Council of Metropolitan Area Leagues of Women Voters, 1966), 36 pages; <u>Metropolitan Maze . . . The Council-Watcher's Guide</u> (Minneapolis: Council of Metropolitan Area Leagues of Women Voters, December, 1967), 8 pages.

97. Olsen, Interview, April, 1969.

98. Anderson, Interview, June, 1969.

99. Tilton, Interview, June, 1969.

100. Olsen, <u>loc. cit</u>.

101. <u>Ibid</u>.

102. <u>Ibid</u>.; Peter Vanderpoel, "Officials Oppose State Metro Unit," <u>Saint Paul Pioneer Press</u>, March 28, 1967. Quote is from the Bloomington Chamber of Commerce in the <u>Saint Paul Pioneer Press</u>.

103. Peter Vanderpoel, "Suburb Stand on Metro Plan Leads to Hot Legislative Hassle," <u>Saint Paul Dispatch</u>, February 14, 1967.

104. <u>Ibid</u>. Quote is Vanderpoel paraphrasing John Pidgeon, Bloomington City Attorney, before the legislature.

105. "Dakota Municipal League Opposes Metropolitan Sewer Bill," <u>Saint Paul Dispatch</u>, April 18, 1969.

106. Betty Wilson, "Commissioners Plan to Organize Area Council," <u>The West Saint Paul Booster</u>, October 6, 1965.

107. <u>Ibid</u>., quoting Robert Janes, Hennepin County Board Chairman.

108. Wilson, <u>loc. cit</u>.

109.   "Controversies May Lie Ahead as Council Deals with Specifics," _Minneapolis Star_, August, 1968.

110.   _Ibid_.

111.   Anderson, _loc. cit_. The 1969 legislature did divide responsibilities for these programs, substantially as the counties hoped and without council opposition.

112.   Tilton, _loc. cit_.

113.   John E. Tilton, ". . . and a Vote Against It," _Minneapolis Star_, March 14, 1967. Reprint from the _Minnesota Herald_, March, 1967.

114.   Tilton, Interview, June, 1969.

CHAPTER **6** FOUR MEASURES

FOR CHANGE

While the metropolitan consensus was being
formalized during the years 1964-1967, four events
of critical importance occurred. They were not
planned as part of any overall strategy and, except for the final one, they were not counted upon
to help bring a metropolitan council into being.
These four events--legislative reapportionment,
special censuses of Twin Cities area suburbs in
1965, the Demonstration Cities and Metropolitan Development Act of 1966, and the virtual elimination
of home rule in the state--were mutually reinforc-
ing elements which came along at the right time to
create, along with the consensus, an irresistible
force for metropolitan change.

LEGISLATIVE REAPPORTIONMENT

On the eve of the metropolitan discussion, the
Minnesota legislature was overwhelmingly dominated
by outstate representatives--both the Senate and
the House of Representatives--despite the fact that
the population of the Twin Cities metropolitan area
constituted 44.8 percent of the state total.[1] Outstate representatives in January, 1963, held 42 of
67 seats in the Senate and 87 of 135 seats in the
House.[2] This was the case even though the legislature had just been reapportioned following a court
decision in 1959.[3] Senatorial districts, according
to the 1960 census, varied from a high of 100,520
to a low of 24,428.[4] Only twenty-one of the sixty-
seven districts were within 10 percent of the average (state population divided by the number of

districts) of 50,953 people. In the House, districts varied from a high of 56,076 to a low of 8,343. Only forty-three House districts were within 10 percent of the average 24,288 persons per district. The 1959 reapportionment, which was based on the 1950 census, when the area comprised only 38.6 percent of the state, added two seats in the Senate and four seats in the House for the Twin Cities area following the general elections of 1962.[5] The 1959 reapportionment was the first in the state since 1913, even though the state constitution required the legislature to be reapportioned after each census and for it to be "apportioned equally throughout the different sections of the State, in proportion to the population thereof."[6]

In June, 1964, a group of Twin Cities officials, led by Honsey and Wolfe, instituted suit in federal district court to have the 1959 reapportionment declared unconstitutional because of district population imbalance.[7] Shortly after, in July, 1964, Governor Rolvaag, also doubtful of the reapportionment's constitutionality, established a Bipartisan Reapportionment Commission to study the problem and to prepare a draft reapportionment plan to submit to the 1965 legislature.[8] In December, 1964, the three judge federal court declared the 1959 reapportionment to be unconstitutional because it violated the equal protection clause of the Fourteenth Amendment. The court then noted recent United States Supreme Court decisions in the Baker v. Carr case and six other reapportionment cases, which declared that both houses of state legislatures must be apportioned according to population, i.e., "one man, one vote."[9] The following January, the Reapportionment Commission proposed a unanimously adopted plan to the Governor, but one which was not seriously considered by the legislature. Indeed, the conservatively oriented 1965 legislature passed a reapportionment bill which the Governor called "gerrymandered" and vetoed. That November, the Minnesota Supreme Court upheld the veto, leaving the state without a valid reapportionment law.[10]

In December, the Governor reconvened the Reapportionment Commission, to prepare a new districting plan, using as criteria population devia-
tions within 5 percent, compactness of districts
and conformity to political boundaries, fairness to
political groups and preservation of communities of
interest, and criticisms of the initial plan. A
revised plan was completed and submitted to the
Governor on March 7, 1966.[11]   In the meantime, the
Honsey-Wolfe group, because of the Governor's failure to call a special session of the legislature to
pass a valid reapportionment law, had filed a new
suit in federal court, asking it to reapportion the
state.[12] The court, in January, 1966, withheld action of its own pending a possible special session
of the legislature to enact the required law. In
March, the Governor did call a special session of
the legislature which passed an "acceptable" reapportionment law the following May.[13]

The reapportionment, the first major one in
over a half century, was based on the 1960 census
of population and provided for a complete redistricting of the state, without adding seats as did
the 1959 act. It gave the seven-county Twin Cities
area 6 additional seats in the Senate, or 31 out of
67 seats, and 11 new seats in the House, or 59 out
of 135 seats, all in the suburbs. Honsey and company had sought to have the reapportionment based
on the area's population in 1965 (almost one half
of the state's) which would have given it 33 out of
67 senators and 66 out of 135 representatives, and
only reluctantly accepted the 1960 base.[14] They
looked to the 1970 census and a new reapportionment
for complete satisfaction.[15]

SPECIAL CENSUS OF TWIN CITIES
AREA SUBURBS IN 1965

During the spring and summer of 1965, fifty-
eight Twin Cities suburban communities paid for
and received special censuses of population. The
primary reason, as with many growing suburban communities throughout the country, was to secure

additional revenues from the state, which returned
certain funds to communities on a per capita basis.
A further reason was to establish accurately the
size of the area's population so as to put greater
pressures on the legislature to reapportion itself,
hopefully based on the 1965 figures.[16]

The new censuses showed the suburban area to
be the fastest growing area in the state, with an
increase of more than 32.7 percent since 1960, or
an increase of 180,000 persons.[17] The increased
figures, when coupled with the central cities' populations of 1960, showed the Twin Cities area to
have a total population of some 1.7 million, about
one-half of the state's. Such a population base
for a reapportionment would have given the Twin
Cities area virtually one-half of the representation in the legislature. While this line of thinking did have an impact on the legislature, it did
not succeed in forcing a 1965 base to the new reapportionment. It was recognized as unrealistic
because not all of the area had grown or been
counted, e.g., Minneapolis and Saint Paul. It did,
however, "persuade" the legislature and its leadership to act more effectively and quickly.[18]

One significant result of the 1965 special
censuses of Twin Cities suburbs, therefore, appears
to have been increased pressure to give the area a
proper and increased voice in the 1967 legislature
--the first to experience the reapportionment--so
essential to the successful passage of any metropolitan council legislation.

THE DEMONSTRATION CITIES AND METROPOLITAN
DEVELOPMENT ACT OF 1966

Section 204 of the Demonstration Cities and
Metropolitan Development Act,[19] which as of July 1,
1967, provided for the review and coordination of
federal assistance to qualifying programs in metropolitan areas, had an important, though not vital,
influence on the legislation establishing the Twin

Cities Metropolitan Council. Its influence was not
so much in bringing the Council about, but rather
in determining the nature of the review powers it
was to possess and possibly the speed at which the
Minnesota legislature was to act to create it. Local pressures and needs already in existence, including a recognized need for effective review of
local plans, even if not federally assisted, had by
themselves predetermined some kind of metropolitan
body with major planning and review functions.[20]
The MPC, which qualified under the 1966 federal act
and which for five weeks possessed metropolitan review powers authorized by it, had been subject to
major criticism for its general lack of power.
This was indeed one of the major reasons for creating a new body, one which not only was responsible
for metropolitan planning, but also had effective
powers to implement plans, including the coordination of local plans and programs having impact beyond immediate governmental boundaries.

The 1966 Demonstration Cities and Metropolitan
Development Act did force the Minnesota legislature
to take note of its provisions so that a mechanism
adequate to meet federal review requirements as
well as local demands was created. The state legislature took equal cognizance of Section 205 of
the Act. It provided bonus grants for

> metropolitan development projects
> meeting the requirements of . . .
> satisfactory metropolitanwide compre-
> hensive planning and programming. . .
> [for which] adequate metropolitanwide
> institutional or other arrangements
> exist for coordinating . . . local
> public policies and activities affect-
> ing the development of the area, [and
> which] are, in fact, being carried out
> in accord with such metropolitanwide
> comprehensive planning and programming.[21]

Under earlier state legislation, the MPC did have
limited review powers over local plans and projects,

provided they had an area-wide impact. However,
the determination as to whether they did have such
an impact was left to the local units of government,
and in the ten years of MPC operation none ever
voluntarily submitted a plan or project to it.[22]
Metropolitan council legislation completely reversed the situation so that the council determined
whether or not a local plan or project had a metropolitan or intermunicipal effect.[23]

Until the Federal Aid Highway Act of 1962 and
the Demonstration Cities and Metropolitan Development Act of 1966 were passed, the federal government had done little to "encourage area-wide jurisdiction over the planning and administration of
urban developmental programs. . . ."[24] Beginning
with the passage of Section 701(g) of the Housing
and Urban Development Act, which authorized grants
"to organizations composed of public officials
representative of the political jurisdictions within the metropolitan area . . ."--COGs--the federal
government began to push this device as the model
for metropolitan reorganization and review.[25] This
policy led to a major problem for the Minnesota
legislature, one which only recently has been resolved.

From the very beginning of the metropolitan
discussion, the COG concept had been discarded as
an inadequate mechanism for metropolitan reorganization. (Virtually all persons interviewed were of
this opinion, including Kolderie, Honsey, Johnson,
Boezi, Hetland, Wolfe, etc.) A voluntary cooperative organization, even if authorized by state legislation, could not do the job. The 1966 Demonstration Cities and Metropolitan Development Act, however, gives statutory though not exclusive preference to such an organization. It provides for a
review function to be exercised by an area-wide
agency, "which is, to the greatest practicable extent, composed of or responsible to the elected officials of a unit of area-wide government or of the
units of general local government within whose jurisdiction such agency is authorized to engage in

such planning. . . ."[26] Section 208(7) specifically describes COGs, as defined under Section 701(g)
of the 1954 Housing Act, as acceptable area-wide
agencies. Because of implications of the policy
inherent in this legislation, the Twin Cities proponents of a different kind of metropolitan mecha-
nism--whether it be elected or appointed--felt they
might be pressured into creating either a mechanism
which was inadequate to their needs or one which
would not qualify for federal review functions and
grants.[27] With this in mind Representative Donald
Fraser (DFL, Minneapolis) revised the 1966 legislation before enactment in the House to enable metropolitan agencies constituted differently from COGs,
so long as they were specifically authorized by
state legislation, to qualify as the metropolitan
(now "area-wide") review body.[28]

Early U.S. Department of Housing and Urban Development (HUD) regulations, unfortunately, again
beclouded the issue by pushing COGs to the apparent
near exclusion of other metropolitan mechanisms.
They stated:

> In order to have an effective dis-
> trict planning program, it is essen-
> tial that the local elected officials
> who will have the primary responsibil-
> ity for carrying out the District
> Agency's recommendations also have
> direction over the policies and ac-
> tivities of the Agency. Therefore,
> it is HUD's policy that voting mem-
> bership on the District Agency's
> policy-making body must, to the great-
> est practicable extent, be composed
> of, or responsible to, the elected
> officials of the units of general lo-
> cal government in the district. As a
> minimum, at least two-thirds of the
> voting membership must be distributed
> among units of general local govern-
> ment which together represents at
> least 75 percent of the aggregate

> population of the District. Units of
> general local government shall be rep-
> resented by elected officials. If an
> elected official representing a unit
> of general local government wishes to
> designate an non-elected official as
> his alternate, the designee must be a
> top administrative officer appointed
> by and responsible to the elected of-
> ficials of that unit of government and
> must vote in the name of the elected
> official.[29]

This was modified somewhat in a following paragraph
as follows:

> Where state law is explicit regarding
> the composition of the Board, state
> law prevails. However, the policies
> set forth . . . above shall be fol-
> lowed to the extent . . . allowed; and
> if state law precludes the minimum
> level of . . . representation of elect-
> ed officials . . . , HUD will require
> assurance that the District's activi-
> ties will be [made] responsible to
> the elected officials.[30]

These regulations were subsequently changed in
March, 1969, to require "voting membership on the
Council's policy-making body . . . [to] be as prescribed by state law." Where state law was not
specific, however, at least two-thirds of the body
would be composed of elected officials of constituent local governments or chief appointed officials
comprising three-fourths of the area's population.[31]

THE VIRTUAL ELIMINATION OF HOME RULE

In May, 1967, just a few short days before
passage of the Metropolitan Council Act, the legislature modified the home rule provisions of the
Minnesota constitution to prevent possible local

government veto of pending metropolitan enact-
ments.[32] Home rule, or "local consent" as it is
commonly called in Minnesota, first became operative
in the state in 1898 when special legislation deal-
ing with local government was prohibited. Under
Minnesota law, special legislation applies only to
specific units of government in contrast to general legislation, which applies state-wide without
specific reference to any local unit of government.
Since 1898, the legislature has used various devices, such as classification of local units by
population, area, assessed-valuation, etc., to pass
special laws, evading a constitutional question.[33]
The Minnesota constitution, to overcome this situation, was amended in November, 1958, to provide
increased protection to local units of government
from arbitrary special legislation. It stated:

> Every law which upon its effective
> date applies to a single local govern-
> ment unit or to a group of such units
> in a single county or a number of con-
> tiguous counties is a special law and
> shall name the unit or, in the latter
> case, the counties, to which it ap-
> plies. The legislature may enact
> special laws relating to local govern-
> ment units, but a special law, unless
> otherwise provided by general law,
> shall become effective only after its
> approval by the affected unit ex-
> pressed through the voters or the
> governing body and by such majority
> as the legislature may direct. Any
> special law may be modified or super-
> seded by a later home rule charter or
> amendment applicable to the same lo-
> cal government unit, but this does
> not prevent the adoption of subsequent
> laws on the same subject.[34] (Italics
> added.)

The amendment, as noted, continued to recognize
that "under Minnesota doctrine, the legislature is

supreme" and may override the provisions by "general law."[35]

Because of this amendment, any kind of legislation establishing a metropolitan council would have been virtually impossible. Such legislation would have been a special law subject to referendum or approval by each local council in the area, and there were suburban communities opposed to the metropolitan reorganization as envisaged. Similar provisions of law had thwarted metropolitan government elsewhere in the country.[36] The only way to solve this dilemma was to pass a general law which would eliminate the provision.

Ever since the 1958 amendment was passed, conservative-traditionalist forces in the legislature, headed by Senator Rosenmeier, had regretted the limitation that had been placed on the legislature and had sought to revise it.[37] The amendment itself, at the Senator's insistence, had provided the "out" to achieve renewed legislative primacy, but he lacked sufficient votes to pass the required general law. The pressures for the Twin Cities Metropolitan Council had finally given him the lever by which this could be done. At the same the proponents of a council, who now comprised some 45 percent of the legislature, realized that the home rule provision of the constitution had to be modified if they were to achieve their goals.[38] However, the Citizens League, the League of Minnesota Municipalities, and officials throughout the area wanted only such revision of the constitution to enable passage of the desired legislation without complete loss of local consent.[39] Therein lay the foundations of a deal.

Council proponents had sought consistently to create an operating body which included a mass transit function. (An ad hoc Metropolitan Transit Commission was created by Minneapolis, Saint Paul, and more than twenty suburban communities in 1965, under the "joint powers" provision of state law, wherein two or more communities can exercise together powers that each can

do separately. The area had tried since 1963 to
establish such a commission in the legislature, but
failed; the 1965 commission primarily worked to
prepare draft legislation and plans for 1967 legislative consideration.) However, those representatives who were particularly interested in creating
a permanent Metropolitan Transit Commission (MTC)
were somewhat dubious about the success of metropolitan council legislation in 1967, its first appearance before a conservatively dominated legislature, and were reluctant to tie their bill to
that for a council. During the course of the legislative battle for a council, particularly with
respect to operating powers, they found their anxieties confirmed. When Senator Rosenmeier promised
support for the MTC bill in return for votes to
change local consent as he wished, they agreed and
an effective united front for metropolitan reorganization was prevented.[40] (For a fuller discussion, see Chapter 8.) Part of the agreement was
to act upon the MTC bill before that of the Metropolitan Council to prevent proponents of the latter
from tying the former to it. Revision of local
consent was to come first as both a matter of necessity and good faith. Then in May, prior to
acting upon the MTC bill, the legislature, through
general law, changed--in effect, eliminated--the
constitution's provision authorizing local consent.
It provided that "a special law enacted pursuant
to the provisions of the Constitution, Article XI,
Section 2, shall become effective without the approval of any affected local government unit or
group of such units in a single county or a number
of contiguous counties."[41] Local consent still applies if the provisions of the general law require
it.

   The loss of local consent or home rule, while
considered unfortunate, was not thought to be a
major loss by the proponents of the Metropolitan
Council. They acknowledged and generally agreed
with the Minnesota doctrine of legislative suprema-
cy, that local government was the creature of the
state. They knew also that the loss was minor in

comparison to the establishment of the Metropolitan
Council, even if only in embryo form.

NOTES

1. Metropolitan Population Study: Part II
(Saint Paul: Twin Cities Metropolitan Planning
Commission, February, 1961), p. 11.

2. William Frenzel, Interview, June, 1969.
(Interviews cited are with Stanley Baldinger, unless otherwise stated.)

3. Minnesota Statutes Annotated, Extra Session, 1959, Chapter 45, paragraph 2.02 to 2.715 in-
clusive.

4. Report of Bipartisan Reapportionment Commission (Saint Paul: State of Minnesota, March 7,
1966), p. 1.

5. Frenzel, loc. cit.; Metropolitan Population Study, loc. cit.

6. Minnesota State Constitution, Article IV,
Section 2.

7. Honsey et al. v. Donovan, 236 F. Supp. 8D
Minn. (1964).

8. Report of Bipartisan Reapportionment Commission, loc. cit.

9. Baker v. Carr, 369 U.S. 186 (1962); Reynolds v. Simms, 377 U.S. 533 (1964); WMCA, Inc. v.
Lomenzo, 377 U.S. 633 (1964); Maryland Committee v.
Tawes, 377 U.S. 656 (1964); Davis v. Mann, 377 U.S.
678 (1964); Roman v. Sinock, 377 U.S. 695 (1964);
Lucas v. Colorado General Assembly, 377 U.S. 713
(1964).

10. Duxbury v. Donovan, 138 N.W. 2d 692 Minn.
(1965).

11. Report of the Bipartisan Reapportionment Commission, op. cit., p. 2.

12. "Judges Asked to Reapportion State," Minneapolis Star, December 28, 1965; Milton Honsey, Interview, April, 1968.

13. 1967 Minnesota Session Laws, 66 Extra Session, Chapter 1 at p. 14ff.

14. Honsey, loc. cit.

15. Journal of the House, Sixty-sixth session (Saint Paul: State of Minnesota, May 26, 1969), p. 18. On the last day of the 1969 session, May 26, 1969, the House of Representatives and the Senate passed concurrently and without dissent a resolution authorizing a reapportionment study, and the preparation of a redistricting plan for the 1971 session.

16. Honsey, loc. cit.; Frenzel, loc. cit.

17. U.S. Bureau of the Census, Current Population Reports: Special Census, Series P. 28, No. 420 (Washington, D.C.: U.S. Government Printing Office, June 22, 1966), Table 1.

18. Frenzel, loc. cit.; Honsey, loc. cit.

19. Public Law 89-754, 80 Stat. 1255.

20. Metropolitan Policy and Metropolitan Development (Minneapolis: Citizens League, October 14, 1968), pp. 5, 29.

21. Gordon Rosenmeier, Interview, April, 1969; Public Law 89-754, 80 Stat. 1255, Section 205a and b.

22. Metropolitan Policy and Metropolitan Development, op. cit., p. 29.

23. 1967 Metropolitan Council Act, Minnesota

Sessions Law, Chapter 896, Section 6, Subdivisions
6, 7, 8; 1967.

24.   Norman Beckman, "How Metropolitan are
Federal and State Policies?" Public Administration
Review, XXVI, 2 (June, 1966), 99.

25.   Section 1102 (c) (2), Housing and Urban
Development Act, Public Law 89-117, 79 Stat. 451 502,
1965.

26.   Section 204(a)(1), Public Law 89-754, 80
Stat. 1255.

27.   Reynold Boezi, Interview, March-April,
1969.

28.   Iric Nathanson, staff member, Rep. Donald
Fraser, Interview, September, 1969 and April, 1970;
Section 208 (7), Demonstration Cities and Metropoli-
tan Development Act.

29.   Comprehensive Planning Assistance, Handbook 1: Guidelines Leading To A Grant, MD6041.3
(Washington, D.C.: U.S. Department of Housing and
Urban Development, January 1, 1969), p. 5, paragraph 11a.

30.   Ibid., p. 6, paragraph 11c.

31.   Ibid., p. 41, paragraph 8b.

32.   Minnesota Constitution, Article XI, as
amended.

33.   Orville Peterson, Toward More Effective
Home-Rule (Minneapolis: League of Minnesota Municipalities, September, 1957), pp. 1,3,5. (Mimeographed.)

34.   Article XI, Section 2.

35.   Peterson, loc. cit.

36. <u>Factors Affecting Voter Reactions to Gov-</u>
<u>ernmental Reorganization in Metropolitan Areas</u>
(Washington, D.C.: Advisory Commission on Intergovernmental Relations, May, 1962).

37. Rosenmeier, <u>loc. cit</u>.

38. <u>A Metropolitan Council for the Twin Cities</u>
<u>Area</u> (Minneapolis: Citizens League, February 9,
1967), pp. 10 and 47; William Kirchner, Interview,
April, 1969; Kolderie, Interview, April and June,
1969.

39. <u>A Metropolitan Council for the Twin Cities</u>
<u>Area</u>, p. 48.

40. Kirchner, <u>loc. cit</u>.

41. Minnesota Statutes 1967, Chapter 645.023,
Subdivision 1.

CHAPTER **7** THE LEGISLATIVE

BATTLE

The advocates of a strong metropolitan council came to the legislature in January, 1967, with a remarkably high degree of consensus. In the three years of metropolitan discussion, they had achieved a great measure of agreement on the need and kind of body required for meeting the area's metropolitan problems. The council should be an elective, operating, and multi-purpose agency exercising those functions authorized by the legislature that the local units of government could not do adequately by themselves. Equally important, the consensus had apparent wide support throughout the Twin Cities area community, with little or no real opposition. The "informal coalition," therefore, should have been optimistic about the chances for getting the kind of metropolitan reorganization it sought, but it recognized that a difficult battle faced its forces. Agonizing memories of earlier battles over efforts to create a metropolitan sewer system still loomed in peoples' minds. And despite recent legislative reapportionment, rural and outstate men, jealous of their state prerogatives, still controlled the legislature.[1] These apprehensions were to prove justified. The effort to create a metropolitan council was to be long and arduous and, at times, so frustrating as to appear almost impossible. Not until the very end of the session did council advocates achieve a measure of success. The force they had built was sufficiently great that, though their proposal would be modified and significantly so, it could not be stopped.

THE OGDAHL AND FRENZEL BILLS

Early in February, Senator Ogdahl and Representative Frenzel introduced their nearly identical bills into the state legislature. They were the first of four bills--one of two major pairs--that were to be submitted to the legislature on metropolitan reorganization. (See Table 5 for a comparison of the bills and Table 4 for a comparison of other proposals.) Shortly afterwards, hearings before the House Metropolitan and Urban Affairs Committee and the Senate Metropolitan Division of the Civil Administration Committee began, with testimony from the LMM, the Citizens League, business leaders, local officials, and other participants in the metropolitan discussion.[2] The testimony, as noted in Chapter 5, was overwhelming in its agreement to support an elected and operating body as called for by Ogdahl and Frenzel. Over the course of the next three months, however, substantial Twin Cities-outstate and intraparty acrimony was to arise over the issues of metropolitan council election versus appointment and operation versus coordination.

Minneapolis Tribune political reporter, Jonathan Friendly, characterized the supporters of the Ogdahl-Frenzel approach as being "Conservatives with strong ties to the Republican Party and . . . from most of the DFLers in the Legislature."[3] The opposition was largely "independent Conservatives . . . the 'establishment' which has called the shots in the Legislature for many sessions."[4] The Twin Cities-outstate and inter-Conservative splits were to reach an early climax when on February 23 Senator Rosenmeier and Representative Howard Albertson, in anticipation of the forthcoming Ashbach-Newcome bills to be introduced within the next few weeks, announced their "concepts on a Metropolitan Council."[5]

TABLE 5

Comparison of Bills in the Minnesota Legislature
To Establish the Metropolitan Council of the Twin Cities Area, Spring, 1967

	OGDAHL 15 members	FRENZEL 29 members	ASHBACH 15 members	NEWCOME 15 members
COUNCIL SIZE				
METHOD OF SELECTION	Directly-elected by the people from combinations of state legislative districts in Nov., 1970, and thereafter; appointed by legislators in those districts from July 15, 1967, until 1970 election.	Same as Ogdahl except first election is in fall of 1968.	Appointed at-large by governor with senate's approval from entire metropolitan area.	Appointed at-large by governor with senate's approval—four from Mpls; three from St. Paul at-large; one from each of seven suburban-rural districts formed from combinations of state legislative districts.
COMPENSATION	$35 per meeting.	$300 per month.	Same as Ogdahl.	Same as Ogdahl.
TERMS	Four years.	Two years.	Six years.	Six years.
CHAIRMAN	Council appoints.	Council appoints.	Appointed by governor with senate's approval, serves at governor's pleasure.	Same as Ashbach.
CONTROL OF METRO FUNCTIONS	*Absorb Metropolitan Planning Commission (MPC) Aug. 1, 1968; assume operating control of transit, sanitary sewerage and mosquito control Jan. 1, 1971.	*Absorb MPC July 1; assume operating control of transit Sept. 1, 1967; sewerage and mosquito control Jan. 1, 1968.	Absorb MPC immediately. Coordinate long-range, comprehensive plans of metropolitan special service districts; suspend such plans indefinitely if they are not in accord with council's metropolitan development guide; legislature settles disputes.	Same as Ashbach, except separate sanitary sewer district board would retain authority to decide location of regional treatment plants and expansion of Pig's Eye plant.
PLANNING AUTHORITY	Adopt plans for "physical, social and economic development of the metro area (to obtain) coordinated and harmonious development."	Same as Ogdahl.	"Adopt a comprehensive development guide for the metro area . . . encompassing physical, social, or economic needs . . . for an orderly and economic development, public and private, of the metro area."	Same as Ashbach.
CONTROL OF MUNICIPAL FUNCTIONS, PLANNING	*None except the general authority to specifically operate transit, sewerage and mosquito control. Strong authority in those three fields.	Same as Ogdahl.	No operating power; indefinite suspension of municipal long-term, comprehensive plans or portions of them, if they would affect neighboring municipalities or metro development; legislature to settle disputes if council and municipality cannot agree.	None.
AUTHORITY IN FEDERAL GRANTS	Comment on whether projects for which municipalities apply for federal grants are consistent with the metro development guide.	Same as Ogdahl.	Same as Ogdahl.	Same as Ogdahl.
TAXING POWER	*Levies of a half-mill for administration; one-third mill for planning; one-half mill or 50 cents per capita for mosquito control; $1 an auto for transit.	*Same as Ogdahl.	Not specified; presumably one-third to one-half mill for planning and administration.	Same as Ashbach.
BONDING AUTHORITY	May issue an unlimited amount of bonds without a referendum "for acquisition or betterment of any system or facility which will be used to perform" sewerage, mosquito control or transit services.	Same as Ogdahl.	None.	None.
OTHER POWERS	1. Appoint one of its members to all governing units in area except municipalities, counties and school districts.	1. Same as Ogdahl.	1. Appoint a member to Metro. airports cmsn., mosquito control dist. and any sewerage district operating.	1. None.
	2. Allocate funds given by the legislature to redistribute.	2. Same as Ogdahl.	2. Approve or disapprove of use of money given municipalities and counties by state or federal government for park acquisition.	2. Same as Ashbach.
	3. Accept state and federal grants.	3. Same as Ogdahl.	3. Same as Ogdahl.	3. Same as Ogdahl.

*Only those operating districts which the legislature has created or will create in separate acts would be absorbed by the metropolitan council. Taxing power of the council to operate those districts would be prescribed in the separate acts, and mill levy increases could be made only by the legislature. The planning commission and mosquito control district exist; the legislature is considering transit and sewerage bills.

Source: St. Paul Dispatch, April 28, 1967.

THE ROSENMEIER-ALBERTSON APPROACH

The fears of the Twin Cities advocates of a strong, locally responsive metropolitan council regarding outstate opposition were realized when the two Conservative leaders in the legislature--Rosenmeier and Albertson--released their ideas on metropolitan reorganization. In an effort to preserve an element of control over Twin Cities development, these two leaders sought to avoid, as they described it, "an 'urban Minnesota' separate from a 'rural Minnesota.'"[6] To do so, they wished to create an administrative arm of the state responsible to the governor and legislature, with emphasis on coordinating area-wide functions and comprehensive planning.[7] Briefly, their plan proposed a fifteen-member council selected from the Twin Cities area by the governor and, except for its chairman, confirmed by the Senate. The council, which would be nonpartisan and at-large, would absorb the MPC, review long-term local development plans and applications for federal grants, study a wide range of area-wide problems including environmental pollution, solid waste disposal, local fiscal disparities, and the structure of local government, and prepare a comprehensive development guide to cover elements such as sewage collection and disposal, transportation, regional parks and open space, and land use that special districts would have to follow. In connection with this last point, the proposal envisaged separate special districts with their membership selected, at least in part, by the council. Differences between the council and local governments or special districts, if mutually irreconcilable, were to be settled by the legislature.[8] These concepts were spelled out in particular terms three weeks later when parallel bills, nominally sponsored by Senator Robert Ashbach and Representative Thomas Newcome (both suburban Saint Paul Conservatives), were introduced in the legislature.[9]

TWIN CITIES AREA REACTION

There was an immediate and vociferous response
to these proposals and bills from all elements of
the Twin Cities area community, particularly from
among suburban officials. Almost to a man they opposed, in the most vigorous terms, the concept of a
state agency controlling the development of their
Twin Cities area. Typical comments were as follows:
(1) "It is difficult to find very much merit in the
Rosenmeier approach. This bill in . . . creating a
state rather than local agency completely ignores
the carefully considered views of municipal officials, citizens of the area, and the business community."[10] (2) "One of the basic essentials of
metro government is that it be genuinely local in
character--the object is to strengthen, not to
weaken, local government."[11] (3) "We oppose Rosenmeier coming down here from Little Falls and at-
tempting to tell us in the metropolitan area just
how we are to run our local government."[12]
(4) ". . . the council ought to be elected and
based on a one-man, one-vote principle. . . . no
nonelected council should have any power to approve
the plans of local government. . . ."[13] (5) "It is
a fundamental principle that policymaking bodies
should be elected, not appointed. . . ."[14] (6) "Show
us you are great leaders . . . delegate to us a metropolitan council of the people, by the people, for
the people . . . the same people who elect local
officials and state legislators can be trusted to
elect metropolitan council members."[15]

Perhaps the most significant statement, one
that summed up the feelings of the Twin Cities officials, was made by Al Illies, Mayor of Minnetonka
and Chairman of the Hennepin County League of Municipalities, at a hearing of the Senate Committee on
Civil Administration on the Ogdahl-Frenzel bills.
He said: "Gentlemen, we look on metropolitan government as local government."[16] Both the central
cities and suburbs over the four preceding years
had come to realize that many of the problems they
faced were equally metropolitan and local. Local

officials now understood that their choice in resolving area-wide problems was to be either state-
wide or metropolitan. They chose the latter as
being closer to home and therefore "local."

Rosenmeier, reacting to this flurry of statements, said, "the one-man, one-vote principle,
which they [proponents of an elected council] often
cite, is 'irrelevant,' since we're not talking
about a political institution--we are talking about
an administrative branch of the legislature."[17]
Yet, what he and Albertson proposed was a policymaking body, an inherently political institution.
The only hesitant word from the area's leadership
was one of omission in the testimonies of Donald
Dayton, Earl Ewald, and Philip Nason before the
legislature when they carefully avoided any position on an elected body; the important thing was
that it be able "to do the job."[18] This omission
was noted by the legislature's Conservative leadership and may have blunted the effect that a more
united front could have achieved.[19] With the introduction of the Rosenmeier-Albertson approach to a
metropolitan council for the Twin Cities, the proponents for an elective and operating council grew
anxious over possible success.[20] They then looked
to a compromise, hoping to achieve some measure of
success.

A MOVE TO COMPROMISE

Senator Ogdahl, author of one of the bills of
the "informal coalition" metropolitan council, was
chairman of the Metropolitan Problems Division, the
Senate subcommittee considering metropolitan council legislation. The subcommittee, however, was a
division of the Civil Administration Committee, on
which Rosenmeier was a most influential member.
During the fall of 1966, Ogdahl had tried and
failed to have his division organized as a new committee in order to bypass the Civil Administration
Committee. As a consequence, Ogdahl had to have
the approval of that committee as well as his

division before his bill could even get to the floor
of the Senate. Unfortunately, until late April his
division appeared to be slightly in favor of the
Rosenmeier-Albertson approach. In the House, the
critical committee was the Metropolitan and Urban
Affairs Committee, chaired by Albertson. Strangely
enough, Albertson's committee appeared to favor
slightly the Ogdahl-Frenzel bill. Thus, for several weeks in March and April, 1967, neither chairman was anxious to bring his respective bill to a
vote.

In late March, to put pressure on the Ogdahl-
Frenzel forces, Albertson expressed the hope of
moving sewer and transit bills from his committee
to the House floor--separate from any council legislation.[21] About the same time, Ashbach and Newcome offered a compromise--to permit possible appointment of council members by state legislators
or local officials within specified districts and
to consider election of council members after an
anticipated reapportionment of the legislature in
1971 following the 1970 census.[22] Ogdahl, while
willing to postpone elections until after 1968,
wanted a commitment to an eventual elected council,
which was not forthcoming, and therefore rejected
the compromise offer.[23] Both he and Frenzel continued to maintain that they were open to compromise. Rosenmeier, in contrast to the other legislative participants, was noncommittal, but colleagues said that he was not "inflexible." It was
still too early to compromise.[24]

To get off dead center and move his bill forward (as well as to avoid an open battle within the
Conservative caucus), Ogdahl in late April proposed
his own compromise, which in effect was a new bill.
He proposed to reduce the number of council members
from twenty-nine to fifteen, to permit the council
to appoint only one member to special districts,
and to have the council members appointed by legislators until 1970 when they would be elected. Except for the election of council members, these provisions were part of the Rosenmeier-Albertson

approach. Newcome and Ashbach agreed that these
amendments made the Ogdahl bill less objectionable,
but the essential dispute over an elective council
remained. Rosenmeier, keeping his "cool," remained
quiet; it was still too early for him to compromise,
although it was reported that he could accept all
of Ogdahl's proposals except an elected council.[25]
Ogdahl was not satisfied. One week later, Representative Newcome announced three amendments to his
(Rosenmeier-Albertson) bill to make it more palat-
able to the Ogdahl-Frenzel forces. He moved to
strike provisions giving the council a veto over
all municipal plans; to permit the operating board
of any metropolitan sewer district, rather than the
council, to determine the location of treatment
plants; and to have council members "appointed from
combinations of legislative districts," rather than
from at-large.[26]

LEGISLATIVE BATTLES

On May 5, Ogdahl's Metropolitan Affairs Division voted against his proposal for an elected and
operating metropolitan council, by a margin of
eight to six.[27] Three days later, Representative
Albertson's Committee on Metropolitan and Urban Affairs voted seventeen to fifteen to reject a new
"compromise bill" offered by Representative Robert
Renner, chairman of the House Civil Administration
Committee. The compromise, in effect, was a combination of the two opposing bills and provided initially for an appointed and coordinating council
which would in 1970 become elected and operating.[28]
In rejecting the compromise, Albertson's committee
in effect endorsed a state agency for the metropolitan area, an action which unwittingly required it
to be sent to the House Civil Administration Committee where William Frenzel was co-chairman with
Renner. House rules required that any legislation
proposing a "new department . . . of state government . . . shall [be] referred to the committee on
civil administration."[29] Frenzel and Renner hoped
in this way to amend the Newcome bill to make it

more like the Renner bill. On May 10, two days
later, the House Civil Administration Committee,
contrary to the hopes of Frenzel and Renner, voted
sixteen to thirteen against the Renner compromise
and moved the Newcome bill to the House floor.[30]
The very next day, the House version of the bill
was approved by a voice vote by the Senate Civil
Administration Committee.[31]

Just eight days after the first House committee voted on a metropolitan council, the House of
Representatives passed the Newcome-Ashbach bill
103 to 20. This apparently overwhelming vote was
in reality very much closer than it first appears.
Backers of the Ashbach-Newcome bill had to fight
off a last minute floor amendment to make the council an elected body. The proponents of an elected
council lost on a 66 to 62 vote, with 7 members ab-
staining.[32] As was expected, the amendment had the
bipartisan support of most--42 of 58--of the 7
counties representatives. It was supported by 32
Conservatives and 30 Liberal-DFLers.[33] The performance of the House was repeated on May 19, when
the Senate overwhelmingly passed the Ashbach-Newcome
bill 46 to 18. Again, it did so only after a bitter, two and one-half hour fight by the proponents
of an elected council, who lost on an amendment to
make the council elective in 1971 by a vote of 33
to 33.[34] Again, as expected, the amendment had bipartisan support from 19 of the area's 21 senators
and 21 of 22 Liberal-DFLers. An anticlimactic motion to reconsider failed 36 to 30, when one
Ashbach-Newcome and four Ogdahl-Frenzel supporters
switched their votes. The lone senator who did not
vote in the 33 to 33 tie was William Kirchner, sponsor of the successful MTC legislation, who was
home ill.[35]

Governor LeVander signed the metropolitan
council legislation on May 26, along with three
other pieces of legislation which were to have significant area-wide effect--a metropolitan transit
commission act, a law establishing an office of
local and urban affairs within the State Planning

Agency, and a law creating a pollution control
agency. (The Pollution Control Agency replaced a
much weaker and more limited Water Pollution Control Agency.) While he would have preferred an
elected and operating council, the Governor considered the creation of another kind of council as
"significant and gratifying."[36] Its record in the
future would determine whether or not it should be
an elected body.

LEGISLATIVE POST MORTEM

     With the closeness of the last-minute votes in
both the House and Senate, the proponents of an
elected and operating metropolitan council realized
they had been panicked and "outfoxed" in their legislative strategies. Their position was really
much stronger than they had thought.[37] Senator
Ogdahl, in reflecting on the votes, maintained that
had he and his colleagues worked harder, they might
well have carried the day and achieved an elected
council with more power than authorized in the
Ashbach-Newcome bill.[38] The Minneapolis Tribune,
in an editorial of May 22, 1967, noted an equally
unfortunate element among the supporters of an
elective council. Governor LeVander, despite his
known preference for an elected body, had done virtually nothing to help garner votes for its support.
In view of the closeness of the House and Senate
votes, even minimal help from the Governor, claimed
the Tribune, "could almost have had the Council in
the form he said he preferred it."[39] Yet, the
creation of a metropolitan council was a real and
substantial victory for the forces of metropolitan
reorganization in the Twin Cities. The legislature
had created a council possessing many of the powers
it needed if it were to effectively plan and coordinate the area's development.[40] More important,
the council would possess a structure admirably
adaptable to the eventual needs of the Twin Cities.
New functions may be readily added as required.
Representation is by districts of equal population
size and reflects the composition of the whole area.

As such, it should be responsive to the community's
aspirations. Ultimately, it can be an elected body--
one on which the people of the Twin Cities area can
build for the future.

THE TWIN CITIES METROPOLITAN COUNCIL

The Metropolitan Council is the most ambitious
attempt at metropolitan reorganization in the United
States in over seventy years. The Twin Cities metropolitan area comprises the largest number of governmental units, including two major central cities,
in more (seven) counties, and having the largest
number of people (1.9 million) yet brought together
under one structure in a major American metropolitan
area in this century. A noted observer of the metropolitan scene calls it "a long step beyond the
Toronto Metro," the best-known and most respected
experiment in metropolitan government in the western hemisphere.[41]

The Metropolitan Council is a fifteen-man
broad policy-planning body designed to coordinate
the planning and development of the seven-county
metropolitan area. Fourteen members are appointed
by the governor on a nonpartisan basis for staggered
terms of six years each (after the initial appointment terms) from specific districts based on combinations of two state senatorial districts of equal
population size. The Senate ratifies the appointments after consultation with area legislators.
The fifteenth member, the chairman, serves as the
chief executive officer of the Council, at the
pleasure of the governor, with the Senate's advice
and consent. He is responsible for organizing the
work of the Council, leading the Council in establishing advisory committees to assist it in performing its duties, preparing biennial reports to
the legislature, preparing studies and plans, and
supervising the Council's staff, a task it assumed
when the Council absorbed the MPC. The Council may
hire staff or contract for consultant services, accept gifts and appropriations from the state,

MAP 3

LOCATION OF THE 14 DISTRICTS
OF THE METROPOLITAN COUNCIL

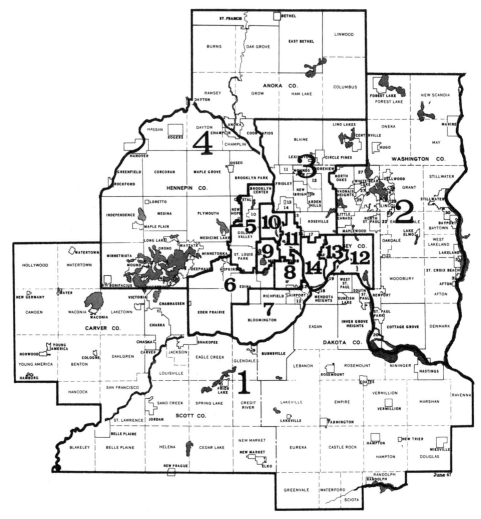

The councilmen and their districts are as follows:
Chairman — James L. Hetland, Minneapolis.

1. Marvin F. Borgelt, West St. Paul.
2. Milton L. Knoll, Jr., White Bear Lake.
3. Joseph A. Craig, Coon Rapids.
4. Donald Dayton, Wayzata.
5. George T. Pennock, Golden Valley.
6. Dennis Dunne, Edina.
7. Clayton L. LeFevere, Richfield.
8. Glenn G. C. Olson, Minneapolis.
9. E. Peter Gillette, Jr., Minneapolis.
10. James L. Dorr, Minneapolis.
11. George W. Martens, Minneapolis.
12. The Rev. Norbert Johnson, St. Paul.
13. Mrs. James L. Taylor, St. Paul.
14. Joseph A. Maun, St. Paul.

Source: Metropolitan Council of the Twin Cities Area.

federal government, and other sources, and must prepare and adopt a comprehensive development guide
consisting of policy statements, goals, standards,
programs, and maps prescribing the orderly development of the area.

COUNCIL POWERS

The Council reviews all metropolitan plans and
projects of special districts--independent commissions, boards, and agencies--and may "indefinitely
suspend," in total or in part, any which it finds,
within sixty days of submission, to be inconsistent
with its development guide.[42] In this event, the
only course open to a special district for redress
is application to the Council for reconsideration
or appeal to the legislature--through the Council.
It also reviews and comments on long-term municipal
comprehensive plans and "any matter which has a substantial effect on metropolitan area development."[43]
Local plans are not subject to a veto, but must wait
at least sixty days before being implemented to permit the Council to inform contiguous and other concerned governments of the proposals. If a local
unit objects to a plan of another unit, the Council
may hold a hearing and mediate any differences.
The decision as to whether a plan has a metropolitan or intergovernmental effect is the Council's.
It also reviews and comments on applications for
federal grants emanating from local governments,
commissions, boards, and agencies, but such action
under Section 204 of the Demonstration Cities and
Metropolitan Development Act of 1966 is only advisory to the applying unit and concerned federal
agency. In contrast, all applications for grants
under federal and state open space land acquisition
programs are subject to unqualified Council approval or disapproval.[44]

The Council may individually or in association
with other agencies of the state develop a data and
research center, conduct research, coordinate civil
defense shelter planning, levy a tax to finance its

operations, and participate with the Municipal Commission in proceedings on municipal incorporation, annexation, and consolidation. It may also appoint one nonvoting member to each board of an area-wide special district. Finally, the Council engages in continuous programs of research and study with respect to (1) air pollution, (2) regional parks and open space, (3) water pollution, (4) the development of long-range planning in, but not for, the area, (5) solid waste disposal, (6) area-wide tax disparities, (7) metropolitan tax assessment practices, (8) storm water drainage facilities and needs, (9) the need to consolidate common services of local government, (10) advance public land acquisition, and (11) government organization, including recommendations on the mechanisms most suitable to accomplish all the above.

The Twin Cities Metropolitan Council officially came into being on August 8, 1967, upon appointment of the fifteen members of the Metropolitan Council by Governor LeVander after consultation with state legislators in each Council district. The appointments were acclaimed by virtually all segments of the Twin Cities community for their high quality of demonstrated capability, leadership, and involvement in community affairs. Many were activists in the "informal coalition" pushing for creation of the Council, including Chairman Hetland, member of the Citizens League, and law professor at the University of Minnesota. Other members include the former mayor of a large Saint Paul suburb, two former presidents and members of the Minneapolis City Council, the Chairman of the Board of the Dayton Corporation, two bankers, a minister, a staff member of the Saint Paul Hallie Q. Brown House, and several businessmen and lawyers. The only criticism (and it was minor) leveled at the appointments was that nearly all of them were Republicans; but membership followed closely the political makeup of the districts that members were to represent.

NOTES

1.   Verne Johnson, Interview, April, 1969 (interviews cited are with Stanley Baldinger, unless stated otherwise); Peter Vanderpoel, "Citizens League's Metro Government Plan Draws Legislators' Praise, Condemnation," Saint Paul Dispatch, February 15, 1967.

2.   Ibid.; Peter Vanderpoel, "Officials Oppose State Metro Unit," Saint Paul Pioneer Press, March 26, 1967; "City Behind Metro Council, Says Byrne," Saint Paul Pioneer Press, February 28, 1967; Peter Vanderpoel, "Ramsey League Urges Creation of Metro Unit," Saint Paul Dispatch, February 23, 1967; "C. of C. Aides Back Elective Metro Council," Minneapolis Tribune, March 3, 1967; Peter Vanderpoel, "Area Groups Push for Elected Metro Unit Bill," Saint Paul Pioneer Press, March, 1967; Peter Vanderpoel, "Officials Give Big Pitch for Metro Government Plan," Saint Paul Dispatch, February 18, 1967.

3.   Jonathan Friendly, "Conservatives Splitting Over Metro Bills," Minneapolis Tribune, April 9, 1967.

4.   Ibid.

5.   Gordon Rosenmeier and Howard Albertson, Concepts on a Metropolitan Council (Saint Paul, February, 1967). pp. 1-7. (Mimeographed.)

6.   Howard Albertson, Memorandum to Committee on Rules, Minnesota House of Representatives (Saint Paul: Howard Albertson, Chairman of the House Committee on Metropolitan and Urban Affairs, February, 1967), p. 1. (Mimeographed.)

7.   Ibid.

8.   Rosenmeier and Albertson, loc. cit.

9. Jonathan Friendly, "Metropolitan Council Bill Offered," _Minneapolis Tribune_, March 18, 1967.

10. James Dalglish, Saint Paul Commissioner of Finance and Chairman, Metropolitan Section, League of Minnesota Municipalities, quoted by Peter Vanderpoel, "Officials Oppose State Metro Unit," _Saint Paul Pioneer Press_, March 26, 1967.

11. Arthur Naftalin, Mayor of Minneapolis, quoted by Peter Vanderpoel, "Metro Unit Compromise Seen," _Saint Paul Pioneer Press_, March 24, 1967.

12. Milton Honsey, Mayor of New Hope, _ibid_.

13. Thomas Byrne, Mayor of Saint Paul, "City Behind Metro Council, Says Byrne," _Saint Paul Pioneer Press_, February 28, 1967.

14. Charles Clay of the Citizens League, quoted by Peter Vanderpoel, "Agency Foes Fear Metro Rule by State," _Saint Paul Pioneer Press_, March 28, 1967.

15. Stanley Olson, Mayor of Richfield and Chairman of the League of Minnesota Municipalities, _ibid_.

16. Jim Boland, "Twin Cities Metro Council Carved Order Out of Chaos," _Dayton Daily News_, November 21, 1968; Peter Vanderpoel, Interview, June, 1969.

17. Peter Vanderpoel, "Appointive Agency Urged for Metro Council," _Saint Paul Pioneer Press_, March 4, 1967.

18. "NSP Head, Dayton Urge Metro Plan," _Minneapolis Star_, February 27, 1967; Dennis W. Dunne, Interview, June, 1969.

19. Dunne, _loc. cit_.

20. _Ibid._; "No Approval in '67 for Metro Plan," _Minneapolis Star_, March 21, 1967.

21. Friendly, "Conservatives Splitting Over Metro Bills," <u>loc. cit</u>.

22. Peter Vanderpoel, "Metro Unit Compromise Seen," <u>Saint Paul Pioneer Press</u>, March 24, 1967; Jonathan Friendly, "Metro Compromise Indicated," <u>Minneapolis Tribune</u>, March 25, 1967.

23. <u>Ibid</u>.; Peter Ackerberg, "Ogdahl Rejects Metro Council Compromise," <u>Minneapolis Star</u>, March 25, 1967.

24. Peter Vanderpoel, "Delayed Compromise on Metro Bill Likely," <u>Saint Paul Pioneer Press</u>, March 26, 1967.

25. Peter Ackerberg, "Metro Council Bill Shifted But Deadlock Sticks," <u>Minneapolis Star</u>, April 19, 1967; Jonathan Friendly, "Metropolitan Council Plan is Amended," <u>Minneapolis Tribune</u>, April 19, 1967.

26. Peter Vanderpoel, "Major Changes in Metro Bill Will Be Made," <u>Saint Paul Dispatch</u>, April 26, 1967.

27. Peter Vanderpoel, "Elected Metro Council Vetoed by House Unit," <u>Saint Paul Pioneer Press</u>, May 11, 1967.

28. <u>Ibid</u>.; Peter Ackerberg, "Metro Council Bill Clears Committee," <u>Minneapolis Star</u>, May 9, 1967.

29. <u>Ibid</u>.

30. Peter Ackerberg, "Both Sides Say House Will Pass Metro Plan," <u>Minneapolis Star</u>, May 11, 1967; Jonathan Friendly, "Elected Metro Unit Dies in House," <u>Minneapolis Tribune</u>, May 11, 1967.

31. Peter Vanderpoel, "Senate Unit OKs Metro Planning Bill," <u>Saint Paul Pioneer Press</u>, May 12, 1967.

32. Frank Wright, "Metropolitan Council Bill Passed by House," _Minneapolis Tribune_, May 16, 1967.

33. _Ibid_.

34. Peter Vanderpoel, "Metropolitan Agency Bill Passes in Senate," _Saint Paul Pioneer Press_, May 20, 1967.

35. _Ibid_.

36. Jackie Germann, "LeVander Signs 4 Metro Bills," _Saint Paul Pioneer Press_, May 26, 1967.

37. Harmon Ogdahl, Interview, April, 1969.

38. _Ibid_.

39. Editorial, "Two Cheers for the Metropolitan Council," _Minneapolis Tribune_, May 22, 1967.

40. 1967 Minnesota Sessions Law, Chapter 896 (Codified as Chapter 473 B). See Appendix A, Sections 5-9, for details of powers.

41. John Fischer, "The Minnesota Experiment: How to Make a Big City Fit to Live in," _Harper's Magazine_, CCXXXVIII, 1427 (April, 1969), 12; John Fischer, "Innovations in Government," speech delivered at 1969 National Planning Conference of the American Society of Planning Officials in Cincinnati, Ohio, April 21, 1969.

42. 1967 Minnesota Session Laws, Section 6, Subdivision 6(2), Chapter 896. The MSSD and the NSSSD were excepted. As a result of the 1969 metropolitan sewer act, this restriction has been eliminated.

43. _Ibid_., Subdivisions 7 and 8.

44. _Ibid_., Subdivision 12.

PART III

THE METROPOLITAN COUNCIL IN OPERATION

CHAPTER **8** THE METROPOLITAN
COUNCIL: THE
FIRST TWO YEARS

A planner or political scientist from outside
Minnesota would have been somewhat astonished at
the tributes praising the achievements of the Metropolitan Council on its first anniversary in August, 1968. After all, the Council, as established,
was essentially an advisory and coordinating body.
It lacked operating powers; it possessed only limited powers to prevent development not in confor-
mance with its development guide. And the development guide was still to be prepared. Consequently,
there could be little opportunity to please the
general public or local officials, or to rub them
the wrong way. No great controversies could seemingly be generated or conflicts of local interest
created. And it would take many months before the
Council's review functions could get off the ground
sufficiently to antagonize anyone. One, therefore,
would have expected the public officialdom to be
quite moderate in its praise or criticism of Council achievements. It was really too early to appraise its work objectively. Yet, local comments,
as noted above, were nearly unanimous in their
praise.

In August, 1968, Twin Cities newspapers--cen-
tral cities and suburban press alike--were filled
with accolades for the Council and its achievements,
many coming from its severest opponents of just one
year before. Examples are numerous. Senator
Thomas E. Greig, Conservative from suburban Fridley,
in 1967 had characterized metropolitan government
as a "cancerous growth"; one year later, he said,
"the Council has done a much better job than I

thought it would . . . ; in fact, I think they've
done a pretty darn good job."[1] Representative
Ralph P. Jopp, Conservative from Mayer, in 1967 had
voted against both approaches to the Council, but
one year later called it a "high caliber" body that
had "acted expeditiously" in preparing a metropolitan sewer plan.[2] An editorial in the suburban
Anoka County Union stated,

> We must point out that none of the
> dire things predicted for the metro-
> politan area by the formation of this
> first attempt at metro concept for
> guidance and direction of area plan-
> ning have come to pass. . . . [o]n
> the contrary, the record of the Coun-
> cil the past year has led many oppo-
> nents of metropolitan government,
> including us, to realize that the
> Council, as now constituted, does
> need more authority and greater lee-
> way in its operation. . . .[3]

This acknowledgment was to be the guidepost and
basis for later Council success with the 1969 legislature. The Council's most ardent admirers had
their views summed up in the words of Frenzel,
House author of an elected and operating council
bill: "I can't imagine a more productive first
year."[4] These statements were neither idle comments, wishful thinking, nor without foundation.
They were based upon a surprisingly good record,
achieved quickly, and without great controversy or
animosity in diverse areas of strong local interest
and augmented Council power.

GEARING UP

The first months of the Council's life were
spent largely in organizing itself to assume the
responsibilities authorized by the legislature.
Within two weeks after council members were named
by the Governor, they had revised the budget for

the rest of 1967 and were involved in preparing a
budget and work program for 1968.[5] The work program, as required by the enabling legislation, included a series of seven priority study projects to
be presented to the 1969 legislature, continuing
work on the projects of the now defunct MPC, establishing referral procedures for plans of planning
and research. The seven priority study projects
were as follows: (1) a metropolitan zoo, (2) a
metropolitan open space system, (3) a sewage plan
to help solve the area's critical water pollution
problems, (4) a solid waste disposal plan, (5) a
mass transit plan, (6) a method of resolving highway planning disputes, and (7) a metropolitan development guide.[6]

In carrying out the foregoing and other projects, the Council operated at a variety of levels.
It established a series of citizen advisory committees to work with it on the specific studies, and
purposefully involved other local officials, citizen groups, and other agencies in its deliberations.
The aim was to bring about a high degree of community participation in the development of plans to
help ensure that the plans considered local interests and that they would be understood and acceptable.[7] Collateral with this, as a first step in
coordinating metropolitan developments, the Council
assigned members to act as liaisons, to attend
meetings of other area agencies, and to serve on
the boards of special districts. In addition, the
Council contracted with a number of consultant
firms to study particular technical problems, e.g.,
provision of metropolitan sewer service. Council
members spent a great deal of time with the staff,
reading and talking with local officials and community representatives to educate themselves on the
area's problems and plans.[8] They expected to be
directly involved in council work beyond that directly assigned to them.

The Council also organized the staff taken over
from the MPC. In December, 1967, it appointed Robert T. Jorvig as its chief administrator--Executive

Director. Jorvig came to the Council from service
as Minneapolis' City Coordinator. Previously, he
had served as Director of the Minneapolis Housing
Authority after coming from a similar position in
Saint Paul. The Council, further, established two
departments--one for planning and the other for
community services. The Planning Department is responsible for comprehensive planning "in the areas
of government and social, economic, and physical
development."[9] The Community Services Department
"maintains contacts with Area communities, government officials, civil leaders, and the public; ad-
ministers the Council's referral operations; and
conducts special projects."[10] It also set up staff
units responsible for administrative services and
public information. In April, 1968, it published
the Metropolitan Development Guide "to fulfill a
contractual obligation" of the MPC, while beginning
work on its own Guide as required by the 1967 legislature.[11] Up to this point, nothing the Council
did had created any controversy, stepped on local
sensibilities, or conflicted with parochial interests. This was not to last much longer.

A HEADQUARTERS CONTROVERSY

One of the first real problems that the Council faced should seemingly have been one of relatively minor import--the selection of a headquarters
location. However, it was an inauspicious start,
yet one that may have been fortunate in shaking
down the Council by permitting its members to become more quickly acquainted with each other while
subduing inherent parochial interests. At the
start of its work in August, 1967, the Council set
up an office space committee to study needs and to
decide whether it should move from the old MPC offices to more suitable and convenient quarters.
Within a few weeks, the committee reported that improved headquarters space was necessary and reduced
potential locations to three sites: (1) the existing MPC offices to be expanded and remodeled, (2)
the Minneapolis Public Health Building; and (3) a

CHART I

Organization Chart
Metropolitan Council of the Twin Cities Area

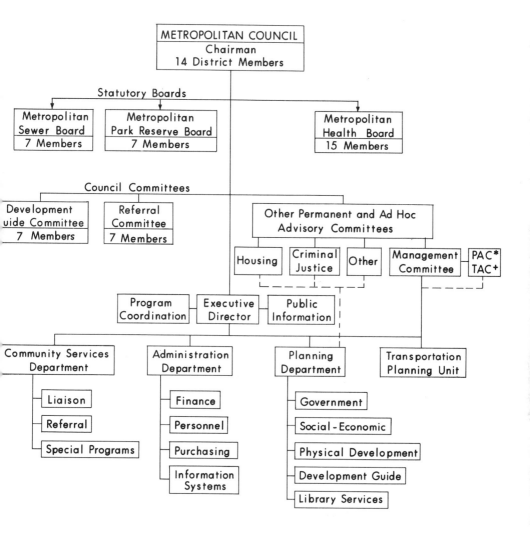

*Policy Advisory Committee of the Transportation Planning Program.
+Technical Advisory Committee of the Transportation Planning Program.

Source: Metropolitan Council of the Twin Cities Area.

new office building in downtown Saint Paul adjacent
to the state office complex and the Capitol. Each
site had obvious merits and supporters. The Minneapolis location was modern and the least costly,
but the amount of space barely met council needs.
The existing MPC space in Saint Paul was somewhat
more expensive, but equidistant from the downtowns
of both cities. The downtown Saint Paul location
was most expensive, but was convenient to state offices and to the intercity freeway. Complicating
the selection was the Minneapolis City Council proposal to have the Metropolitan Council make its
permanent headquarters in that city's new civic
center as Minneapolis, being the center of the metropolitan area, was "the only logical site."[12]

Within a few weeks, it became apparent that
the Council was sharply divided between the Minneapolis and downtown Saint Paul sites. The site
selection committee favored the Minneapolis location three to two, with the three Minneapolis area
members voting in its favor and the two Saint Paul
members voting against it; the final selection was
to be made by the full Council.[13] Because of what
appeared to be rising parochial interests, the
mayors of both Minneapolis and Saint Paul proposed
"neutral" sites--Saint Paul Mayor Byrne suggested
Fort Snelling (between both cities) and Minneapolis
Mayor Naftalin nominated the University of Minnesota. Chairman Hetland replied that "entire seven-
county area is neutral ground."[14] He further denied that the split represented parochial geographical blocks as the divergent views were based on
objective reasoning.[15] The situation unfortunately
persisted into mid-November before Chairman Hetland
broke a full Council, seven-to-seven deadlock, voting against the Minneapolis site.[16] Seven Minneapolis area members supported the committee's recommendation favoring the Minneapolis site; five
Saint Paul and two Minneapolis area members opposed
it. The Chairman's tie-breaking vote against the
Minneapolis site, however, did not by itself assure
selection of the downtown Saint Paul site. This
was accomplished on the following ballot when three

Minneapolis area members switched their votes to
join those of one Minneapolis area and four Saint
Paul area members for an eight-to-six majority in
its favor.[17]

The initial reaction in the press and outside
community was that the vote was a victory over nar-
row parochial interests.[18] One member indeed indicated that the Minneapolis area members had
switched, in part, in hopes of stimulating Saint
Paul to a "more active and pro-metro position."[19]
As noted before, Saint Paul leaders in government,
business, and the community were more conservative
and generally followed the initiatives of suburban
and Minneapolis leaders; such a prodding just might
have been necessary. However, to view the Council
split as a Saint Paul versus Minneapolis issue is a
gross overstatement. A more accurate explanation
appears to be that the split in good measure reflected anti-Minneapolis sentiments or fears on the
part of the rest of the Twin Cities area community.
(The resentments and fears by Minneapolis suburbs
are noted in Chapter 2, pp. 26-57.) Evidence of
this lies in the initial council ballot where two
members from suburban Minneapolis voted against the
Minneapolis site and later in favor of the downtown
Saint Paul or old MPC location, also in Saint Paul.
This may also explain the apparent lack of antago-
nism that a more parochial battle might have been
expected to generate. Subsequent discussions on
various issues were "low key and undramatic, with
no close votes."[20] Fortunately, too, the difficulties involved in making what should have been a
relatively minor decision did not carry over to
more important issues.

METROPOLITAN REVIEW AND
COMMUNITY RELATIONS

Perhaps the most delicate, if not controversial, area of council operations--one which touches
upon the widest range of local government sensibilities and interests--is that involving the review
of local and special district plans and applications

for federal and state grants. Local comprehensive
plans and matters having a metropolitan or intergovernmental effect, as noted in the last chapter,
are submitted to the Council for review and comment.
All such plans, matters, and grant applications,
save those for open space land acquisition, receive
only positive or negative comment for the information of concerned federal agencies. Open space
land acquisition applications, however, are subject
to an unqualified council veto. Special district
plans inconsistent with council development standards may similarly be vetoed, in total or in part.
It is in these delicate dealings that the Council
has seen need to maintain a high level of good intergovernmental relations.

From the beginning, the Council had recognized
the need to improve relations with the area's local
units of government. The old MPC had set up in
1966 only a modestly manned staff to handle intermunicipal relations; its review powers, although
authorized by law, were ignored by local units, who
were jealous of their planning prerogatives. The
Council, with much more effective powers authorized
by both federal and state law, immediately organized
a Referral Committee of seven members aided by its
new Community Services Department. It then began
to work out referral procedures, published in March,
1968, and effective avenues of liaison and communications, using the services of the Metropolitan
Section of the LMM and local county Leagues of Municipalities.[21] Special efforts were aimed at the
counties and the more rural suburbs, centers of the
area's principal opposition to the Council, particularly Carver, Scott, and Washington Counties which
have no residents serving on the Council.[22] (Their
districts are represented by nearby residents of
other counties.)

This more concerted effort to improve community relations, however, was hampered by a number of
factors. The Community Services Department did not
have a director until August, 1968, when Robert

Nethercut, former mayor of second tier Saint Paul
suburb of Arden Hills, was promoted to the position.[23] The department's staff also is small--only
seven persons--and referrals and the need for better communications are growing. Thirdly, Council
members serving on boards of special districts cannot vote. They may participate fully in all other
activities of the boards, but they have no real
power and may therefore be ignored.[24] Further, as
the Council moves into more sensitive efforts, such
as social considerations, major public investment,
and proposals to share local tax revenues, the potential for increased conflicts of interests
grows.[25]

    Directly related to these difficulties and
severely hampering the Council in its efforts to
coordinate area development intelligently is the
lateness of its involvement in the review process.
Too often it has been forced to act unfavorably or
to give qualified approval to plans that had progressed so far that unfavorable action would have
created undue cost, legal, or development problems.[26] Too often commitments on projects have been
made before the Council is brought in to coordinate
or review. The Council, in its report to the 1969
legislature, noted the problems involved in effective coordination

> . . . after final local or agency
> action has been taken and commitments
> made. If the Council is to effec-
> tively determine policy and coordi-
> nate overall development . . . and
> ensure that the expenditure of public
> funds will be directed toward the
> most economical and socially desir-
> able uses, some form of more effec-
> tive review power must be developed
> and some form of initiatory power be
> granted to the Council. . . . Review
> without an opportunity to determine
> priorities often is wasteful. . . .

The Council [must have the] power to
provide needed policy solutions.[27]

To help meet the demands of this situation, the
Council asked the 1969 legislature to authorize its
involvement in the review process at an earlier
stage of planning,[28] and revised its referral policies in January, 1969, to permit its staff to discuss preliminary findings with applicants prior to
formal action by the Referral Committee.[29] Referral procedures on municipal plans and highways were
revised in April, 1969, to reflect the change in
policy.[30] The hoped-for goal is to achieve reasonable, not necessarily agreeable, solutions.

    Despite these difficulties, relations between
the Council and municipalities and special districts for the most part have been good. Conflicts
inherent in the review process have been minimal.
Municipalities and special districts realize that
council review, in contrast to that of the MPC, is
mandatory under both federal and state law; that it
is necessary for orderly development, even if they
do not like it; and that the Council has carried
out this function responsibly.[31] Moreover, the
Council has acted unfavorably on very few referrals.
Between August, 1967, and January, 1969, the Council completed review of 132 of 167 plans and grant
applications. Only two were acted upon unfavorably,
four were approved with critical comments to serve
as guides in future planning, and two others were
either withdrawn or returned to the applicant.[32]
In view of the implications for effective metropolitan planning required under council legislation,
it is worthwhile commenting on Section 204 of the
Demonstration Cities and Metropolitan Development
Act of 1966.

    Section 204 was designed to provide informa-
tion--review comments--to involved federal agencies
about "the relationship of the proposed project to
comprehensively planned development of the area"[33]
so that the agency would be more knowledgeable when
it was approving or disapproving an application.[34]

Simultaneously, the review process was to serve as
a clearing house for other federal and state agencies and local governments so that they might be
informed when planning activities were of concern to
them and be better able to coordinate their respective development programs, particularly at the local and metropolitan levels. Section 204 was not
to serve as a means to reject an application that
the metropolitan review agency believed incompat-
ible with area-wide considerations, even though this
could happen.

While negative comments are important to influence necessary change in local plans, rejection
could involve a great waste of time, effort, and
money already invested. The ideal is to avoid this
through early involvement of the review body in the
planning process and early notification of state
and local governmental units when activities are of
concern to them so that their interests may be adequately considered. Initial experience with metropolitan review between July 1, 1969, and December
31, 1969, showed that in only three cases out of
sixty did federal agencies approve applications
having negative review comments.[35] This could indicate that negative review was likely to cause rejection of a local application as unsatisfactory
and thereby persuade local authorities to give more
consideration to metropolitan and intermunicipal
consequences of their plans. However, during the
next six months, twenty-eight applications out of
forty-seven receiving negative comments were federally approved, showing this not to be the case.[36]
There is, therefore, no assurance that negative review, by itself, can be the "big stick" of metropolitan planning. (For examples of the Metropolitan Council's review of local and special district
plans, see Appendix B.)

NOTES

1.   "Legislators Pleased With Action So Far,"
Minneapolis Tribune, August 8, 1968.

2.   Ibid.

3.   "Metro Council's First Year," Anoka County
Union, August 16, 1968.

4.   "Legislators Pleased With Action So Far,"
loc. cit.

5.   "Council's First Months," Metropolitan
Council Newsletter, I, 1 (December, 1967), 1.

6.   1967-1968 Biennial Report (Saint Paul:
Metropolitan Council of the Twin Cities, January,
1969), p. 4.

7.   James Hetland, Jr., Interview, April, 1969;
Reynold Boezi, Interview, April, 1969. (Interviews
cited are with Stanley Baldinger, unless otherwise
stated.)

8.   "Council's First Months," loc. cit.

9.   1967-1968 Biennial Report, loc. cit.

10.   Ibid.

11.   The Joint Program, Twin Cities Area Metropolitan Development Guide (Saint Paul: Twin Cities
Metropolitan Planning Commission, April, 1968), p. 1.

12.   Dennis W. Dunne, Interview, June, 1969;
"Thinking Big in Minneapolis," Saint Paul Pioneer
Press, October 17, 1967.

13.   Peter Ackerberg, "Metro Council Office Site
Choice Delayed," Minneapolis Star, October 27, 1967.

14.   Ibid.

15.   Ibid.

16. George McCormick, "Downtown St. Paul Location Selected by Metro Council," Minneapolis Tribune, November 10, 1967.

17. Ibid.; "Saint Paul to House Metro Council,"
Saint Paul Pioneer Press, November 10, 1967

18. Peter Ackerberg, "Met Council Geared Up
During First Year," Minneapolis Star, August 7, 1968.

19. Dunne, loc. cit.

20. Ackerberg, "Met Council Geared Up During
First Year," loc cit.

21. Robert Nethercut, Director of Department
of Community Services, Interview, June, 1969; Referral Manual (Saint Paul: Metropolitan Council,
March, 1968), pp. 1-12.

22. Ibid.

23. 1967-1968 Biennial Report, loc cit.;
Nethercut, loc. cit.

24. Alan J. Wilensky, "The Twin Cities Metro-
politan Council: A Case Study of the Politics of
Metropolitan Cooperation (unpublished senior thesis,
Princeton University, Princeton, N.J.), April, 1969.

25. Ibid.

26. Nethercut, loc. cit.; David Rubin, Metropolitan Council Transportation Planner, Interview,
June, 1969.

27. 1967-1968 Biennial Report, op. cit., p. 12.

28. Ibid.

29. James Hetland, Jr., Memorandum (Saint
Paul: Metropolitan Council, January 23, 1969).
(Mimeographed.)

30. Hugh C. Faville, Memorandum: Suggested Procedure for Certain Types of Highway Referrals (Saint Paul: Metropolitan Council, April 10, 1969); and Memorandum: Revised Procedures on Handling Comprehensive Municipal Plans (Saint Paul: Metropolitan Council, April 29, 1969). (Mimeographed.)

31. Nethercut, loc cit.

32. 1967-1968 Biennial Report, op. cit., pp. 19-25.

33. Section 204--The First Year (Washington, D.C.: The Bureau of Budget, September 24, 1968), p. 1. (Mimeographed.)

34. William Brussat, Bureau of the Budget, Interview, May, 1969; Charles M. Haar, Metropolitan Development and Budgeting: A Step Toward Creative Federalism, speech delivered at Columbia University (Washington, D.C.: U.S. Department of Housing and Urban Development, September 21, 1967), pp. 9-10. (Mimeographed.)

35. Meeting with William G. Colman, Executive Director of the U.S. Advisory Commission on Intergovernmental Relations, on Monday, June 24, 1968, at Gannon's Restaurant in St. Paul (Minneapolis: The Citizens League, 1968), p. 3. (Mimeographed.)

36. Section 204--The First Year, op. cit., p. 3.

9

METROPOLITAN TRANSPORTATION PLANNING

Under the legislation which established it,
the Metropolitan Council possesses ultimate responsibility for all comprehensive planning bearing on
area-wide development, including authority to prepare a transportation plan together with the Minnesota Highway Department (MHD) and the MTC. This
authority evolves from the requirements of the law
"to coordinate the planning and development of the
metropolitan area," the grant of power to veto unacceptable transit and airport location plans, and
the requirement and authority to review highway
plans.[1] Augmenting these is the MTC legislation
requiring that body to prepare and implement a
transit plan in cooperation with the Council and
MHD.[2] Complicating this situation is a welter of
federal laws, including the Federal Aid Highway Act
of 1962 and the Urban Mass Transportation Act of
1964, that require a continuing, comprehensive
transportation planning process to be carried out
cooperatively between state and local governments
and direct assistance to states and their agents.[3]

It was in response to this tangle of laws that
a series of proposals to establish a principal
transportation planning body began to emerge toward
the end of 1967. The first to appear was that of
the Coordinating Committee of the newly defunct
Joint Program of the MPC, the MHD, and representatives of each of the seven counties and the two
central cities. The Coordinating Committee proposed

a nineteen-member body, including the chairmen of
the Metropolitan Council, the MTC, the MAC, the
commissioner of the MHD, representatives of county
boards, the mayors of Minneapolis and Saint Paul,
representatives of the central cities' councils,
and four representatives of suburban communities.
The proposed Joint Transportation Program policy
committee would study area transportation needs and
prepare recommendations for the Council, the MTC,
and the MHD, but only on an advisory basis. The
Council, the MTC, and the MHD would have the sole
power to make decisions. The proposal was even
weaker than the preceding ungainly Joint Program,
possessing no decisionmaking power or responsibility, though each agency in its own right could implement parts of a plan if it so wished. The major
goal, however, was to involve local units of government in the policymaking process at the earliest
stage, while recognizing the ultimate responsibilities of the three policy bodies.

In response to this, Council Chairman Hetland
proposed a three-man policymaking board consisting
of himself, the chairman of the MTC, and the commissioner of the MHD. Municipal and county officials would participate through committees representative of the Metropolitan Section of the LMM
and of the MICC. This structure would focus policy
and decisionmaking authority in the three empowered
bodies while permitting balanced participation of
local government. Local officials would be represented further through membership on the MTC as
stipulated by its law.[4] The private sector would
be represented also by an advisory group. Because
of its triple-headed policy composition, the proposal was popularly dubbed the "troika."

The MTC, in August, 1968, endorsed the Hetland
proposal without opposition, and with only one ab-
stention.[5] The MHD and local officials took exception to it.[6] Both maintained that counties and
municipalities planned and built roads and should
therefore be included in the policymaking process.
The MICC circulated a resolution opposing the

"troika" and called for full and equal participation of the counties in the policy board; by early October, all seven area counties had endorsed the MICC proposal.[7] The Metropolitan Section of the LMM rejected the council plan, calling for a popularly elected agency to carry out transportation planning for the area.[8] Hopefully, this would be the Metropolitan Council, but in the event it did not become elected in 1969, another body would be necessary. Local representation was a requirement of such a policy body. The Highway Department believed that representation from the counties, particularly Hennepin and Ramsey, and from the two central cities was desirable.[9] It hoped that with their full participation the problem of "local consent" on highways, which enabled local units to veto most highway plans within their territory, could be avoided. (For a discussion of highway local consent, see pp. 195-96.) Hetland's reply was that the MHD approach would give local government an even more effective veto.[10]

By November, county, municipal, and MHD pressures had persuaded the Council and Hetland to modify their plan for a transportation policymaking body to include one representative for the counties and one for the municipalities.[11] The MICC and the Metropolitan Section of the LMM each would select a representative. This closely approximated a plan put forth by the Hennepin County Board in early October.[12] The modified proposal, now dubbed the "troika-plus-two," then became the center of renewed controversy.

In December, the MTC, on a six to two vote, endorsed a proposal "which designated the Metropolitan Council as the transportation decision-making organization in the seven-county area."[13] It opposed the five-man committee as intruding "another layer of government between the making of plans and the actual construction of a . . . system."[14] The MTC continued to oppose the "troika-plus-two" until it was also modified. In late January, 1969, the Council, somewhat reluctantly, voted eleven to two

to adopt the five-man transportation policymaking
body.[15] The proposal, as approved by the Council
(and later by the MHD), provided no power to implement adopted plans or to require other governmental
units to do so. The only significant power within
it was the authority of the Council to veto the
policy committee's plans if it deemed them unacceptable.[16] In such an event, the Council would be
able to adopt its own plan independent of the policy
committee's proposals. As noted earlier, the Council's enabling act requires it to have a transportation plan as part of its Development Guide.

As winter and spring dragged on, the participants in the discussion realized they had reached
another impasse. The Council, the MHD, and counties and municipalities had achieved agreement on
what they considered an acceptable policymaking
body; the MTC, on the contrary, opposed it. While
the MTC might accept the simple "troika," it continued to prefer to have the Council alone have the
responsibility to establish policy.[17] It had primary legislative responsibility in the planning
area. The MTC was supported in concept by the Citizens League and the Minneapolis newspapers.[18] Not
until late April was there a satisfactory compromise reached. The Council, the MHD, counties and
municipalities moved one step back, making the Metropolitan Council the policymaking body, but with
the five-member committee becoming the Management
Committee, which as its name implies, manages,
adopts, and operates the work programs for the metropolitan transportation system plan and program as
recommended by the Council.[19] The Council has final
authority, including a veto over the committee's actions. Its review and comments are final and may
constitute a veto over local plans if other than
strictly local or federal funds are used.

In an agreement between the Council and the
MHD signed in April, 1969, the MHD designated "the
Council as the area agency pursuant to the requirements of the Highway Act of 1962 to establish and
maintain a continuing, comprehensive and cooperative

transportation planning process in the Metropolitan
Area. . . ."[20] The MHD as final authority over
highway matters as required in the State Constitution and federal and state law, however, remains un-
affected.[21] Similar agreements or resolutions with
the MTC, the seven counties, and the municipalities
were signed in the weeks following.[22] By early
June, a transportation planning staff was being
assembled as part of the Council, but with the members of the Management Committee funding it.[23] The
agreement to make the Metropolitan Council the
policy body follows the path of such areas as Milwaukee and Seattle, where regional planning bodies
have received state responsibilities, though not
final authority, for area-wide transportation planning.[24]

The final, agreed proposal for a metropolitan
transportation policymaking body was a compromise
with the ideal, i.e., complete centralization of
this responsibility and authority in the Metropolitan Council. But this compromise was inevitable.
From the very nature of the diffuse and disparate
planning and development authority granted by law--
federal and state--to the governmental units in-
volved--the Council, MHD, MTC, municipalities, and
counties--there could be no other kind of solution.
Moreover, to endow the Council with the ultimate
authority over highway planning in the metropolitan
area would have raised serious legal problems and
would have placed a quasi-local body over a state
agency, which is an unlikely, if not illegal, situation.[25] Compounding the complexity of the problem were the different approaches to bring order
out of an unclear, or, more accurately, near anar-
chic transportation planning situation, caused by
"local consent" or local veto of highway proposals.
The MHD sought to overcome it by bringing local government into the planning process at an early stage;
local units, because of the pending elimination of
local consent by the 1969 legislature, sought direct
policy involvement to protect their interests. The
MTC, on the other hand, sought to centralize the
process entirely within the Council. The Council,

recognizing the merits of each position and the
realities of the situation, worked for a workable
compromise. The compromise agreement when finally
announced was subject to considerable criticism for
being watered down. Yet, the surprising thing is
that the Council was able to obtain basic responsibility for comprehensive transportation planning in
the seven-county area, albeit this was not entirely
of its own doing, and despite a position of relative political weakness in comparison with the other
participants. In final analysis, it was the skill
of Chairman Hetland and the respect of the area-wide
political community for the Council and its goals
that enabled the Council to achieve primary responsibility for the area's transportation planning.

A METROPOLITAN SEWERAGE PLAN

Of the ten studies that the legislature required of the Metropolitan Council, none was more
sensitive or controversial than that of sewage collection and treatment. The issues involved in
creating a metropolitan system had confronted and
divided the community for almost a decade, not only
frustrating the attempts, but at times coloring
other metropolitan proposals.[26] The Council recognized that its sewage plan, as such, was both the
key to the legislative success of its other proposals and the key to its future as a successful metropolitan body.[27] Failure on this issue could adversely affect its effort to resolve other metropolitan-
wide problems. Adding to the urgency of the situation was the requirement of the HUD that an acceptable area-wide sewage plan be adopted, or be under
active preparation, by July 1, 1968.[28]

At the same time complicating efforts of the
Council were the deliberations of the state Pollution Control Agency (PCA) which was considering two
suburban applications to build sewage treatment
plants before the Council had formulated its plan
for an area-wide system. As it turned out, the PCA
approved construction of a plant which the Council

termed "unfortunate" because it restricted the development potential for sewage disposal and other
uses.[29] The PCA's prime concern was the control or
prevention of pollution; the Council's was an integrated metropolitan system making use of the
area's rivers for a variety of uses. To avoid further recriminations and to promote internal and
community-wide agreement, the Council organized itself as a "committee of the whole," foregoing an
advisory committee, and proceeded to work quietly
and forthrightly away from public view. Work was
carried out, with the help of its staff and the consulting firm of Metcalf and Eddy of Boston, Massachusetts (which had not previously been involved
with the sewer issues), at informal and nonpubli-
cized meetings.[30] After five months of concerted
work, on July 1, 1968, the Council announced its
"preliminary concept plan" for an area-wide sewer
system.[31] The plan, subsequently, was to serve as
the focus of discussion and feedback so that a
final plan and recommended legislation could be
prepared in anticipation of the 1969 session of the
legislature.

The major stumbling block to previous attempts
to create a metropolitan sewer system was that of
distribution of costs, particularly between the central cities with their existing facilities and the
suburbs where new facilities had to be built. An-
cillary to this were such considerations as acquisition and cost of existing facilities, the use of
one or more treatment plants, the costing of new
facilities by service district or area-wide considerations, and the cost of service in general. The
preliminary concept plan called for the creation of
a "total metropolitan sewerage system" based on a
network of seven watersheds, or combination of watersheds, each with at least one major "treatment plant,
interceptors, and tributary service area."[32] The
Council would establish "broad policies, the system
plan, fiscal policy, bonding, capital budgeting,
and approval of facilities. . . ."[33] It would also
appoint a separate, but dependent, Administrative
Board of seven members, one from each service

district (a combination of two council districts),
to administer the Council's policies, design, con-
struct, operate, and maintain the system, as well
as prepare an annual budget.[34] To finance the system, each service district would be established as
a taxing unit to spread normal local costs in a manner similar to the way municipalities routinely
charge construction and operating costs for collection and treatment. Costs of facilities having
metropolitan characteristics, e.g., major interceptor sewers, would be spread throughout the area by
a tax levy. There would be no required purchase of
existing facilities, although ownership of the system would reside in the Council.[35] The concept
plan was a "total water resources program," tying
pollution control to natural resource development
and recreation.[36]

In view of the controversial nature of the issues involved, the Council's concept plan was surprisingly well received. The PCA and suburban officials were generally pleased.[37] Senator Rosenmeier
called it "an imaginative plan," and said he would
consider it sympathetically.[38] The only significant
reservations came from the officials of Minneapolis,
Saint Paul, and South Saint Paul. They felt that
the financial arrangements favored the suburbs at
their financial expense.[39] Over the next six
months, these and other comments, suggestions, proposals, and criticisms were evaluated, incorporated,
or dismissed, and a final Metropolitan Sewerage Plan
developed in time for the 1969 session of the legislature.[40] The final plan, in most respects, was a
more detailed presentation of the "concept plan."
Only in the manner of financing was there a significant change. Instead of recommending that
"both the collection and treatment facilities be
charged back to communities by service area" as
proposed in the concept plan, the Council now recommended that the goal of uniform rates for treatment
be established on a metropolitan basis, with adjust-
ments for relative strength and volume.[41] Otherwise, desired "differential water control standards
would be too difficult to achieve" and could result

in inequitable rates. Communities using existing
facilities owned by other communities would pay a
rental fee to the latter, based on replacement
costs, less depreciation, federal grants, and out-
standing debt of the facilities.[42]   In addition,
service areas would be established through which
the cost of the metropolitan interceptor systems
would be charged back to the communities in each
service area on a user, future-user basis. It was
still a policy plan, rather than a procedural manual, but with sufficient detail so "that government
units and residents of the Area have the information they need to make decisions affecting the
Area's total development."[43]   Legislation to create
the proposed plan was introduced early in the session by Senator Ashbach, who had sponsored attempts
to set up a metropolitan system since 1961.

    The reactions of the Twin Cities community to
the final report and proposed legislation was, as
expected, much the same as that received by the
Council's preliminary concept plan. The suburbs
were in general agreement with it; the central
cities were dissatisfied for the same reason--the
estimated high cost to them. Rather than fight and
hold each other off, as in previous sessions of the
legislature, central cities and suburban interests
engaged in a series of dialogues which resulted in
three compromises in the manner in which sewage
treatment and metropolitan costs would be apportioned. First of all, the Council's goal of uniform rates, in concept, would be retained but modified for treatment charges to consider the following:

> (1) The extent of treatment which must
> be given sewage from each municipality;
> (2) the extent to which sewage has been
> diluted by water from storm sewers;
> (3) the extent to which sewage has been
> diluted by surface water; (4) and the
> amount of error in calculating volume
> during previous years.[44]

Secondly, a formula was worked out which would ap-
portion costs for interceptor sewers and special

facilities of particular benefit to the metropolitan area as a whole, and for deferred payment, when
communities could not afford costs initially, on a
basis of one-half according to the assessed value
of property and one-half according to population of
communities within the system area.[45] Finally,
shortly before the full Senate considered the bill,
it was further amended to enable the Council to ad-
just the formula to provide relief from unusually
high and burdensome costs to a given community.[46]
In only one other major way was the Council's plan
amended. The legislation provided that ownership
of the system would reside in the Sewer Board rather
than in the Council. Chairman Hetland, speaking for
the Council, objected that this could prove adminis-
tratively awkward, but reluctantly agreed to it.[47]

Despite these changes, many suburban and central cities partisans were not satisfied; they
still believed that the plan and its cost alloca-
tions were unsatisfactory. This was particularly
true of South Saint Paul and the NSSSD.[48] As the
session moved into the spring, it became apparent
that the legislature would no longer be hung up on
purely parochial considerations. The Council's
proposal was well considered and supported both in
the legislature and by the great majority of local
officials, including the Metropolitan Section of
the LMM. On April 18, 1969, the Senate passed the
Council's bill with only four dissenting votes,
three of them from suburban districts.[49] On May 12,
the House similarly passed the bill, 116 to 15.[50]
Shortly after, the Governor signed the bill into
law creating a metropolitan-wide sewage collection
and treatment system administered by a separate but
dependent board appointed by and responsible to the
Metropolitan Council.[51] After close to a decade of
work, education, and proselyting, the advocates of
a metropolitan sewer system were successful. They
had built upon the same general consensus generated
to create the Metropolitan Council two years before.
And the legislature, pleased with the Council's record and performance since its creation, was receptive to that body's plan, viewing it as the product
of truly representative metropolitan interests.[52]

A LEGISLATIVE DELUGE

The sewer bill, as noted early in the previous section, was the key to the success of the Council's legislative program. If it were to fail, enactment of other council proposals would also be in jeopardy.[53] Equally important, if the Council had failed there would have been serious questions about its general effectiveness as a metropolitan planning and coordinating body. But the Council did not fail. It achieved almost everything it asked for in the sewer bill and received at least part, if not all, of every proposal in each piece of legislation it sponsored or supported. The 1969 legislature gave the Council significant planning and service power with respect to solid waste disposal, regional parks and open space, a state zoo, mediation of the local veto over highway proposals, airport zoning and development, and metropolitan transit.

Solid Waste Disposal

The Council, with the assistance of a citizen advisory committee, proposed joint action by the Council, the seven area counties, and the state PCA to plan, develop, and operate a solid waste disposal system throughout the seven-county area. The Council would prepare and adopt a comprehensive system plan, including a statement of goals and policies, the general locations of disposal sites and facilities (based on sanitary land fill), site and capacity criteria, operating regulations and disposal techniques, and the kinds of waste to be disposed of at given sites. It would also review the counties' operational plans to determine if they were in accord with the system plan.

The counties would operate the system, owning and operating the disposal sites and facilities or regulating private operators, pursuant to the Council's plan. In doing so, they would prepare and submit to the Council for its approval their plans to acquire, finance, develop, and operate sites and

facilities, including ultimate use and disposition
of sites. In the event of the failure of a county
or counties to act in accordance with the system
plan, the Council would assume their powers to acquire, finance, and operate necessary sites and
facilities. The PCA would establish air and water
pollution standards and issue licenses.[54] The 1969
legislature authorized the solid waste disposal system, substantially as recommended by the Council,
save that the "standby" powers requested by the
Council in absence of county action were denied.[55]

Metropolitan Park Reserve Board

The Council, with the assistance of a citizens'
advisory committee, proposed that the legislature
establish a Metropolitan Park Reserve Board of
seven members under the Council "to acquire . . .
open space, prepare site and facility plans and de-
signs, develop sites and facilities, operate and
maintain facilities, and prepare an annual budget."[56]
The Council would prepare the system plan, providing
"standards, criteria and guidelines" for the acquisition, preservation, and regulation of system elements.[57]

The 1969 legislature authorized a more limited
Park Board than requested by the Council. The Park
Board would purchase and own the properties and
would contract, when feasible, with units of local
government, to acquire, develop, and maintain them
in the name of the Park Board.[58] Two million dollars are to be provided from part of the proceeds
of a four cent per package increase in the tax on
cigarettes to purchase state and metropolitan park
land. None of these funds, the Park Board's only
source of direct revenue, however, can be used for
administrative purposes. In addition, the Park
Board does not have the power of eminent domain although this was requested by the Council.[59] Local
government will continue its present park and open
space activities and advise the Council on its
long-range plans. The Council will also have the
power to veto Park Board annual capital and operating

budgets which do not conform to the council approved
parks and open space system plan.

Zoological Gardens

The Council, also with the assistance of a
citizens' advisory committee, proposed to the legislature the establishment of a seven-member zoo
board to "maintain and operate" a major metropolitan zoological garden, including the study and
preparation of the site, engineering, and design
plans.[60] The Council would "appoint the Board members, prepare [the] system plan and capital improvement program with [the assistance of the zoo board],
review and approve site . . . engineering and design plans, approve annual operating budgets, etc."[61]
Ownership of land and facilities would reside in the
Council. The legislature, instead of creating a
metropolitan zoo under the Council, authorized a
state zoo to be acquired, constructed, and operated
by an eleven-member board appointed by the governor.
The zoo will still be located in the seven-county
metropolitan area, and the Council must review the
location and development plans before they can be
implemented.[62] Any development plan or zoo site
that is unacceptable to the Council may be vetoed.

Highway Local Consent

The Council, again with the assistance of a
citizens' advisory committee, proposed that existing law, permitting municipalities to veto state
and federal trunk highways (excluding interstate
systems and local roads), be rewritten to provide
better and more expeditious highway planning. It
would establish a procedure (1) to involve municipalities at earlier stages of highway planning;
(2) to require municipalities to commit themselves
to plans that would be binding later on; and (3) to
rework and resubmit for approval any plans disapproved by the Highway Department or governmental
unit involved, or submit them to a proposed Highway
Appeal Board whose decision would be final. The
community or communities involved and the governor.

would each select one member; these two would select
the third.   The legislature authorized almost everything that the Council proposed, but expanded the
law's application state-wide.   In the metropolitan
area, the Council and the MTC became participants.[63]
The law, in effect, gave the Council much the same
rights as local government in highway planning and
approval, involving it at early stages of the process.

Airport Zoning and Development

The Council, together with the Metropolitan
Airports Commission (MAC), early in the session,
prepared legislation to resolve problems connected
with the new international airport proposed for the
area.   The legislature subsequently authorized the
Council to establish criteria and guidelines for
proper land use and development within three miles
(five if a special natural resource is involved) of
the new facility to protect people and natural resources.   Concerned municipalities must then incorporate these criteria into their zoning ordinances,
subdivision regulations, official maps, and building codes, and submit them to the Council for approval.   Any local controls and plans not conform-
ing to council airport development criteria and
guidelines, the Council may amend as necessary.
These local controls must be put into effect; no
other than the approved uses will be permitted.
The Council also will determine permitted noise
levels and zones from standards developed with the
MAC.   The affected units of government within the
noise zones must adopt appropriate land use and development controls as approved by the Council.

The law gives the Council important powers
with respect to property diminished in value because of limited permitted development.

> If a court determines that application
> of the [above] . . . controls within
> the airport development area consti-
> tutes a taking, . . . MAC is author-
> ized to purchase the property. . . .

> The acquisition of such land must be
> exercised if the Commission has or
> will have the necessary funds and if
> the Council determines that it is
> necessary to protect the airport from
> encroachment, or protect the resi-
> dents of the area, or encourage the
> most appropriate use of property in
> the airport development area, or pro-
> tect and conserve the natural re-
> sources of the . . . area. After
> . . . acquisition . . . MAC would pre-
> pare a plan for its use in accordance
> with the land-use controls and dis-
> pose of the land in the same manner
> as a housing and redevelopment agency.[64]

Presumably, damages will also be payable where the
concerned property is not purchased. This, however,
is still somewhat vague.[65] As these controls will
affect the amount of tax revenues that would otherwise accrue to involved communities from development in the area controlled, tax revenues from permitted development may be shared among them, according to a mutually agreed upon apportionment formula.[66]

Metropolitan Transit

The basic law governing the creation of the
MTC was amended to permit the MTC to acquire the
existing Twin Cities public transportation system
by condemnation. The Council, however, must approve
any such purchase before it can take place. Beginning in June, 1969, the MTC must submit, with comments, its capital expense and capital improvement
budgets to the Council for approval or disapproval.
The Council and the MTC are instructed to cooperate
and furnish information to each other for meaningful evaluations.[67] A Council proposal to approve
MTC system plans was withheld, although under the
1967 Metropolitan Council Act, the Council has the
power to veto an unacceptable MTC systems plan.

Other Legislation

The work of the Council and its citizen advisory committees favorably influenced several other pieces of legislation, including state-wide flood plain management,[68] shoreland zoning,[69] creation of a new state park in the area,[70] and the preservation of open space.[71]

OTHER ACTIVITIES

The Council since its inception has been involved in a number of functions and activities that will increase in importance over the next few years. Among the most significant of these has been the Council's involvement in social considerations such as low income housing, criminal justice planning, and area-wide health and hospital planning. The housing study began in 1968 under a 100 percent HUD grant to determine the area's needs for low and moderate income housing, in the context of the area's current housing activity, and to recommend ways to make such housing more readily available.[72] The criminal justice planning program is being developed in conjunction with the State Planning Agency under provisions of the federal Omnibus Crime Control and Safe Streets Act of 1968.[73] The program covers such elements as law enforcement, court procedures, radio communications, recordkeeping, and a metropolitan police academy and detective force; the effort is to design such a program and not, at this time, to carry it out. The Council, as with other sensitive projects, is being assisted by a citizens advisory committee of thirty-three members.[74] The health study has been under way since 1968, spurred by a federal requirement for metropolitan coordination of federal health program grants and loan expenditures.[75] The goal is to develop a comprehensive and unified area-wide planning system, replacing the present two local ones to meet future area-wide needs.[76]

The Council gave preliminary approval to a
1969-1970 work program calling for the Council to
study and prepare recommendations to the 1971 legislature on metropolitan finance and tax disparities to reinforce "highway and mass transit programs," to flesh out the metropolitan park and open
space system and its financial resources, and to
prepare its own Development Guide.[77] In addition,
it would complete its low and moderate income housing study, crime prevention and criminal justice
planning study, health and hospital planning; implement the provisions of the 1969 sewer bill; and work
with the MAC in selecting the site of the new airport.[78] The most sensitive of the projects to be
taken up is preparing a plan to help equalize the
area's tax revenues or to compensate for local tax
disparities as a means to achieve area development
goals. This study, required by the 1967 council
legislation, was deliberately put off for two reasons. First of all, its controversial nature could
have threatened the success of metropolitan considerations of equal importance, e.g., the passage of
a sewer system.[79] Secondly, there was not enough
time to properly prepare a recommendation for the
1969 session of the legislature.[80] During the 1969
session, Senator Rosenmeier proposed an elected metropolitan fiscal agency, separate from the Council,
to control the fiscal aspects of area-wide government.[81] In theory it would carry out the policies
of the Council; but it is generally recognized that
such a body, elected and separate from the Council,
could in effect become the locus of metropolitan development power and all but completely undercut the
current position of the Council.[82] Certainly, local
units of government and boards would listen very
carefully to a new agency if they depended on it for
their funds. And such a body would have definite
policy views; the powers to tax and carry out policy
decisions, as the Minneapolis Tribune noted, are in-
separable.[83]

A limited tax-sharing mechanism--really a
formula--proposed by the Citizens League and endorsed by the Metropolitan Council was approved by

the Minnesota House but failed of action by the Senate. It provided for the sharing of the growth in
nonresidential property valuations, with 40 percent
of funds going into a metropolitan pool to be allocated to all parts of the area on a per capita
basis; 60 percent would be retained locally within
the jurisdictions where the buildings are located.[84]

A SUCCESSFUL THREE YEARS

The accomplishments of the Metropolitan Council--the 1969 legislative program, the extra-legal
augmentation of authority and responsibility for
transportation planning, earlier involvement and
review in local and district plan referrals, etc.--
have been most impressive. They indicate a promise
for the future far greater than one would have
thought possible. There are several reasons for
this. Perhaps most important has been the uniformly high level of the council members--a quality
that has determined an equally high quality of performance and that in turn has engendered an unusual
degree of respect throughout the metropolitan community and the legislature. In the forefront of
the Council's work has been its Chairman Hetland,
respected both for his capabilities and his long
experience in metropolitan activities. He has
played the major role in establishing the council
policy of proposing to do only those functions that
the local units could not effectively do themselves
and then to share new responsibilities with local
units when practicable. This, as much as anything,
has created a confidence within central cities and
suburbs that the Council does not constitute a danger to their interests and local government, but is
instead a logical extension of it.

Complementing the Council has been its good
fortune of inheriting immediately a highly competent and respected staff from the MPC and adding
to it a staff of equal competence. Equally important to the Council's legislative success was the
ability to persuade important community persons to

become involved in the Council's projects. Typical
of this was the naming of John Tilton, former publisher of the suburban <u>Sun</u> newspapers and critic of
the original proposals for a metropolitan council,
to be chairman of the Metropolitan Zoo Advisory Committee. Over the course of the six months of his
involvement in council work, his doubts and reservations were transformed into a warm regard and
strong support for council proposals. He deemed
them to be responsible and thought they did not go
beyond what was necessary to meet area-wide needs
properly.[85] Finally, in exercising its authority
responsibly, the community led a renewed metropolitan discussion which lacked the fears and apprehen-
sion that characterized the pre-1967 period and
which has permitted it to move quickly and far
ahead in just three years.

A MINOR CONTROVERSY

       During the spring and summer of 1969, the Coun-
cil and elected local officials became involved in
a minor controversy--the composition of dependent
administrative boards under the Council. In establishing a metropolitan sewer system, the legislature
called for membership of the system's governing
board to be drawn exclusively from the area's private citizenry; dual service of elected local officials on the Sewer Board was prohibited. The legislation establishing the Park Reserve Board, in
contrast, was not specific on membership. Through
the course of the discussions of the 1969 legislative session, many local officials had pushed for
their representation on both boards. Only reluctantly did they accept the legislature's decision
on the Sewer Board. Though they strongly differed
with it, they recognized that the establishment of
a metropolitan sewer system was too important to
jeopardize over the issue of representation. In
addition, the system itself was a very sensitive
issue in some communities; dual service, therefore,
could compromise necessary decisions on system policies and operations.[86] The community--officials

and public alike--all too well remembered the general inability of local officials who served on the
old MPC to make basic decisions because of conflicts
of interests. Local official views with respect to
representation on the Park Reserve Board, however,
were another matter. Elected local officials were
intimately involved in area park activities, they
argued, and their views should be formally represented on the Park Board. To get their support for
the creation of a metropolitan park reserve system,
particularly that of county officials, Frenzel,
House sponsor of the bill, agreed to leave the composition of Park Board membership open. As a result, local officials held high hopes for greater
influence in council activities.[87] When Chairman
Hetland, in late August, announced that council
policy on the Park Board would follow the legislative mandate for the Sewer Board--membership would
be composed of private citizens only[88]--the issue
was set.

     Local officials felt that to deprive elected
officials of membership on the Park Board constituted unwarranted discrimination; all citizens, not
just private ones, should be eligible to serve on
the Council and its administrative boards.[89] They
noted that one council member, Milton Knoll, served
at the same time as mayor of the City of White Bear
Lake (suburban Saint Paul) for two years. The issue of elected officials on the Council had not
arisen before for a variety of reasons. Elected
officials did not oppose the practice and the area
had hoped the Council would be an elected body.
Even when the legislature made it appointive, the
metropolitan community overwhelmingly believed its
eventual election a certainty.

     Council policy on the Park Board as stated in
its resolution of August 28, 1969, called for board
membership to be consistent with the legislature's
requirement on membership for the Sewer Board. Persons with backgrounds of elected public service
would be desirable on the board, but not while they
were serving also in local capacities.[90] Elected

officials could serve on the Board, but only after
they officially terminated their relations with the
local unit. As private citizens, hopefully, they
would have a more metropolitan outlook and fewer
parochial interests. Further, the excessive time
demands of dual service would be eliminated.[91] The
emphasis was to be on metropolitan and district
constituencies and council authority. Local officials were more than slightly annoyed with this decision. Municipal officials, through the Metropolitan Section of the LMM, in June, 1970, formally
called for all citizens of the metropolitan area to
be eligible to serve on "any appointive body or organization which exists or is created in the metropolitan area."[92] County officials, through the
MICC, similarly reasserted that there was need for
greater participation of elected local officials in
metropolitan affairs and that county officials were
prepared to cooperate fully with the Council in doing so.[93] Fortunately for the Council and the Twin
Cities community, despite the strong feelings generated over the issue of representation, there is
no significant residue of hard feelings.[94]

      Council policy on this issue seems to be basi-
cally sound. It is consistent with what the legislature and the Twin Cities community as a whole
felt desirable with respect to the Sewer Board.
The views of elected local officials were important
to the Council, but the potential conflicts of interest were too great to chance. The issues that
the Council faced were largely metropolitan and membership on administrative boards should reflect
this. Local officials were indeed involved in metropolitan as well as local park activities, as they
had noted. Their sympathies and outlooks might be
similar for both; however, their responsibilities
and obligations for each might well be different,
even antagonistic. The Council's policy should
even be further reinforced by preventing dual service on the Council itself. Local views could be
taken into consideration through the establishment
of formal advisory boards composed of elected local
officials under the Council. This issue will

shortly be faced when the Council formally establishes a Twin Cities area Health Advisory Board;
elected officials are being considered, but they
have as yet to be elected.

POSTLUDE

The next few years will be as critical for the
Metropolitan Council as the last three. The next
sessions of the legislature will have to come to
grips with vital issues that could immutably change
the character of the Council. The Council now is
deeply involved in the study of area fiscal disparities and will propose recommendations on how to
share area-wide revenues. How the legislature re-
sponds--in augmenting the Council's responsibilities or in setting up a separate body to handle
such a function--may, as noted earlier, profoundly
affect the Council, possibly even destroy it.
Should the Council continue as an effective metropolitan body, the community and legislature must
contend with the issue of making it elective. During the 1969 session, most of the advocates of an
elective Council did not vigorously push the issue
for fear of jeopardizing other proposals considered
equally important, but this holding off cannot continue for long, particularly if the Council ac-
quires more authority and greater responsibilities
as it has since its creation in 1967.

In anticipation of such a contingency, the
Council is actively preparing and adopting a Metropolitan Development Guide (a major concern in the
years ahead), in the form of a series of platform
planks or issues that council members could run
on.[95] The planks or issues would be prospective
council policies which for the most part would not
be subject to frequent change as development programs could be. Policies would be spelled out in
sufficient detail to include such elements as
standards, principles, and systems plans. These
policy statements could be timed to come out at
moments convenient for elections.

Another major issue the Council will increasingly face as time goes on is the proper distribution of functions between itself and local units (and the state). Presently, it is involved in only those functions obviously essential for orderly metropolitan development that the community has agreed upon--sewage and solid waste disposal, parks and open space, transit and transportation planning, local and district plan review, etc.--and that local units cannot adequately do alone. But it can be expected that in the not too distant future it will have to face the issue of whether it should handle those functions that can be carried out best, rather than only, at the metropolitan level. Such issues as police service and low income housing will then come under close scrutiny. A poll by the Minneapolis Star indicates that such consideration is not yet close at hand; only an elected Council, transit, airport location, and sewage disposal are presently of major community concern.[96] And which of those functions can local units carry out adequately, but refuse to do? As noted before, the recent legislation which set up a metropolitan solid waste disposal system refused to grant the Council back-up powers if counties failed to carry out their responsibilities. Depending on how local units will exercise their responsibilities, the Council and legislature may well face this issue again in 1971.

NOTES

1. 1967 Minnesota Session Laws (hereafter cited as MSL), Chapter 896 (codified as Chapter 473B).

2. 1967 MSL, Chapter 892 (codified as Chapter 473A).

3. Federal Aid Highway Act, 1962, Public Law 87-866, 76 Stat. 1145; Urban Mass Transportation Act, 1964, Public Law 88-365, 78 Stat. 302.

    4.   James Hetland, Jr., <u>Chairman's Analysis of</u>
<u>Proposal by Joint Program Coordinating Committee for</u>
<u>Continuing Transportation Planning</u> (Saint Paul:
Metropolitan Council, July 25, 1968), pp. 1-6.
(Mimeographed.)

    5.   "MTC Backs Troika Plan for Policy," <u>Minne-</u>
<u>apolis Star</u>, August 29, 1968.

    6.   Peter Ackerberg, "Counties Objecting to
3-Unit Agency to Plan Metro Transit," <u>Minneapolis</u>
<u>Star</u>, October 10, 1968.

    7.   <u>Ibid</u>.; Wilfred "Andy" Anderson, Interview,
June, 1969. (Interviews cited are with Stanley
Baldinger, unless otherwise stated.)

    8.   Ackerberg, <u>loc. cit</u>.

    9.   Peter Ackerberg, "Conflict Arises Over
Transportation Program for Cities," <u>Minneapolis</u>
<u>Star</u>, October 26, 1968.

    10. <u>Ibid</u>.

    11. Peter Ackerberg, "More Transit Planners
Urged," <u>Minneapolis Star</u>, November 26, 1968.

    12. <u>Ibid</u>.

    13. Jerry Montgomery, "MTC Wants Metro Coun-
cil to Set Policy," <u>Saint Paul Pioneer Press</u>, December 19, 1968.

    14. <u>Ibid</u>.

    15. Peter Ackerberg, "Creation of Transit
Planning Unit Backed," <u>Minneapolis Star</u>, January
24, 1969.

    16. <u>Ibid</u>.

    17. Lester Bolstad, Jr., Interview, June,
1969.

18. Ted Farrington, "Metropolitan Decisions on Transportation in Conflict," Minnesota Valley Sun, December 12, 1968; Editorial, "Metropolitan Transportation Planning," Minneapolis Tribune, December 26, 1968.

19. James Hetland, Jr., Interview, June, 1969; Gene Avery, Transportation Planning Director, Interview, June, 1969.

20. Agreement Between Metropolitan Council and Minnesota Highway Department (Saint Paul: Metropolitan Council, April 10, 1969), p. 2. (Mimeographed.)

21. Ibid.

22. Resolution for Seven Counties, April-June, 1969; Agreement Between Metropolitan Council and Metropolitan Transit Commission, May 13, 1969 (Saint Paul: Metropolitan Council). (Mimeographed.)

23. Avery, loc. cit.

24. David Rubin, Interview, June, 1969.

25. James Hetland, Jr., Interview, June, 1969.

26. George McCormick, "Metro Sewer Bill Goes to Governor," Minneapolis Tribune, May 13, 1969.

27. Boezi, Interview, March-April, 1969.

28. Housing and Urban Development Act of 1965, Public Law 89-117, 79 Stat. 451, 502.

29. Peter Ackerberg, "OK on Sewerage Plant Permit Criticized," Minneapolis Star, May 5, 1968.

30. 1967-1968 Biennial Report, op. cit., p. 6; Peter Ackerberg, "Met Council Geared Up During First Year," Minneapolis Star, August 7, 1968.

31. *Metropolitan Sewer Plan: A Preliminary Concept Plan* (Saint Paul: Metropolitan Council, July 1, 1968).

32. *Ibid.*, p. 6.

33. *Ibid.*, pp. 6, 26.

34. *Ibid.*

35. *Ibid.*, p. 6.

36. *Ibid.*, pp. 4, 5.

37. "State Agency Backs Metro Sewer System," *Minneapolis Tribune*, July 10, 1968.

38. "Legislators Pleased with Actions So Far," *Minneapolis Tribune*, August 8, 1968.

39. Boezi, Interviews, March-April, 1969, and June, 1969.

40. *Metropolitan Sewerage Plan* (Saint Paul: Metropolitan Council, January 30, 1969).

41. *Ibid.*, pp. 7, 8, 39-41.

42. *Ibid.*, p. 41.

43. *Ibid.*, p. i.

44. Terry Borman, "16 Municipalities Vote to Support Metro Sewer Bill," *Saint Paul Dispatch*, March 6, 1969.

45. Boezi, Interviews, March-April, 1969, and June, 1969.

46. *Ibid.*

47. "Sewer Bill Amendment Would Shift Ownership," *Minneapolis Star*, February 18, 1969.

48. "Metro Sewer Bill Foes Meet to Plan Stand," Minneapolis Star, March 9, 1969; Peter Ackerberg, "Met Council Sewer Bill Revisions Urged," Minneapolis Star, March 5, 1969.

49. "State Senate Passes Bill Creating Metro Sewer System," Saint Paul Dispatch, April 18, 1969.

50. Peter Ackerberg, "Metro Region Sewer Bill Passed by State Senate [sic, should be House]," Minneapolis Star, May 13, 1969.

51. 1969 MSL, Chapter 449.

52. George McCormick, "Metro Sewer Bill Goes to Governor," Minneapolis Tribune, May 13, 1969.

53. Peter Ackerberg, "Met Council Sewer Bill Revisions Urged," Minneapolis Star, March 15, 1969. These views were expressed by several council members.

54. Solid Waste Disposal Advisory Committee, Recommendations for Solid Waste Disposal in the Twin Cities Area (Saint Paul: Metropolitan Council, November 14, 1968), passim.

55. 1969 MSL, Chapter 847.

56. 1967-1968 Biennial Report, Addendum B, Recommendations for Metropolitan Area Legislation (Saint Paul: Metropolitan Council, January, 1969), p. 7.

57. Ibid.

58. 1969 MSL, Chapter 1124.

59. 1969 MSL, Chapter 879; 1967-1968 Biennial Report, Addendum B, op. cit., p. 17. This legislation was passed on what has been traditionally the last day of the legislative session which, normally, would make the act illegal; the legislature, however, termed it as not the last day as deemed by

law by virtue of that body's failure to meet on a number of days nominally considered legislature days by law. A test case is pending before the State Supreme Court.

60. 1967-1968 Biennial Report, Addendum B, op. cit., p. 4.

61. Ibid.

62. 1969 MSL, Chapter 868.

63. 1969 MSL, Chapter 312.

64. Summaries of Acts (Saint Paul: Metropolitan Council, July, 1969), p. 1.

65. Reynold Boezi, Interview, May, 1970.

66. 1969 MSL, Chapter 1111.

67. 1969 MSL, Chapter 625.

68. 1969 MSL, Chapter 590.

69. 1969 MSL, Chapter 777.

70. 1969 MSL, Chapter 979 (Afton State Park in Washington County along the St. Croix River).

71. 1969 MSL, Chapter 1039 (Green Acres tax concessions).

72. 1967-1968 Biennial Report, op. cit., pp. 10, 14.

73. Public Law 90-351, Section 522 (82 Stat. 197, 208). This was part of an amendment of the Demonstration Cities and Metropolitan Development Act of 1966.

74. Hetland, Interview, June, 1969.

75. 1967-1968 Biennial Report, op. cit., pp. 10, 14.

76.   Ibid.; Robert Pratzman, "Metro Hospital
Agency Merger Plans Advance," Saint Paul Pioneer
Press, March 26, 1969.

77.   Steve Dornfield, "Metro Unit Plans Finance
Studies," Saint Paul Pioneer Press, June 27, 1969.

78.   Ibid.; Hetland, Interview, loc. cit.

79.   Ibid.

80.   Reynold Boezi, Interview, May, 1970.

81.   Al Eisele, "Rosenmeier Asks Metro Fiscal
Unit," Saint Paul Dispatch, March 25, 1969; Rosenmeier, Interview, April, 1969.

82.   Hetland, Interview, June, 1969.

83.   Editorial, "Is a Metro Funding Authority
Necessary?" Minneapolis Tribune, March 31, 1969.

84.   Ted Kolderie, note to Stanley Baldinger,
May, 1970; Minnesota House bill, H.F. 2871.

85.   John Tilton, Interview, June, 1969; John
Tilton, "An Experiment in Self-Government Unfolds,"
The Sun, February 10, 1969.

86.   Dean Lund, Interview, June, 1970.

87.   Wilfred Anderson, Interview, June, 1970.

88.   Metropolitan Council Resolution No. 69-11
of August 28, 1969.   (Mimeographed.)

89.   Lund, loc. cit.

90.   Metropolitan Council Resolution, loc. cit.

91.   Boezi, Interview, May, 1970.

92.   A Government Structure Program (Minneapolis: Metropolitan Section of the League of
Minnesota Municipalities, June, 1970), p. 2.

93.   Anderson, <u>loc. cit</u>.

94.   Lund, <u>loc. cit</u>.

95.   Robert Einsweiler, Interview, June, 1969.

96.   "Elected Met Council Favored," <u>Minneapolis Star</u>, January 28, 1969.

PART IV

PRESCRIPTIONS FOR CHANGE

CHAPTER **10** SUMMING UP

The Twin Cities area has developed the most
promising and innovative means yet to plan and gov-
ern major metropolises. Not enough time has passed,
however, to appraise completely the full potential
and accomplishments of the Metropolitan Council.
Despite this limitation, there is still much to
gain and learn from its experience. This case
study has been undertaken to explain in some detail
the kind of government the Council is and how and
why it came about. The Metropolitan Council, hopefully, can serve as an example for change in the
pattern of government in other major metropolitan
areas. From the experience of the Council, we are
able to draw a number of conclusions that may explain it more fully and help others to meet the
challenge of metropolitan growth.

THE WHAT, WHY, AND HOW OF THE COUNCIL

A Hybrid Government

The Metropolitan Council is a cross between a
full metropolitan government and a state agency.
It is a compromise between the true metropolitan
government sought by the people of the Twin Cities
area and the state agency preferred by outstate
legislators. (For background on this compromise,
see Chapter 7.) Consequently it possesses powers
and attributes of both. It is a metropolitan government in that it has solely area representation,
represents area interests, performs area services,
makes area decisions, responds to area needs and
wishes, and levies an area _ad valorem_ tax to finance

its activities. It is a state agency in that the
governor appoints all council representatives and
the legislature assigns to it specific powers, controls its finances, determines its structure and
continued existence, and requires it to make peri-
odic reports. It should be noted that the gubernatorial appointments are made only after consultation with area legislators and local officials and
interests; similarly, council powers are assigned
only after prior agreement by local officials and
interests. The Council, even if it were a full
metropolitan government, would have no home rule
privileges (they were not sought by council advocates), and, consequently, it would have had to return in any case to the legislature to alter its
powers or structure.

The Council also resembles a multi-purpose
special district in that it is responsible for providing area-wide services, e.g., sewer collection
and treatment, solid waste disposal, regional parks
and open space, etc., and financing some of its operations through user charges. It differs, however,
in that it does not directly exercise functional
powers even though it is responsible for them; it
is more responsive to the area's political processes,
and it plans and coordinates development for a particular area. The Minnesota Attorney General, in
an opinion, states "that the Council is a unique
governmental unit standing a step above local governmental units and a step below state agencies and
that it is clothed with certain attributes and powers of each."[1] Local officials and interests would
more likely call it an extension of local government.

The Structure of the Council

The form of the Council--a strong legislative
body--is directly attributable to the traditional
structure of government and the political environment of the state. Legislative bodies in Minnesota--
the state legislature and local councils--are strong
in contrast to executives who are weak. Minneapolis
has a "weak mayor" form of municipal government;

Saint Paul has the commission form. The suburbs
have the council-manager form and the counties are
governed by a board. This is an inheritance from
the Populist period of the late nineteenth and
early twentieth centuries when strong executives in
government were suspect. It was only natural, therefore, that the Metropolitan Council be established
with a strong council and with the executive selected from among its membership. Further, as the legislature sought to maximize the state aspect of the
Council, it (the legislature) structured the Council along the lines of a state commission or board
and made it an appointed body. The part-time character of its membership also harks back to the
Populist period. Politics and government should be
an avocation for the public spirited rather than
the province of the full-time, professional politician who is subject to financial and partisan in-
fluences.

While the Council is not an elected body, representation is so constructed that it can readily
be made so any time in the future. The 1966 Demonstration Cities and Metropolitan Development Act
also influenced the council-enabling legislation,
making it able to accept federal responsibilities
and grants. The Act, however, was not a decisive
force in bringing it about or shaping it. In fact,
the Twin Cities proponents of the Metropolitan Council pointedly rejected the proposal of the Act to
have area-wide bodies composed largely of elected
public officials; they had much too frustrating an
experience under the old MPC which closely resembled
a COG.

The area's reaction to the inadequate responsiveness and independent operations of metropolitan
special purpose districts was also an important factor in determining the Council's form and powers.
They now come under either the Council's direct administrative responsibilities or its development
controls, which include possible indefinite suspen-
sion--really veto--of district plans that are not
consistent with its plans for the area. In addition,

the Council appoints the full membership of its dependent service boards and one member to each independent district. In the future, metropolitan special district functions will likely be authorized
under the Council as were the recently created Metropolitan Sewer Board and Metropolitan Park Reserve
Board. The council structure is admirably flexible
and capable of assuming such functions with ease.

    As a consequence of the close integration of
the political and planning functions and of its
qualities as a strong legislative body without a
separate executive, the Council closely resembles
a British local planning authority. Enhancing this
structural similarity are the Council's new powers
with respect to airport zoning, acceptable land use,
and compulsory purchase of a property which has suf-
fered a loss in value resulting from limited or acceptable development. Upon the finding of a competent court that the Council's airport development
controls (which, together with council stated goals
and policies, are analogous to a "development plan")
constitute a taking of a property ("planning blight"),
the Council can determine that the property be bought
("compulsory purchase") through eminent domain by
the MAC to ensure proper development of the airport
area or protection of its residents. While these
powers are not identical to those of a local planning authority in the United Kingdom, the similari-
ties are remarkable.[2]   (See Chapter 9, pp. 196-97,
and this chapter, pp. 226-27.)

Policy Planning

    The primary reason for the creation of the
Metropolitan Council was the need for area-wide
policy planning joined with adequate power to coordinate the area's development. That is, the leadership of the community--government, business, civic
affairs, newspapers, political parties, the MPC,
etc.--believed that the entire area required a
single unit of government to direct development
taking place if existing metropolitan problems were
to be resolved and future ones avoided or minimized.

The leadership was reacting against piecemeal and uncontrolled area planning, particularly of metropolitan special districts insulated from the local political process and other area-wide considerations. The Council, as a result, would not only determine area-wide policies and plans, but also approve or veto special district plans, review local government plans and programs, and be responsible for necessary area-wide services, etc. No one considered that the Council would replace local planning and governmental functions. Rather, it would coordinate local and metropolitan planning and functions more rationally through knowledgeable and effective decisionmaking in a combined planning and political body. Both area-wide and local service needs and systems planning, such as that involved in the controversy over suburban sewer needs in the early 1960's, were intimately related to policy planning. Only a combined political and planning body could, therefore, interrelate them properly and assure success of the community's hopes.

Why in the Twin Cities First?

It is difficult if not impossible to define the precise reasons why the Twin Cities area has led the nation in metropolitan reorganization, particularly as the area is a place where the pressures and problems of urban growth--congestion, waste disposal, pollution, transportation, etc.--are not generally as critical as in other major centers, e.g., New York, Los Angeles, Philadelphia, Chicago, et al. Indeed, it may be that these lesser pressures and problems have enabled the leadership of the community, both public and private, to come to a more substantial understanding and a common approach to the area's problems and to minimize the passions which often restrict compromise and cooperation. As two central cities were involved, there was little fear of domination by either a single central city or suburbs that characterizes most metropolitan areas. Equally important are the long and strong traditions of good government and citizen participation in public affairs which have made government readily

accessible and responsible even to the individual
citizen. This has created a political environment
which militates against popular fear of metropolitan ("big") government and is conducive to change
and innovation. An interesting aspect of this was
the lack of opposition to metropolitan reorganization by the area's Black community. This was in
part, no doubt, due to its relatively small size--
less than 2 percent of the total population. It
had acquired, as a result, little of the political
bloc power that Black communities elsewhere possess
and that has thwarted other attempts at reorganization. It would have had little to lose even if it
had significant political power. Federation does
not involve the consolidation of local governments
which can result in dilution of political bloc
power.

Consensus

The amazing degree of consensus achieved in
the Twin Cities area is testimony to the fact that
if a community wants something strongly enough and
is prepared to act, it will be successful.[3] This,
perhaps, is the most important conclusion that can
be drawn from the Twin Cities experience. With de-
sire and the will to act, obstacles confronting reorganization can be swept aside, not necessarily
with ease, but certainly with assurance.

The consensus in both central cities and suburbs reached a remarkable degree of agreement not
only on the need for a metropolitan governmental
structure to resolve area-wide problems, but also
on the responsibilities, powers, and form it should
have. The consensus was neither highly organized
nor elitist--university, foundation, etc.--led. It
was rather an informal but close coalition which
crystallized and formalized existing ideas and
thoughts into a precise statement of goals and
wants. It amounted, in effect to a popular demand
for change--a change that could be and was modified, but that could not be denied.

Instrumental in achieving the consensus was the
MPC which had worked ten years to educate the Twin
Cities community to accept metropolitan solutions to
metropolitan problems. It actively participated and
often initiated discussions on issues vital to the
well-being of the area and even proposed its own replacement with a body similar to that of the Metropolitan Council as an alternative to the existing
situation. Moreover, Minneapolis, Saint Paul, and
their suburbs came to realize that many of the problems they faced individually were area-wide as well.
They understood that certain ones--transportation,
sewage disposal and pollution control, open space,
etc.--required more than local attention. They
chose a metropolitan rather than a state solution
because it was "closer to home" and, therefore, essentially local in nature and more responsive to
their needs and wishes. They stressed a federal approach, avoiding consideration of consolidation,
that allayed central cities resentment of their
"subsidization" of suburbs and mitigated suburban
fears of central cities' domination. The business
community realized that its continued growth and
prosperity depended more upon cooperation than upon
competition within itself. Citizen groups, newspapers, and other concerned interests advocated metropolitan reorganization--federation--because it
seemed the only logical solution to recognized area
problems while safeguarding local values. Opposi-
tion--Bloomington and some of the rural, outer-ring
suburbs, the counties, and certain suburban news-
papers--appeared too late to be effective. It sur-
faced only on the eve of the Council's creation,
and then offered no adequate alternatives.

The Role of the Minnesota Legislature

The proponents of the Metropolitan Council
looked to the legislature to authorize its creation
in both form and power. At no time did they advocate or contemplate a structure for the Council
which would give it home rule, i.e., exempt it from
returning to the legislature for authorization of

new powers or change. In Minnesota, as in other
states of the Union, the state, particularly the
legislature, is the source of sovereign power with
municipalities, counties, special districts, commissions, boards, and state departments alike exercising only those powers that have been delegated to
them by the constitution and legislature. The Council, even as a pure metropolitan government, consequently, would still have been responsible to the
legislature for those powers and functions which
the Twin Cities community had agreed upon and had
requested. The rural dominated legislature, in
recognizing the increasingly dominant role that the
Twin Cities area played in the economic well-being
of the state, resolved that the area's problems
would best be solved on an area-wide basis. The
legislature waited only for the area to agree upon
the necessary solution, e.g., the Metropolitan
Council. But in doing so, the rural and conservative legislators felt they had a substantial stake
and role to play in the future of the Twin Cities
area. The legislature, therefore, sought to maximize the state's role in the operations of the
Council by making it an appointed rather than an
elected body. A more local (elected) Council might
not be as responsive to the needs of the rest of
the state or to the wishes of the legislature.

COUNCIL INNOVATIONS

Integrating the Political and
Planning Processes

The most important innovation of the Metropolitan Council of the Twin Cities Area is its
close integration of the political and metropolitan planning processes into one governmental structure. In so doing, it at once authors the area's
plans, i.e., making the political decisions, and is
responsible for implementing them. Its decisionmaking powers ensure that a plan or program, once
approved, will be undertaken. This linking of the
two processes was deliberately done. Its advocates

sought to assure that metropolitan planning was not
frustrated through execution in the abstract or
through fragmentation among a score of area-wide
governmental bodies and that development should be
responsive to the political process. Such a development runs contrary to the traditional concepts of
local government and of those reformers of the
1920's and 1930's who called for the separation of
planning and functional services from politics. It
may have promoted efficiency and honesty of the independent planning commission, but it also weakened
the policymaking machinery of local government and
functionally fragmented local and area services.
The multiplicity of jurisdictions, gerrymandered
local units, and lack of broad geographic jurisdiction have compounded local problems and inhibited
"the kind of long-range planning and decisionmaking
essential to effective local government."[4] The
Metropolitan Council, by closely integrating the
political and planning processes, by sharing development powers with local governmental units, by
controlling special districts, and by providing a
geographic jurisdiction that encompasses the entire
Twin Cities metropolitan area, has reversed this
tradition with its problems and has tied together
in one structure those functions not manageable at
the local level.

Council Representation

The Metropolitan Council is composed of fifteen members appointed by the governor, fourteen of
whom represent districts of equal population size
(based on state senatorial districts rather than
units of local government) and are confirmed by the
state Senate. Each member must reside in the district which he represents. District boundaries do
not coincide with any existing governments, but
break up the two central cities, combine the suburbs, and in one case combine portions of Minneapolis with suburban communities. Moreover, Council
and subordinate board members are private citizens,
with the one brief exception noted earlier. The
intention is to minimize the possible division of

loyalties that occurs when local public officials
also serve on a metropolitan body. There was surprising agreement within all segments of the community on this. No one wanted to repeat the frustrating experience of the MPC on which local public
officials with their parochial interests served.
An additional, collateral benefit, one which should
become more apparent with time, is the decreased
importance of incorporated boundaries to area residents. They will (or should) think increasingly of
their governmental services and problems in metropolitan, as well as in local, terms.

Control Over Special Districts

The Council's powers to review and veto unacceptable area plans and projects of independent
metropolitan special purpose districts go a long
way toward making them more responsive and closer
to area political processes and development plans.
The Council can veto--wholly or in part--any plan
or project inconsistent with its plans or guidance.
In addition, the Council appoints a member, with
full powers save voting, to the governing board of
each independent metropolitan special purpose district. The only recourse that an independent special district has with respect to a veto is to appeal to the Council for reconsideration and, upon
failure of redress there, to appeal to the state
legislature--through the Council. It should be
noted that one of the major reasons for establishing the Council with its review and veto powers was
to resolve area conflicts without having to go to
the legislature. The one major case where a special district plan was vetoed--the proposal to
build a new international airport (see Appendix B
for a discussion of this case)--avoided the latter
possibility when the applicant asked the Council to
involve itself from the beginning in the selection
of another, appropriate site. This case does point
up the limitations of the review/veto power; the
Council legally becomes involved only in the final
stages of the planning process. Too often the Council has been forced to veto, or comment unfavorably,

or give qualified approval to plans for which expenditures or commitments have already been made.

The establishment of administrative boards
directly under the Council is a major breakthrough
in stopping or minimizing the proliferation of independent functional local government--metropolitan
special purpose districts. The administrative
boards are really subordinate metropolitan special
purpose districts over which the Council exercises
virtual complete control. It appoints all members
(with full powers), establishes policies, approves
or vetoes board plans and budgets, and determines
their relations with other units of government.
This innovation may be the harbinger of future complete control over still existing independent special purpose districts. Precedent was established
in 1969 when the Council took complete control over
the area's special service sewer districts and established a single subordinate Metropolitan Sewer
Board and System to provide area-wide service.
(For a full discussion, see Chapter 9, pp. 188-92.
For a discussion of council review powers, see
Chapter 8, pp. 175-79, and Appendix B.)

Center of Comprehensive
Transportation Planning

The Metropolitan Council has the responsibility for determining the area's comprehensive and
continuous transportation policy, including that
for public transportation, highways, etc. It has
final authority, including possible veto, over any
unacceptable system plan developed by its Transportation Management Committee, which is composed of
representatives of the Council, the MHD, the MTC,
the Metropolitan Section of the LMM, and the MICC.
The director and staff of the committee are employees of the Metropolitan Council.

A major element of the Council's responsibilities and powers is the assignment to it by the MHD
of the latter's responsibility to maintain a comprehensive, continuing, and cooperative highway

planning function for the seven-county metropolitan
area. Such a transfer is not new in the United
States; regional planning bodies in other areas,
e.g., metropolitan Milwaukee and Seattle, similarly
possess comprehensive highway planning powers which
have been transferred to them by their respective
state highway departments. The innovation in the
exercise of this transportation planning function,
however, is that it resides in a body with so many
other major planning, coordinating, and development
responsibilities and powers. The other responsibilities and powers specifically include: legal
authority to prepare a metropolitan transportation
plan with the MTC and the MHD; veto power over unacceptable plans and capital expense and capital
improvement budgets of the MTC; veto power over unacceptable plans of the MAC; federal highway plan
review; veto over any unacceptable local highway
plan if it uses other than local or federal highway
funding; and ultimate responsibility for all comprehensive planning bearing on area-wide development.

The package of transportation planning responsibilities and powers is a compromise between those
who hoped to see all transportation planning powers
centered in the Council and the political and legal
realities of other concerned units of government involved in transportation planning--the MTC, the MHD,
the Metropolitan Section of the LMM, the MICC, and
federal legislation. (For a discussion of the development of the Council's transportation planning
responsibilities, powers, and machinery, see Chapter 9, pp. 183-88, 197.)

Other Governmental Powers

The Council possesses a catalogue of other
significant powers which make it even more effective. As with metropolitan transportation planning, they are not necessarily unique to the Council. But they are innovative when considered in
the context of the broad range of powers within a
metropolitan planning body. Under the recent Metropolitan Sewer Act (Chapter 449, 1969 Sessions Law),

the Council has the power to levy a property tax to
service the debts of the sewer system, to levy a
tax (through county auditors) on the property own-
ers of a local government delinquent or deficient
in its sewer payments, and to issue bonds against
the revenues of the system. The Council's trustees,
the sewer board, can acquire all necessary property,
easements, and water and air rights, etc., through
a variety of means, including condemnation.

The Council's determination that property reduced in value by its airport area development controls be purchased to ensure proper development is
a significant innovation in metropolitan planning.
Other than urban renewal, this is the first open
reliance on the use of eminent domain and the payment of compensation to go along with the use of
traditional police powers to control development.

The Council also participates in proceedings
of the Minnesota Municipal Commission on matters
concerning changes in municipal boundaries and
studies of the feasibility of enlargement, annexation, or consolidation of units of local government
within the metropolitan area. It has, further, the
right to approve or disapprove without qualifica-
tion, any local government application for federal
or state funds to acquire land for open space or
conservation purposes that do not conform to council policy standards, priorities, or guidelines.

REPLICABILITY

The Twin Cities Metropolitan Council has been
called a "model" for reorganizing metropolitan
America.[5] Since its creation in 1967, it has been
the center of ever increasing nation-wide attention
that has focused on its ability to control multi-
jurisdictional metropolitan growth and problems.
It has been widely recognized as a major innovation
in metropolitan government, but the question remains
as to whether it can be used--duplicated--in a meaningful way elsewhere. Recently, the National Service

to Regional Councils has offered it to members for
consideration as a new prototype regional council.[6]
Many problem-racked areas have sent representatives
to the Twin Cities to study the Council to learn if
and how it can be used back home. The San Francisco-
Oakland, Denver, and Atlanta areas are actively considering state legislation which would create counterpart councils for their areas. Because of the
great interest in its possible adoption elsewhere,
some brief comments on its replicability and useful-
ness are in order.

A Nation of Twin Cities Councils

There is no question that the Metropolitan
Council of the Twin Cities area can be reproduced
in every detail for any metropolitan area. All
that is required is preference for it, and the will-
ingness to work to achieve it. It is unlikely, however, that an exact reproduction would work well
everywhere, or that it would be necessary or even
desirable. As pointed out in the introduction to
this study, each metropolitan area is different.
The problems confronting each vary both in magnitude and kind. The reorganization of our metropolitan areas, therefore, must be tailored in each case
to meet the specific area's needs and goals. There
is no single model or approach which fits all or
most of our expanding metropolises. The Twin Cities
Council is a landmark innovation, a breakthrough,
in metropolitan reorganization, but it is valid only
for a limited group of the nation's metropolitan
areas. It is most suitable to intermediate and
larger multi-county areas. In contrast, those metropolitan areas which are completely or largely en-
compassed within a single county--approximately
one-half of the SMSA's--should probably look to the
urban-county approach to achieve similar ends. As
noted earlier, a fully developed urban county, such
as Dade County, Florida, possesses many of the qualities of a federal metropolitan council and might be
easier to achieve as it utilizes an existing familiar and accepted unit of government--the county.

While all metropolitan areas differ in make-up, certain of them share with the Twin Cities similar qualities which would enable them to reorganize more easily. Many medium-sized metropolitan communities such as Seattle, Denver, and Milwaukee share with the Twin Cities a tradition of good government, largely homogeneous populations, a high degree of education and home ownership, and little poverty, etc. Just last year, in 1969, the Colorado House of Representatives passed a bill (which died in the Senate) to create a near identical counterpart to the Twin Cities Council for the Denver area. The bill differed only in that the council members were to be appointed by county commissioners in each metropolitan county, that suspension of district and local plans would be for a maximum of six months, and that dissolution of the council would take place in the event a multi-purpose district were established covering the same area.[7] The original bill was even closer to the Twin Cities model. The governor would have appointed the council members and there was no provision for dissolution of the council.

Overcoming Obstacles to Metropolitan Reorganization

All obstacles to metropolitan reorganization, as noted in Chapter 1, are determined by popular attitudes toward local government in this country, the rules by which our political system operates, and the structure of the political system itself. Political bloc interests, popular suspicion of "big" government, and the American attachment to small, more intimate government are typical obstacles generated by popular attitudes; accountability, nonpartisan elections, and referenda are some examples of the rules of our local politics; home rule, limitations on annexation and incorporation, and interstate compacts are measures of the political system--all are considerations which the advocates of metropolitan reorganization must deal with successfully if they are to achieve their

goals. All these measures, and more, are firmly
rooted in the American political system. So en-
trenched are they "that those who attempt to alter
the system," as Bollens and Schmandt have noted,
"must be prepared to face charges of removing government from the people, infringing on basic human
rights, and destroying local self-rule."[8]

The Twin Cities area proponents of the Metropolitan Council were amazingly successful in over-
coming a wide range of obstacles. Over a period of
a decade, the people had been taught to think in
metropolitan terms for solutions to their metropolitan problems. Political responsiveness and an in-
tense adherence to the philosophy of small government gave rise to the concept of a federal mechanism
to resolve metropolitan problems in a local way,
rather than area-wide consolidation into a massive
monolithic structure. The Council would do only
those things that had to be done, but that local
units could not do, or could not do adequately, on
their own. The issues of home rule and the referendum, they recognized, were critical to success;
to achieve their goal, they accepted limitations on
home rule and elimination of a referendum on the
Council because these are the issues on which most
attempts to reorganize an area's metropolitan structure have, up to now, failed. To be sure, council
proponents did not achieve 100 percent of their
goal--an elected body with more operating powers--
but they did achieve most of it and, equally important, they won a mechanism which they could adapt,
build on, and elect for the future. The three
years of council life have shown this to be true.
The 1969 legislature greatly expanded council powers and responsibilities; the years ahead promise
even more.

If other areas are to achieve necessary reorganization, they must follow the lead of the Twin
Cities. All of the obstacles confronting them can
be overcome to one degree or another; certainly, to
the extent necessary to achieve reorganization.
First of all, the citizenry must be made to realize

that their metropolitan problems can best be solved
in a metropolitan way. There need be no significant loss of home rule if the federation or urban-
county approach is followed, particularly if the
mechanism undertakes only those functions local
units cannot do. This approach would even enhance
the quality of local government by giving it a
greater role in metropolitan-wide affairs. As such,
popular fears of big government, loss of local and
individual rights, and higher taxes (the principal
criticism of opponents) could be diminished.[9] The
people would have two equally responsive "local"
governments: the one they have always had and the
new metropolitan one. Taxes might indeed go up as
area-wide programs are undertaken, but they should
be materially lower than if each individual unit
were to undertake adequate similar programs on its
own.

As the nation becomes more urbanized, the
present machinery of local government will become
increasingly inadequate to meet area-wide problems
of congestion, transportation, sewage and trash disposal, open space, and finances, etc. Consequently,
pressures for change and reform will mount. It will
become increasingly clear to all that these problems
can be met best on a metropolitan basis, rather than
through the use of expedient solutions such as the
special district of the past. The question raised,
then, is not whether metropolitan reorganization
will come about, but by whom and how. Demands for
higher quality of service, public health, and finance will force it. The choice is whether reorganization will be accomplished by the area through
its own initiative, by the states, or called for by
the federal government. Since 1962, when the Supreme Court decided in _Baker_ v. _Carr_ that both
houses of state legislatures must be apportioned
according to population, most metropolitan areas
have (or should have) the legislative votes to
bring about their preference in metropolitan reorganization. The only prerequisite--the one in-
dispensable ingredient--is a unified will of the
metropolitan community to act. If public officials,

community leaders, and the general public genuinely
want reorganization and are prepared to go all out
for it, local provincialism and legal-political obstacles can be swept away, not necessarily with
ease, but with certainty. State action is necessary
because only the state can create a political mechanism with necessary powers and jurisdictional
boundaries, determine representation and form of
structure, and establish financing--even when the
initiative for change comes from the metropolitan
area.

Today, the advocates of metropolitan reorganization have a readymade issue--pollution--on which
to build a demand and consensus for their desired
change. It is on the lips of every concerned citizen. He knows that it involves the water he drinks
and the air he breathes. The ever-growing number
of sewer and water service breakdowns has brought
home as nothing else has the immediacy of the problem. The citizen need be shown only that inadequate
service and pollution are but different aspects of
the same problem and that they can be best resolved
through some form of metropolitan government. Neither voluntary intergovernmental agreements nor
special districts are satisfactory; the first is
generally ineffective while the second only further
fragments the planning and development of the area.
Exclusive state action raises problems of local
(metropolitan) control, responsiveness, and funding,
as noted in the discussion of the role of the state.
In the Twin Cities area, public officials and private citizens demanded improved sewer service and,
as a result, were instrumental in creating a consensus conducive to establishing the Metropolitan
Council. Solving their service problem could not
be done piecemeal, voluntarily, or through the
creation of another special district. Only the
area itself, with the help of the state, could do
the job. The area avoided further fragmentation
and created a political and planning structure
which utilized the power of the state, yet was
locally ("metropolitanly") responsive and effective.
Other approaches, such as the transfer of functions

to the state or the county, could prove adequate
for other areas, but they were not for the Twin
Cities.

Community Experiences and the
Metropolitan Council

To metropolitan areas elsewhere wishing to reorganize, the experiences of the Twin Cities com-
munity--officials, business groups, citizens' organizations, political parties, and private indi-
viduals--should be of greater importance than that
solely of the Council. For it was these experiences
that brought about the Metropolitan Council and
largely determined its powers and scope of activities. It will be from these experiences, more than
from the form of the Council, that the leaders of
other areas will find guidance.

The reasons for reorganizing the Twin Cities
area political structure have been described in
some detail--congestion, inadequate services and
transportation, pollution, unresponsive special
districts, frustration and confusion over area-wide
development policies, and many more. All elements
of the community, whether in central cities or suburbs, recognized that they shared a universe of
problems and that each one was both local and metropolitan. If they were to achieve their own particular favorite solution, they had to unite and work
for all of them. It was this recognition that produced the remarkable degree of consensus on goals,
form, and powers of the Council. The actions and
tactics of the major participants (described in
Chapters 2 through 9) are the guidelines that other
metropolitan areas should look to for possible
answers to their problems. They demonstrate that
a tightly organized and/or elitist led movement is
not essential to success; an intent, cooperative,
and highly motivated community is.

Role of the State

The key to the success of any effort to establish a metropolitan council is the state legislature.

It is the only body which has the authority to create supra-municipal governments, i.e., a metropolitan council, with sufficient powers to resolve an
area's problems. For the legislature to authorize
a metropolitan council as a unit of local, general
purpose, and home rule government is an ideal, but
also a problem. In states where a single metropolitan area (like the Twin Cities) is in a position to
dominate a state, a legislature may be reluctant to
create a council. Even when the area demonstrates
a unity of intent for it (again as in the case of
the Twin Cities), there may be legislative fears of
the metropolitan "tail" wagging the state "dog."
Equally important, many states depend on their metropolitan areas for a significant part of their
well-being and therefore, have a legitimate interest or stake in the area's development. The advocates of a council may find it necessary to compromise on issues and hopes to gain needed support of
nonmetropolitan legislators. The compromise may
take the form of creating the council essentially
as a state agency, or as a combination metropolitan-
state body (as is the Twin Cities Council), or as
one of any number of other variations in structure
or ground rules, by which a council would operate.
Such an approach could include the grant of only
specifically authorized powers and responsibilities
that the area and legislature agree upon, rather
than make the council a home rule government. Similar results could occur where there is a lack of
sufficient unity in the metropolitan area. It
might then be necessary or desirable to seek a
coalition with nonmetropolitan interests in the
legislature to bring about the creation of a council. The precise nature of the structure agreed
upon will vary from state to state and from metropolitan area to metropolitan area, depending upon
individual area-state characteristics, needs, problems, and goals.

    In establishing a state agency rather than a
metropolitan mechanism to resolve a metropolitan
area's problems, legislators from both the concerned area and the rest of the state must contend

with the issue: Does this approach commit the resources of the entire state to programs that are
essentially metropolitan? If it does, then a state
agency is a logical mechanism to do the job. If
there is no such commitment and metropolitan operations are financed largely or entirely through the
area's own resources, a state agency could open up
serious problems of responsiveness to area needs
and local control as well as threaten to subvert
the very efforts that the approach is supposed to
sustain.

Upgrading an Existing
Metropolitan Body

The Twin Cities Council is an entirely new,
primarily metropolitan agency that local groups,
leaders, and state legislators deemed necessary to
meet the area's needs and wishes. But the essentially same mechanism could have been achieved by
upgrading the then existing MPC, had the area and
the legislature so chosen. The Council possesses
the same primary purpose--metropolitan policy and
planning--essentially the same staff, and an appointed governing body composed of area representatives. It differs in that it also possesses a different approach to area representation and effective coordinating and development controls, including ultimate responsibility over the administration
of new area-wide functions.

Many metropolitan areas (and states) could
find that upgrading an existing mechanism is a more
expeditious means to acquire a metropolitan council.
A prerequisite to this, of course, is the presence
of a metropolitan agency which lends itself to such
a transmutation, i.e., a metropolitan planning
agency, a regional COG, or a multi-jurisdictional
special purpose district. In so doing, it may be
possible to avoid local referenda and avoid the appearance of radical change, substituting what appears to be the more traditional approach of adding
necessary new powers to existing and accepted units
of government.[10] Presumably, the council would

assume only those functions necessary to do its metropolitan tasks. In addition, this approach also
tends to minimize popular fears that a metropolitan
super-government threatens the qualities of small
local government that so much of the public values
as necessary for democratic living. The tactic of
transmuting an existing metropolitan agency into a
metropolitan council is seriously being considered
in the San Francisco-Oakland area. Legislation has
been introduced to convert the Association of Bay
Area Governments into a council generally patterned
after the Twin Cities experience.[11] Several leaders
and delegations from the Bay area have visited the
Twin Cities to witness metropolitan council operations firsthand.

As an interim or initiatory measure, many communities may wish to establish the more traditional
multi-purpose special district with area-wide planning powers. Political and policy matters would
remain with existing local officials and governments and they could be represented on its governing board. Such a mechanism would share the benefits described above, but on a more limited scale.

Metropolitan Councils and Subregional Reorganization

Interstate political realities--federal requirements for prior congressional approval (an
interstate compact), state reluctance to accept a
reorganization that might subject a portion of its
jurisdiction to the authority of a second state,
local fears of domination by a jurisdiction over
which its states' residents would have only partial
control, etc.--sharpen even more the obstacles to
metropolitan government.[12] Where such a reorganization seems unlikely or impossible, it would still
be advantageous to establish metropolitan councils
in the component parts of the region. Areas like
northern New Jersey or the Maryland and Virginia
suburbs of Washington would benefit greatly from a
more rational governmental structure and development
effort. Such councils would deal more effectively

with subregional or metropolitan problems than
could dozens of independent and competing local governments. They could establish subregional goals
and policies, provide subregional-wide services,
eliminate or minimize overlapping jurisdictions
(mostly special districts), minimize local conflict
and competition hampering area development, and
plan and implement programs more comprehensively.
The federal approach would also enable the normally
conflicting pressures for decentralization and centralization to be accommodated within the same
framework.[13] Moreover, metropolitan councils could
conduct business with their respective states from
a politically stronger position, bargaining for more
financial assistance for local and subregional needs
and for desired legislation. Rather than remaining
a fragmented potential, the combined strength of all
the units would be fully realized.

Subregional councils would also serve as excellent counterparts and/or partners to councils in
the other subregions of the same region. Collabo-
rating closely, they would simplify interstate
negotiations, establish clearer lines of authority
and jurisdiction, provide a generally smoother mesh-
ing of efforts, and obtain agreements more easily
on plans and programs for development of the entire
metropolitan region. In brief, a subregional metropolitan council could do most of the things that
a metropolitan council covering the entire region
could do, but in a smaller geographic area. And
it could do the necessary tasks of planning, establishing, and implementing programs in a far superior
way than they are now being done. A bonus is the
lack of need for uniformity among the subregional
councils of the metropolitan region.

LESSONS FOR PLANNER AND POLITICIAN

The lessons that the planner and politician
can derive from the Twin Cities experience in the
creation and functioning of the Metropolitan Council are important. These lessons, hopefully, will

prove useful to them in effectively managing our
metropolitan environment.

The Planner and the Political Process

The planner must realize that planning is in-
tegrally related to the political process, particularly to the decisionmaking aspect. Intelligent
decisions cannot be made on the variety of economic,
social, and development issues facing our political
leaders without the information that the planner is
able to provide. Metropolitan planning in the Twin
cities has materially benefited--become more effec-
tive--with the close integration of planning and
the political decisionmaking process. Planners
there now have more precise policy direction and
significantly greater powers to implement their
proposals. And Twin Cities planners were instrumental in bringing this about. They both educated
the public to accept metropolitan solutions to metropolitan problems and actively pushed to create
the Council. Once the Council was established they
lobbied before the legislature on behalf of its
bills.[14]

The planner's function should not be merely to
provide a series of requested alternatives to the
decisionmakers and then to implement the one chosen.
He should also initiate the discussion of goals and
issues, and when necessary, actively push, even
lobby for preferred courses of action. By so doing,
he improves the chances of plan success and makes
himself more useful to the decisionmakers. In the
past, the planner either refrained or reluctantly
participated in the political process, considering
himself essentially a technician somewhat removed
from it. As a result, most plans were not implemented; no one listened to the planners. To tie
planning closely to the political process requires
the politician to recognize the intimate relationship between himself and the planners and to uti-
lize more fully the planner's capabilities to meet
area needs.

Planning Issues as Political Issues

Many of the issues facing the planner also face, or should face, the politician. Issues such as community goals and policies, the need for and placement of public facilities, pollution control, area fiscal disparities, transportation needs, and development programs reflect, in general, the quality of life the community wants its leaders to strive to provide. While many aspects of these issues are technical, the decision to follow one course or another is political. Where planning is closely tied to the political process, such planning issues can be valid planks in a political platform on which the politician can or should run for office. In so doing, the politician can help assure that community goals and policies reflect realistically the community's needs and desires and that they will be implemented. In anticipation of the day that the Metropolitan Council will become an elected body, council members and staff are preparing a metropolitan development guide in terms of policies, standards, principles, and plans that members and their opponents may support or oppose.

Citizen and Leadership
Participation in Planning

The planner can improve his effectiveness by establishing a full program of public participation as part of his job. This not only educates the public and its leaders to the need for planned solutions and effective means to implement them, but also involves them in the planning process. Private as well as public leadership at its highest level is of particular importance to the planner. It is this participation which is most influential with legislators; it can virtually assure that proposed plans, legislation, and other desired actions are accepted and undertaken. In the Twin Cities, the commitment of top community leaders was a major factor in persuading state legislators to enact the metropolitan council legislation. The ten solid

years of MPC public information educated the community to accept planned solutions to its problems
and served as the foundation for a broad consensus
and effort.

Real and Realistic Planning

Rather than presenting and promoting ideal
models as urban and metropolitan solutions to problems, the planner must carefully and objectively
match his proposals to the area, its people, its
problems, and to the approach this combination permits. These factors are the determinants of the
success of any course of action. Twin Cities planners, public officials, and citizenry recognized
that consolidation, though perhaps an ideal, was
unrealistic. The people valued the qualities of
small and intimate local government too highly to
give that government up. A federation, therefore,
was the agreed, preferred, and practical approach
to the area's problems. The advocates of the council then used a combination of practical politics,
planning studies, and public pressures to build a
consensus which forced the legislature to face the
area's needs and demands and to come to grips with
them effectively.

Over the first years of its activities, the
Council followed the example of its advocates, establishing a reputation for being practical and
realistic in its approach to planning projects.
Its first major proposal--the metropolitan sewer
system--called for doing only what the local units
of government could not do and for sharing the operations of the system. As a result, the plan was
accepted quickly and with little difficulty.

There need be neither conflict between policy
and project planning nor problems in translating
the former into the latter. The two should comple-
ment one another. Policy planning should establish realistic community goals and approaches;
project planning should achieve them.

Metropolitan Government as an
Extension of Local Government

Luther Gulick has described the various
branches of government in the United States as "ex-
tensions" rather than as levels of government.[15]
Federal, state, and local governments are three
fully equal, collateral partners or aspects of a
single political system which operate parallel to
each other and not in tandem. They are not part
of a hierarchical or "layer cake" system with the
federal position at the top, the states in the
middle, and the local units at the bottom. Carrying this concept one step further, we may view metropolitan government not as a new level interposed
between local units and the state, but rather as a
fuller extension or development of local government.

Of the ten approaches to metropolitan reorganization noted in Chapter 1, only one--the fed-
eration--involves the establishment of a new element of government ostensibly above the area's already existing local units. The other approaches
either do not involve the elimination of existing
units of local government or, in the two where such
elimination is a prerequisite to their success--
annexation consolidation and city-county consolida-
tion--the eliminated units are replaced or absorbed
by other local units. However, federation, whether
it be an area-wide body such as the Twin Cities
Metropolitan Council or the urbanized county approach of Dade County, calls for the new jurisdiction to execute responsibilities of a geographical-
ly broad nature that were either nonexistent before or carried out on a more limited basis. Instead of being a level above local units, however,
the new jurisdiction may be viewed as another form
or extension of local government that possesses a
separate though related set of responsibilities and
operates parallel to or complements, the other,
older local units. The new unit operates those
mutually agreed upon functions which have area-wide

aspects while the previously existing units operate
purely local functions and the local aspects of the
area-wide functions. This constitutes more of a
sharing of powers, as the Committee for Economic
Development recently stated, than a division of responsibilities or a hierarchical relationship.[16]
This sharing of powers further implies, not that
the new jurisdiction possesses a new or separate
set of powers, but that it provides a "completing
component" of powers which are essentially local
in nature even though covering a larger geographic
area.

Mayor Illies of suburban Minnetonka recognized
this when he stated, during the most heated part of
the legislative battle to create the Metropolitan
Council, that he looked upon "metropolitan government as local government."[17] Many of the problems
that he and his colleagues in Minneapolis, Saint
Paul, and the suburbs faced were both metropolitan
and local. And what was needed to solve these problems was a locally responsive unit of government to
handle the metropolitan aspects of services, planning, and coordination, which the existing local
units could not do. The Twin Cities Metropolitan
Council, as noted in the opening section of this
chapter, is a combination of a pure metropolitan
government (federation) and an extension of the
state government. The state extends the legal
power and authority necessary to achieve the desired results; the Metropolitan Council is the
mechanism by which the Twin Cities area finances,
mans, and operates the area-wide services. This
prescription, when combined with the sharing of
responsibilities with existing units of local government, demonstrates that there need be no conflict between the roles of each participant--the
state, the Council, and local units. Each level or
extension of government has a necessary, positive,
and cooperative role to play in solving metropolitan problems in a metropolitan way.

The planning profession should learn from the
Twin Cities experience that the best, perhaps the

only way that metropolitan planning can be effective
is through metropolitan government. And metropolitan government can best be brought about by showing
that it is really a new aspect of local government
rather than a threat to it.

NOTES

1. Douglas M. Head and Will H. Hartfeldt,
Letter to James Hetland, Jr., Chairman, Metropolitan Council, October 6, 1967, p. 12.

2. Town and Country Planning Act, 1968 (Lon-
don: Her Majesty's Stationery Office, 1968);
Desmond Heap, An Outline of Planning Law, 5th ed.
(London: Sweet and Maxwell, 1969).

3. Luther Gulick, The Metropolitan Problem
and American Ideas (New York: Alfred A. Knopf,
Inc., 1962), p. 143.

4. Modernizing Local Government (New York:
Committee for Economic Development, July, 1966),
p. 13.

5. "Minnesota Model," Time, XCIV, 12 (September 19, 1969), 64-65.

6. A Prototype Regional Council (Washington,
D.C.: National Service to Regional Councils,
August, 1969), 2 pages. (Mimeographed.)

7. State of Colorado Engrossed House Bill No.
1085, Sections 4, 7(2)b, and 17, 1969.

8. John C. Bollens and Henry J. Schmandt,
The Metropolis: Its People, Politics, and Economic
Life (New York: Harper & Row, Publishers, Inc.,
1970), p. 375.

9. Ibid., p. 383.

10. James M. Banovetz, Perspectives on the Future of Government in Metropolitan Areas (Chicago: Loyola University, April, 1968), pp. 12-16, 19-22, 23-43.

11. Victor Jones, Interview with Stanley Baldinger, September, 1969; California Legislature Assembly Bill No. 1846, April 7, 1969.

12. For a full discussion of obstacles to metropolitan reorganization, see Thomas P. Murphy, Metropolitics and the Urban County (Washington, D.C.: Washington National Press, 1970), pp. 12-49.

13. Reshaping Government in Metropolitan Areas (New York: Committee for Economic Development, February, 1970), pp. 19, 43-46.

14. Reynold Boezi, Metropolitan Reorganization: Strategies for Action (Saint Paul: Metropolitan Council, April 6, 1970), pp. 1, 8-14. (Mimeographed.) Paper delivered at the 1970 American Society of Planning Officials conference in New York.

15. Gulick, op. cit., pp. 30-31.

16. Reshaping Government in Metropolitan Areas, op. cit., pp. 19-20.

17. See Chapter 7, note 15.

APPENDIXES

APPENDIX A

METROPOLITAN COUNCIL ACT

CHAPTER 473B. METROPOLITAN COUNCIL [NEW]

473B.01 Purpose

In order to coordinate the planning and development of the metropolitan area comprising the counties of Anoka, Carver, Dakota, Hennepin, Ramsey, Scott and Washington, it is in the public interest to create an administrative agency for that purpose.

Laws 1967, c. 896, § 1, eff. May 26, 1967.

Law Review Commentaries
Minnesota's experiment with a metropolitan council. Nov. 1968, 53 Minn.Law Review 122.

Title of Act:
An Act creating a metropolitan council for the counties of Anoka, Carver, Dakota, Hennepin, Ramsey, Scott and Washington; providing for the operation thereof. Laws 1967, c. 896.

Library references
Municipal Corporations ☞53.
C.J.S. Municipal Corporations § 106 et seq.

473B.02 Metropolitan council

Subdivision 1. Creation. A metropolitan council with jurisdiction in the metropolitan area consisting of the counties of Anoka, Carver, Dakota, Hennepin, Ramsey, Scott and Washington, is created. It shall be under the supervision and control of 15 members, all of whom shall be residents of the metropolitan area.

Subd. 2. Terms. The first members of the metropolitan council appointed by the governor shall be appointed as follows: the chairman as provided in subdivision 4; four for terms ending the first Monday in January 1969; five for terms ending the first Monday in January 1971; and five for terms ending the first Monday in January 1973. Thereafter the term of each member shall be for a term of six years and until his successor is appointed and qualified.

Subd. 3. Membership. Fourteen members of the metropolitan council shall be appointed by the governor on a nonpartisan basis, after consulting with all members of the legislature from the area composing the council district for which the member is to be appointed, by and with the advice and consent of the senate. Each such council member shall reside in the council district which he represents. Council districts consist of combinations of legislative and representative districts established by Extra Session

Laws 1966, Chapter 1, as prescribed herein. Each council district shall be represented by one member of the council. Council districts are hereby created as follows:

(1) The first council district consists of legislative district 12, that part of representative district 6A within Dakota county, and representative district 14A, and that part of representative district 14B within Scott county.

(2) The second council district consists of legislative districts 8 and 50.

(3) The third council district consists of legislative districts 49 and 57, and representative district 32B.

(4) The fourth council district consists of legislative district 33 and representative districts 13A and 21A.

(5) The fifth council district consists of legislative districts 30 and 31 and representative district 32A.

(6) The sixth council district consists of legislative districts 29 and 37.

(7) The seventh council district consists of legislative districts 27 and 28.

(8) The eighth council district consists of legislative districts 34 and 35.

(9) The ninth council district consists of legislative districts 36 and 38.

(10) The tenth council district consists of legislative districts 39 and 40.

(11) The eleventh council district consists of legislative districts 41 and 42.

(12) The twelfth council district consists of legislative districts 43 and 44.

(13) The thirteenth council district consists of legislative districts 45 and 46.

(14) The fourteenth council district consists of legislative districts 47 and 48.

Subd. 4. Chairman. (a) Appointment. The chairman of the metropolitan council shall be appointed by the governor as the 15th voting member thereof by and with the advice and consent of the senate to serve at his pleasure. He shall be a person experienced in the field of municipal and urban affairs with administrative training and executive ability.

(b) Duties. The chairman of the metropolitan council shall preside at the meetings of the metropolitan council and shall act as principal executive officer. He shall organize the work of the metropolitan council, appoint all officers and employees thereof, subject to the approval of the metropolitan council, and be responsible for carrying out all policy decisions of the metropolitan council. His salary and expense allowances shall be fixed by the metropolitan council.

Subd. 5. Metropolitan council; duties and compensation. The metropolitan council shall elect such officers as it deems necessary for the conduct of its affairs other than the chairman. A secretary and treasurer need not be members of the metropolitan council. Meeting times and places shall be fixed by the metropolitan council and special meetings may be called by a majority of the members of the metropolitan council or by the chairman thereof. Each metropolitan council member other than the chairman shall be paid a per diem compensation of $35 for each meeting and for such other services as are specifically authorized by the metropolitan council, and shall be reimbursed for his reasonable expenses.

In the performance of its duties the metropolitan council may promulgate rules governing its operation, establish committees, divisions, departments and bureaus and staff the same as necessary to carry out its duties and when specifically authorized by law make appointments to other governmental agencies and districts. All officers and employees of the metropolitan council shall serve at the pleasure of the appointing authority in the unclassified service of the state civil service. Rules promulgated by the metropolitan council shall be in accordance with the administrative procedure provisions contained in chapter 15.

Subd. 6. Executive director. Upon the recommendation of the chairman the metropolitan council may appoint an executive director to serve at his pleasure as the principal operating administrator for the metropolitan

council. He may be chosen from among the citizens of the nation at large, and shall be selected on the basis of his training and experience in the field of municipal and urban affairs.
Laws 1967, c. 896, § 2.

Metropolitan sewer service, see § 473C.01 et seq.
Operative date.
Laws 1967, c. 896, § 9, provides that the metropolitan council shall commence operations when the governor has appointed the members thereof and has proclaimed the organization of the council in writing filed in the office of the secretary of state.

473B.03 Advisory committees

The metropolitan council may establish and appoint persons to advisory committees to assist the metropolitan council in the performance of its duties. Members of the advisory committees shall serve without compensation but shall be reimbursed for their reasonable expenses as determined by the metropolitan council.
Laws 1967, c. 896, § 3, eff. May 26, 1967.

473B.04 Reports

On or before January 15th, of each odd numbered year the metropolitan council shall report to the legislature. The report shall include:

(1) A statement of the metropolitan council's receipts and expenditures by category since the preceding report;

(2) A detailed budget for the year in which the report is filed and the following year including an outline of its program for such period;

(3) An explanation of any comprehensive plan adopted in whole or in part for the metropolitan area;

(4) Summaries of any studies and the recommendations resulting therefrom made by the metropolitan council, and a listing of all applications for federal moneys made by governmental units within the metropolitan area submitted to the metropolitan council;

(5) A listing of plans of local governmental units submitted to the metropolitan council; and

(6) Recommendations of the metropolitan council for metropolitan area legislation, including the organization and functions of the metropolitan council.
Laws 1967, c. 896, § 4, eff. May 26, 1967.

473B.05 Metropolitan planning

Subdivision 1. All the powers, duties, obligations and property now vested in or imposed upon the commission established under chapter 473, for the metropolitan area, are hereby transferred to, imposed upon, and vested in the metropolitan council as the successor of such commission. At the time of such transfer the commission established under such laws is abolished.

Subd. 2. All employees of the commission shall be employees of the metropolitan council without interruption of salaries and employee benefits.
Laws 1967, c. 896, § 5, eff. May 26, 1967.

1. In general
Except for monies controlled by § 473B.06, subd. 4, the provisions of chapter 473B.01, permits the deposit of monies outside the state treasury. Op. Atty.Gen., 8, Oct. 6, 1967. Only the state treasurer must participate in the disbursement of monies which the metropolitan council deposits in the state treasury. Id.

473B.06 Administration of Metropolitan Council

Subdivision I. General powers. The metropolitan council shall have and exercise all powers which may be necessary or convenient to enable it to perform and carry out the duties and responsibilities now existing or which may hereafter be imposed upon it by law. Such powers include the specific powers enumerated in this section.

Subd. 2. Officers and employees. The metropolitan council may prescribe all terms and conditions for the employment of its officers, employees, and agents including but not limited to the fixing of compensation, their classification, benefits, and the filing of performance and fidelity bonds and such policies of insurance as it may deem advisable, the premium for which, however, shall be paid for by the district. Officers and employees of the metropolitan council, however, are public employees. The compensation and other conditions of employment of such officers and employees shall not be governed by any rule applicable to state employees in the classified service nor to any of the provisions of chapter 15A, unless the council so provides. Those employed by the metropolitan council are members of the Minnesota state retirement system. Those employed by a predecessor of the metropolitan council and transferred to it may at their option become members of the Minnesota state retirement system or may continue as members of the public retirement association to which they belonged as employees of the predecessor of the metropolitan council. The metropolitan council shall make the employer's contributions to pension funds of its employees.

Subd. 3. Consulting contracts. The metropolitan council may contract for the services of consultants who perform engineering, legal, or services of a professional nature. Such contracts shall not be subject to the requirements of any law relating to public bidding.

Subd. 4. Gifts and appropriations. The metropolitan council may accept gifts, apply for and use grants or loans of money or other property from the United States, the state, or any person for any metropolitan council purpose and may enter into agreements required in connection therewith and may hold, use, and dispose of such moneys or property in accordance with the terms of the gift, grant, loan, or agreement relating thereto. All moneys of the metropolitan council received pursuant to this subdivision or any other provision of law shall be deposited in the state treasury and the amount thereof is appropriated annually to the metropolitan council for the purposes of carrying out its duties and responsibilities.

Subd. 5. Development guide. The metropolitan council shall prepare and adopt, after appropriate study and such public hearings as may be necessary, a comprehensive development guide for the metropolitan area. It shall consist of a compilation of policy statements, goals, standards, programs, and maps prescribing guides for an orderly and economic development, public and private, of the metropolitan area. The comprehensive development guide shall recognize and encompass physical, social, or economic needs of the metropolitan area and those future developments which will have an impact on the entire area including but not limited to such matters as land use, parks and open space land needs, the necessity for and location of airports, highways, transit facilities, public hospitals, libraries, schools, and other public buildings.

Subd. 6. Council review; independent commissions, boards, and agencies. (1) The metropolitan council shall review all long term comprehensive plans of each independent commission, board, or agency prepared for its operation and development within the metropolitan area but only if such plan is determined by the council to have an area-wide effect, a multi community effect, or to have a substantial effect on metropolitan development. Each plan shall be submitted to the council before any action is taken to place the plan or any part thereof, into effect.

(2) No action shall be taken to place any plan or any part thereof, into effect until 60 days have elapsed after the date of its submission to the council, or until the council finds and notifies the submitting commission, board, or agency that the plan is consistent with its comprehensive guide for the

metropolitan area and the orderly and economic development of the metropolitan area, whichever first occurs. If, within 60 days after the date of submission, the council finds that a plan, or any part thereof, is inconsistent with its comprehensive guide for the metropolitan area or detrimental to the orderly and economic development of the metropolitan area, or any part thereof, it may direct that the operation of the plan, or such part thereof, be indefinitely suspended; provided that the council shall not direct the suspension of any plan or part thereof of any sanitary sewer district operating within the metropolitan area which pertains to the location and construction of a regional sewer plant or plants or the expansion or improvement of the present Minneapolis-St. Paul sanitary district treatment plant. An affected commission, board, or agency may appeal the decision of the metropolitan council suspending a plan, or part thereof, to the entire membership of the metropolitan council for public hearing. If the metropolitan council and the affected commission, board, or agency are unable to agree as to an adjustment of the plan, so that it may receive the council's approval, then a record of the disagreeing positions of the metropolitan council and the affected commission, board, or agency shall be made and the metropolitan council shall prepare a recommendation in connection therewith for consideration and disposition by the next regular session of the legislature.

Subd. 7. Council review; municipalities. Each city, village, borough, and town, all or part of which lies within the metropolitan area, shall submit to the metropolitan council for comment and recommendation thereon its long term comprehensive plans or any matter which has a substantial effect on metropolitan area development, including but not limited to plans for land use. The council shall maintain such plans in its files available for inspection by members of the public. No action shall be taken to place any such plan or part thereof into effect until 60 days have elapsed after its submission to the council. Promptly after submission, the council shall notify each city, village, borough, town, county, or special district which may be affected by the plans submitted, of the general nature of the plan, the date of submission, and the identity of the submitting unit. Political subdivisions contiguous to the submitting unit shall be notified in all cases. Within ten days after receipt of such notice any governmental unit so notified may request the council to conduct a hearing at which the submitting unit and any other governmental unit or subdivision may present its views. The council may attempt to mediate and resolve differences of opinion which exist among the participants in the hearing with respect to the plans submitted.

Subd. 8. Review of federal programs. The metropolitan council shall review all applications of governmental units, independent commissions, boards or agencies operating in the metropolitan area for a loan or grant from the United States of America or any agency thereof if review by a regional agency is required by federal law or the federal agency. Each governmental unit, independent commission, board, or agency, before submitting such an application to the United States government or an agency thereof shall first transmit the application to the metropolitan council for its comments and recommendations with respect to whether or not the project proposed is consistent with the comprehensive development guide for the metropolitan area. The comments and recommendations made by the metropolitan council shall then become a part of the application and if submitted to the United States of America or an agency thereof, such comments and recommendations shall also be submitted.

Subd. 9. Data collection. The metropolitan council in cooperation with other departments and agencies of the state and the regents of the university of Minnesota may develop a center for data collection and storage to be used by it and other governmental users and may accept gifts as otherwise authorized in this section for the purposes of furnishing information on such subjects as population, land use, governmental finances, and the like.

Subd. 10. Urban research. Where studies have not been otherwise authorized by law the metropolitan council may study the feasibility of programs relating but not limited to water supply, refuse disposal, surface water drainage, communication, transportation, and other subjects of concern to the peoples of the metropolitan area, may institute demonstration projects in connection therewith, and may accept gifts for such purposes as otherwise authorized in this section.

Subd. 11. Civil defense. The metropolitan council may coordinate civil defense, community shelter planning within the metropolitan area, accept gifts for such purposes as otherwise authorized in this section and contract with local governmental agencies and consultants in connection therewith.

Subd. 12. Local governmental participation. The metropolitan council may (1) participate as a party in any proceedings originating before the Minnesota municipal commission under chapter 414, if the proceedings involve the change in a boundary of a governmental unit in the metropolitan area, (2) conduct studies of the feasibility of annexing, enlarging, or consolidating units in the metropolitan area, (3) furnish space and other necessary assistance to a metropolitan expeditor assigned to the metropolitan area or any part thereof under the Federal Demonstration City Act of 1966,[1] on condition that such expeditor files monthly reports with the metropolitan council concerning his activities. The metropolitan council shall approve the use of moneys made available for land acquisition to local units of government from the land and conservation fund, the open space program of HUD, the natural resources account in the state treasury, if the use thereof conforms with the system of priorities established by law as a part of a comprehensive plan for the development of parks; otherwise it shall disapprove of the use thereof.

Subd. 13. Participation in special district activity. The metropolitan council shall appoint from its membership a member to serve with the metropolitan airports commission, a member to serve with the mosquito control commission, a member to serve on the Minneapolis-St. Paul sanitary district or any successor thereof, and may appoint a member to serve on any metropolitan area commission or board authorized by law. Each member of the metropolitan council so appointed on each of such commissions shall serve without a vote.

Laws 1967, c. 896, § 6, eff. May 26, 1967. Amended by Laws 1969, c. 9, § 86, eff. Feb. 12, 1969.

[1] 42 U.S.C.A. § 3301 et seq.

Metropolitan sewer service, see § 473C.01 et seq.

1969 Amendment. Correction bill.

1. In general
Only the state treasurer must participate in the disbursement of monies which the metropolitan council deposits in the state treasury. Op.Atty.Gen., 8, Oct. 6, 1967.
Except for monies controlled by subd. 4 of this section the provisions of § 473B.01, permit the deposit of monies outside the state treasury. Id.

473B.07 Special studies and reports

Subdivision 1. The metropolitan council shall engage in a continuous program of research and study concerning the matters enumerated in this section.

Subd. 2. The control and prevention of air pollution.

Subd. 3. The acquisition and financing of suitable major parks and open spaces within and adjacent to the metropolitan area.

Subd. 4. The control and prevention of water pollution in the metropolitan area in conformity with applicable federal and state laws.

Subd. 5. The development of long range planning in the metropolitan area but not for the metropolitan area.

Subd. 6. The acquisition of necessary facilities for the disposal of solid waste material for the metropolitan area and the means of financing such facilities.

Subd. 7. The examination of the tax structure in the metropolitan area and consideration of ways to equalize the tax resources therein.

Subd. 8. Assessment practices in the metropolitan area.

Subd. 9. The acquisition of necessary storm water drainage facilities for the metropolitan area and the means of financing such facilities.

Subd. 10. The necessity for the consolidation of common services of local governmental units and the kind of consolidation most suitable in the public interest.

Subd. 11. Advance land acquisition for development purposes in the metropolitan area and the role of the public in connection therewith.

Subd. 12. All studies shall include recommendations as to the governmental organization, governmental subdivision, or governmental district best suited to discharge the powers recommended.

Laws 1967, c. 896, § 7, eff. May 26, 1967.

473B.08 Tax levy

Subdivision 1. The metropolitan council may levy a tax on all taxable property in the counties named in section 473B.02 to provide funds for the purposes of sections 473B.01 to 473B.08. The tax shall not exceed seven tenths of one mill on each dollar of assessed valuation of all such taxable property, and shall be levied and collected in the manner provided by section 473.08.

Subd. 2. This section applies to taxes levied in 1969 and subsequent years.

Laws 1967, c. 896, § 8. Amended by Laws 1969, c. 1114, § 3.

1969 Amendment. Increased the tax limitation in subd. 1 from one half to seven tenths of one mill and added subd. 2.

APPENDIX B

EXAMPLES OF COUNCIL REVIEW

SPECIAL DISTRICT PLAN REVIEW

Coon Creek Watershed District

In March, 1969, the Metropolitan Council faced
the first open disregard of its review powers. The
Coon Creek Watershed District in Anoka County refused to submit plans to drain a major portion of
the District in order to develop it for truck farm-
ing and housing. The area is close to the proposed
Ham Lake site for a new or second major airport in
the Twin Cities area, which itself has been the
center of major controversy and which sits on a major water recharge area and game refuge. The Council, therefore, passed a resolution without dissent
calling for the District to submit formally its
plans within thirty days so that it could review
its merits in context of area-wide development and
ecological considerations. The District only reluctantly submitted its plans, claiming that they
predated the establishment of the Council, and,
consequently, should not be subject to metropolitan
review. Besides, the District was working against
a late summer, 1969, deadline for start of work.
The Council, in June, after reviewing the plans,
disapproved the project as it involved inappropriate
land use and development standards. It could not
lift the suspension until two issues were resolved.
The District and appropriate governmental agencies
would have to determine acceptable future land uses
throughout the watershed, which was to be treated
as a whole, and they should adopt adequate land use
controls to protect natural resources, particularly

as they relate to the recharge of the watershed's
underground water supply, through a long-term balance between development and preservation. The
Council proposed to cooperate in resolving both issues. The District requested the Council to reconsider its decision the following month, but the
matter was tabled when the District encountered financial problems which delayed the project. In
November, the District again requested reconsideration and submitted proposals on land use controls.
Finally, in September, 1969, the Council lifted its
suspension of the revised plan, provided four conditions were met: (1) construction to be programmed
to ensure compatibility with the proposed airport
should it be built; (2) adequate land use controls,
with respect to planting, drainage, and assurances
against lowering the water table, to be adopted;
(3) effective flood plain regulations for the project area to be developed and adopted; and (4) the
recommendations of the U.S. Fish and Wildlife Service on preservation, maintenance of prescribed
water levels, control of drainage, and elimination
of further development in certain subareas to be
met. Shortly after the first of the year, the District submitted to the Council an outline of the
actions it had taken, asking for plan approval.
Chairman Hetland noted that, in his opinion, conditions 1, 2, and 4 had been met, but that condition 3 was still lacking. The District's plan,
therefore, remained suspended. As of spring, 1970,
the plan was still suspended, pending resolution of
the third Council condition.

The Council, earlier in November, 1968, had
acted on a related District project. The District
had submitted for Council review an application to
the Farmer's Home Administration for a development
loan on which the Council postponed a decision
pending its final decision on the airport at Ham
Lake. The District then withdrew the application
to obtain funds locally. The primary reason for
the District's plan was to encourage private development as a means of enriching the tax base of an
area immediately in the path of urbanization.[1]

A New International Airport
for the Twin Cities

In February, 1969, the Metropolitan Airports
Commission (MAC),[2] a special district, announced
approval of a site at Ham Lake in Anoka County
north of the Twin Cities for a new major airport,
and submitted its plan to the Metropolitan Council
for review. MAC had reached its decision in secret
some months before and without consulting the Council.[3] The MAC announcement followed eleven months
of public hearings on the site recommended by its
professional staff and consultants and based on a
study of eight alternative sites. Its major virtues were that it was the least costly, with minimal residential development, in an area which also
avoided noise pollution. Over the course of the
hearings, substantial opposition and rancor arose.
Among the groups opposed were the State Conservation Department, Northwest Airlines, and community.
groups. The Conservation Department opposed the
site because it would infringe on the Carlos Avery
Wildlife Refuge and would threaten a major area-
wide water recharge resource.[4] Northwest Airlines
opposed it because of major problems arising from
the presence of local fog and birds and because it
preferred a different site; it would be paying a
major portion of the costs for headquarters and
service facilities.[5] Citizen groups and individuals opposed it for a variety of economic, social,
and development reasons, including conservation,
residential disruption, and noise pollution.[6] Support for the MAC plan came largely from local government and business interests in the northern suburbs which would benefit economically from the development.[7] Governor LeVander, in June, 1968, as
the result of the importance of the Council's future decision and the growing controversy, asked
the Council and five state and metropolitan agencies to make an "in-depth appraisal" of the proposed plan. MAC promised cooperation but indicated
impatience and concern that any significant delay
could jeopardize the area's advantageous position
with respect to other Midwest air facilities.[8]

After five months of work, the Council announced
that it could not yet adequately evaluate the site
without further information, including the feasibility of other sites.[9] As of April, 1969, with less
than two weeks to go before the Council would render
its decision, MAC had not yet provided the desired
information to the satisfaction of the Council.

Exactly two months after MAC submitted its
plans for a new international airport for metropolitan review, the Council made its decision, suspend-
ing--really vetoing--it. In justifying its rejection of the plan, the Council stated:

> It is the feeling of the majority of
> members of the council that there are
> enough serious doubts about abusive
> noise, adjacent land development,
> water tables and underground water
> supply recharge to request the MAC to
> examine all available site potential
> so as to find a location which best
> meets all of the criteria for an air-
> port site.[10]

This left open the possibility of an airport being
built at Ham Lake in the future should it prove to
be in fact the best possible site. But this could
be established only after comparative study of all
available sites, using proper development criteria.[11]

The Council also believed that the new airport
should be a replacement for the existing one; it
opposed the operation of two major air facilities
for scheduled commercial and cargo traffic as being
inefficient and as not resolving current "noise"
problems. MAC was ambiguous in its response.[12]
With the Council suspending the MAC plan, a very
delicate political situation arose. Under council
legislation, MAC could either request reconsideration of its plan, comply with the Council's request
to consider alternative sites and submit a new
recommendation,[13] or go to the legislature for

resolution of the impasse. Three weeks later MAC
resubmitted its proposal to use the Ham Lake site
providing further information to prove that other
sites did not have satisfactory air space characteristics. It hoped, too, that pending legislation
(since passed) giving the Council zoning and performance controls over land surrounding airports
would satisfy the development standards the Council
demanded.[14] Complicating the situation were demands from Northwest Airlines for MAC to approve
plans to expand facilities at the present International Airport to enable use of the new Boeing 747
jumbo jets; if they were not forthcoming Northwest
would build elsewhere.[15] With this, MAC approved
Northwest's expansion plan and Governor LeVander
again stepped in to further a solution to the growing controversy. The Council refused to be "pressured into a quick decision" by MAC or Northwest
Airlines.[16] Two weeks after resubmitting its plan
for Ham Lake, MAC withdrew it and called upon the
Council to choose the site for a major new airport.[17] The next day, June 14, 1969, Council Chairman Hetland announced that the Council, MAC, and
carriers would join to study and select the site
for the new international airport.[18] The Council
did not have the right, under law, to select the
site; but it could actively participate in the entire selection process.

The controversy surrounding the selection of
a new international airport again pointed up the
inadequacy of the Metropolitan Council's review
powers. They are essentially negative and come
only in the final stages of the planning process.
Again, as in the case cited with the State Highway
Department, the Council was able to "persuade" a
special district to involve it purposefully at the
earliest possible stage of plan preparation, but
only after almost eighteen months of discussion and
costs in the thousands of dollars. The power of
persuasion, however, has its limits. Experience
has shown that local units of government have re-
linquished prerogatives only when circumstances and
council operations have forced it to do so. This

can hardly be counted upon in all necessary cases.
The Council's request to the 1969 legislature for
augmented review and initiatory powers, involving
it at the earliest possible stage of the planning
process, therefore, seems well taken. Unfortunately, the legislature did not act upon the request
despite widespread public support for such measures,
including porposals to place special districts such
as MAC directly under the Council.[19]

FEDERAL HIGHWAY REVIEW

Burnsville Highway Interchange

    In late 1968, the Minnesota Highway Department
submitted plans for approval to build a complex
highway interchange in suburban Burnsville in Dakota County. Two months later, after some bitter
discussion, the Council's Referral Committee endorsed the design submitted by the Highway Department and demanded by Burnsville. (In Minnesota,
until May, 1969, local governments had the right to
veto highway plans not meeting their approval.)
The suburb insisted on the interchange because of
its need for and commitment to a commercial development.[20] In March, 1969, the Council rejected the
design in a six to five vote after its transportation planner stated that two of the exit ramps were
unsafe. They would require a weaving motion and
give motorists some fifteen seconds to decide to
exit or to change lanes; further, he questioned
whether or not they were even necessary. These
evaluations were again bitterly challenged by the
Highway Department and Burnsville. The transportation planner, backed up by Hetland, claimed that
the unsafe qualities of the interchanges warranted
disapproval. When a council member asked the representative of Burnsville whether the suburb would
want the proposed interchange and shopping center
if there were an area-wide tax sharing scheme, he
replied that the community would then probably prefer to remain residential.[21] The Highway Department, while expressing sympathy for the Council's

stand, noted that the plan had to be a compromise
in view of the politics of local consent and that
plans had been under preparation for over four
years. The Department and Burnsville then asked
the Council to reconsider its decision. At one
point in the deliberations, the Burnsville mayor
threatened to seek help from the state's congressional delegation were the interchange rejected.
In mid-June, the Council offered a compromise solution which, if accepted by the applicants, it could
approve. The solution, creative but simple, called
for adding an additional two thousand feet to the
exit lanes which would give motorists twenty more
seconds to make a decision on whether to exit or
not. The Highway Department and Burnsville indicated acceptance of the compromise, and the Council
approved the plan.[22] This was the first time the
Council could act entirely within federal and state
legislation without necessarily considering outside
factors, such as contractual commitments.[23] It was,
further, a demonstration to the metropolitan community of what intelligent planning and review could
accomplish.

Highway 18 Upgrading

An earlier highway referral even more clearly
shows the difficulties the Metropolitan Council
faced in exercising its review "at the last minute."
In early 1968, Hennepin County requested $293,000
in federal funds to upgrade one mile of County Road
18 to freeway standards as part of a long-range
program to convert it into a freeway. The Council
opposed the plan as a violation of safety and development standards of the Joint Program's Development Guide, adopted by the MPC in 1967 and used by
the Council, pending adoption of its own Development
Guide. At issue was the construction of two dia-
mond interchanges within one mile of each other and
converting a highway into a freeway that would be
within two miles of two other existing freeways.
Two interchanges so close would create a driving
hazard from the weaving of exiting and entering
vehicles, and the very upgrading of the highway

would induce further sprawl in an area already well
developed.[24] Hennepin County representatives differed with the Council, contending that sections of
Highway 18 had already been rebuilt as freeway before adoption of the <u>Development Guide</u>. Equally
important, some communities along its route had at-
tracted commercial development with the promise of
upgrading the road.[25] Several council members considered these as "extenuating circumstances" and
proposed language to this effect be part of its comments. They were outvoted and the Council instead
voted to submit its unrelieved negative comments to
the Bureau of Public Roads.[26] The Minnesota Highway Department then asked the Council to "reanalyze
the proposal" in view of the long-standing plan,
work, and development already undertaken.[27] The
Council was then faced with two disagreeable choices:
(1) It could maintain its position and so further
antagonize local governments whose cooperation was
essential to orderly area-wide development, or (2)
it could alter its comments, softening their impact
on federal authorities, but serving to warn local
units to involve the Council at an earlier stage of
their plans in the future. After a brief, but
heated, debate, the Council decided to follow the
second course, adding an analysis which while re-
affirming its initial stand, noted that, given the
circumstances involved, the upgrading "would appear
to be necessary."[28] Some council members and members of the community viewed this as unfortunate
backing down on a sensitive issue which could set a
precedent, encouraging local pressures and thereby
jeopardizing objective council decisions. Council
Chairman Hetland, however, viewed the action differently. "We are not changing our comment," he
maintained, only "transmitting information that the
federal people can use in evaluating our comment."[29]
In retrospect, both Hetland and council critics appear to be right. The Council did give federal
authorities fuller information on a sensitive and
complicated proposal, but there can be no question
that the added comments on its necessity also
softened their impact. But then there is no assurance of substantial reason to believe that an

unrelieved, unfavorable review would have prevented
the grant. (See discussion in Chapter 8, pp. 175-
79.) The most important aspects of this case demonstrate the difficulties of rendering a "right"
decision when faced with issues only in the last
phases of the planning process and with the possible encouragement of local pressures in support
of vested interests contrary to those area-wide.
The Council's decision, in a way, was unavoidable.
It hoped to be fair in the face of plans and commitments previously made for the road while persuading governmental bodies to involve the Council
earlier in their plans.[30] One significant positive
fall-out, in this respect, was the "agreement with
county engineers and the Minnesota Highway Department to submit highway plans at the earliest possible stage rather than just before bids are to be
let."[31]

NOTES

1. Robert Nethercut, Interview, June, 1969.
(All interviews cited are with Stanley Baldiner,
unless otherwise stated.)

2. The Metropolitan Airports Commission (MAC)
is an independent special district created in 1943
by the state legislature to operate existing airports and develop a comprehensive metropolitan system for the area. It operates six facilities, including the general Twin Cities International Airport, a major airport for freight and corporate
planes, and four satellite fields for private air-
craft. It has jurisdiction over an area extending
in a radius of 35 miles (25 miles before 1969) from
the city halls of Minneapolis and Saint Paul. Commission membership is exclusively from these two
cities, except for a tie-breaking member from outside the area appointed by the governor.

3. "Chronology of Events in Airport Dispute,"
Minneapolis Star, May 21, 1969; Alan J. Wilensky,
"Twin Cities Metropolitan Council: A Case Study of

the Politics of Metropolitan Cooperation" (unpublished senior's thesis, Princeton University, Princeton, New Jersey, April, 1969), p. 166.

4. Editorial, "Airport Decision Nears," <u>Minneapolis Star</u>, February 4, 1969.

5. Edward Schaefer, "Row Looms on Choice of Airport Site," <u>Minneapolis Star</u>, February 4, 1969; Greg Finney, "Metro Council Still Up In The Air About Ham Lake Airport Site," <u>Minneapolis Tribune</u>, April 14, 1969.

6. <u>Ibid</u>.

7. Edward Schaefer, "Airport Panel Renews Ham Lake Site Plan," <u>Minneapolis Star</u>, May 21, 1969.

8. "Chronology of Events in Airport Dispute," <u>loc. cit</u>.; Wilensky, <u>loc. cit</u>.; Finney, <u>loc. cit</u>.

9. "Chronology of Events in Airport Dispute," <u>loc. cit</u>.

10. Dewey Bersheid, "Metro Group Rejects Ham Lake For Airport," <u>Saint Paul Pioneer Press</u>, April 26, 1969.

11. <u>Ibid</u>.

12. <u>Ibid</u>.; Betty Wilson, "New Airport Must Quiet Old Site, Report Urges," <u>Minneapolis Star</u>, May 20, 1969.

13.. Berscheid, <u>loc. cit</u>.

14. Betty Wilson, "MAC Will Ask Metro Council to Reconsider Ham Lake Site," <u>Minneapolis Star</u>, May 20, 1969.

15. "Chronology of Events in Airport Dispute," <u>loc cit</u>.; Dewey Berscheid, "Metro Unit Rejects Pressure," <u>Saint Paul Pioneer Press</u>, May 23, 1969.

16. Ibid.

17. R. J. Johnson, "Site Choice Now Up to Air-
line, Metro Unit, MAC's Hall Says," St. Paul Dispatch, June 13, 1969.

18. Harry Hite, "Hunt For New Major Airport
Site to Begin," St. Paul Dispatch, June 14, 1969.

19. Editorial, "Were They Watching?" Saint
Paul Pioneer Press, May 25, 1969; Editorial, "Change
Needed?" West Saint Paul Sun, June 11, 1969.

20. Peter Ackerberg, "Dispute on Interchange
Ironed Out," Minneapolis Star, June 19, 1969; David
Rubin, Interview, June, 1969.

21. Ibid.; Betty Wilson, "Council State Clash
on Metro Highways," Minneapolis Star, March 6, 1969.

22. Nethercut, loc. cit.; Rubin, loc. cit.

23. Ibid.

24. Peter Ackerberg, "Road Issue May Test Metro Council Power," Minneapolis Star, March 3, 1968.

25. Ibid.

26. Peter Ackerberg, "Met Council Challenges
Hennepin Road Plan," Minneapolis Star, March 15,
1968.

27. George McCormick, "Metro Council Sends
Highway 18 Data to U.S.," Minneapolis Tribune,
April 5, 1968.

28. Ibid.

29. Ibid.

30. Boezi, loc. cit.

31. 1967-1968 Biennial Report (St. Paul: Metropolitan Council, Twin Cities Area, 1969), p. 12.

SELECTED BIBLIOGRAPHY

SELECTED BIBLIOGRAPHY

INTERVIEWS

Albertson, Howard, State Representative, April, 1969.

Altschuler, Alan, Professor, Massachusetts Institure of Technology, November, 1968.

Andersen, Elmer L., former Governor, State of Minnesota, April, 1969.

Anderson, Wilfred "Andy," Director of Metropolitan Inter-County Council, June, 1969, and June, 1970.

Anding, Thomas L., Executive Director, Upper Midwest Council for Research and Development, April, 1969.

Ashbach, Robert, State Senator, April, 1969.

Avery, Gene, Transportation Planning Director, Metropolitan Council, June, 1969.

Boezi, Reynold, Program Coordinator, Metropolitan Council, March-April, 1969; June, 1969; and May, 1970.

Bolstad, Lester, Jr., Chairman, Metropolitan Transit Commission, June, 1969.

Brandt, Lloyd, Manager, Legal Department, Minneapolis Chamber of Commerce, June, 1969.

Brussat, William, U.S. Bureau of the Budget, May, 1969.

Dalglish, James, Finance Commissioner, City of St. Paul, June, 1969.

Dunne, Dennis W., Member of Metropolitan Council, June, 1969.

Durenberger, David, Executive Secretary to Governor LeVander, April, 1969.

Edman, F. Robert, Consultant to Minnesota State Legislature, April, June, 1969.

Einsweiler, Robert, Director, Planning Department, Metropolitan Council, June, 1969.

Finnegan, John, Editor, <u>Saint Paul Pioneer Press</u>, former Member Metropolitan Planning Commission, April, 1969.

Frenzel, William, State Representative, June, 1969.

Grittner, Karl, State Senator, April, 1969.

Hetland, James, Jr., Chairman, Metropolitan Council, April, June, 1969.

Honsey, Milton, Mayor, New Hope, April, 1969.

Johnson, Verne, former Executive Director, Citizens League, April, 1969.

Jones, Victor, Professor, University of California, September, 1969.

Kirchner, William, State Senator, April, 1969.

Kolderie, Ted, Executive Director, Citizens League, April, June, 1969.

Loeks, C. David, former Director, Twin Cities Metropolitan Planning Commission, February, 1969.

Lund, Dean, Executive Secretary, Metropolitan Section League of Minnesota Municipalities, April, 1969, and June, 1970.

Nathanson, Iric, Staff Member, Office of U.S. Rep-
     resentative Donald Fraser, September, 1969.

Nethercut, Robert, Director, Community Services De-
     partment, Metropolitan Council, June, 1969.

Ogdahl, Harmon, State Senator, April, 1969.

Olsen, Raymond, Director, Minnesota State Planning
     Agency, April, June, 1969.

Pickford, James H., Senior Analyst, Advisory Com-
     mission on Intergovernmental Relations, May,
     1969, and June, 1970.

Popham, Wayne, State Senator, June, 1969.

Rasmussen, Bruce, Executive Secretary, Minnesota
     Municipal Commission, June, 1969.

Rosenmeier, Gordon, State Senator, April, 1969.

Rubin, David, Transportation Planner, Metropolitan
     Council, June, 1969.

Tilton, John, Publisher, Suburban Sun Newspapers,
     June, 1969.

Vanderpoel, Peter, Reporter, Saint Paul Pioneer
     Press, and Saint Paul Dispatch, June, 1969.

Whiting, Charles, former head of Metropolitan Coun-
     cil's Public Information Office, April, 1969.

Wolfe, Kenneth, former Mayor, St. Louis Park; State
     Senator, April, 1969.

METROPOLITAN COUNCIL AND METROPOLITAN PLANNING COMMISSION DOCUMENTS

Agreement Between Metropolitan Council and Minnesota
     Highway Department. Saint Paul: Metropolitan
     Council, 1969.

Agreement Between Metropolitan Council and Metro-
    politan Transit Commission. Saint Paul: Met-
    ropolitan Council, 1969.

1965-1966 Biennial Report. Saint Paul: Twin Cities
    Metropolitan Planning Commission, 1967.

1967-1968 Biennial Report. Saint Paul: Metropoli-
    tan Council, Twin Cities Area, 1969.

1967-1968 Biennial Report, Addendum B: Recommen-
    dations for Metropolitan Area Legislation.
    Saint Paul: Metropolitan Council, January,
    1969.

Boezi, Reynold. Metropolitan Reorganization:
    Strategies for Action. Saint. Paul: Metropol-
    itan Council, April 6, 1970. (Mimeographed.)
    Paper delivered at the 1970 American Society
    of Planning Officials annual conference in New
    York, April 6, 1970.

Faville, Hugh C. Memorandum: Revised procedures
    on Handling Comprehensive Municipal Plans.
    Saint Paul: Metropolitan Council, 1969.
    (Mimeographed.)

_____. Memorandum: Suggested Procedure for
    Certain Types of Highway Referrals. Saint
    Paul: Metropolitan Council, 1960. (Mimeo-
    graphed.)

Hetland, James., Jr. Chairman's Analysis of Pro-
    posal by Joint Program Coordinating Committee
    for Continuing Transportation Planning. Saint
    Paul: Metropolitan Council, 1968. (Mimeo-
    graphed.)

_____. Memorandum. Saint Paul: Metropolitan
    Council, 1969. (Mimeographed.)

The Joint Program. 4,000,000 by 2000: Preliminary
    Proposals for Guiding Change. St. Paul: Twin
    Cities Metropolitan Planning Commission, 1964.

_____. Goals for Development of the Twin Cities
     Metropolitan Area. St. Paul: Twin Cities
     Metropolitan Planning Commission, 1965.

_____. Governmental Responsibilities and Re-
     sources. Part D (Draft P. 20 III J). St. Paul:
     Twin Cities Metropolitan Planning Commission,
     1967. (Mimeographed.)

_____. Government-Taxation: Alternatives Paper
     7. St. Paul: Twin Cities Metropolitan Plan-
     ning Commission, 1966.

_____. Governmental Units: A Comparative Study
     of the Twin Cities and Other Metropolitan
     Areas in 1962, Social Studies Paper No. 10GI
     (Draft). St. Paul: Twin Cities Metropolitan
     Planning Commission, 1965. (Mimeographed.)

_____. Social Studies: Population Paper No. 5.
     St. Paul: Twin Cities Metropolitan Planning
     Commission, 1963. (Mimeographed.)

_____. Twin Cities Area Metropolitan Develop-
     ment Guide. St. Paul: Twin Cities Metropoli-
     tan Planning Commission, 1968.

Metropolitan Council, Data-log No. 2: 1968 Popu-
     lation Estimates. St. Paul: Twin Cities
     Metropolitan Planning Commission, 1968.

Metropolitan Council Newsletter. "Council's First
     Months," December, 1967.

Metropolitan Council Resolution No. 69-11, August
     28, 1969. (Mimeographed.)

Metropolitan Population Study: Part II. St. Paul:
     Twin Cities Metropolitan Planning Commission,
     1961.

Metropolitan Sewerage Plan. Saint Paul: Metro-
     politan Council, 1969.

Metropolitan Sewerage Study. St. Paul: Twin
     Cities Metropolitan Planning Commission, 1960.

*Metropolitan Sewer Plan: A Preliminary Concept
     Plan*. Saint Paul: Metropolitan Council, 1968.

Metropolitan Water Study: Parts I and II. St.
     Paul: Twin Cities Metropolitan Planning Com-
     mission, 1960.

Peterson, Barry. *A Brief History of Sanitary Sew-
     age Disposal in the Twin Cities*. St. Paul:
     Metropolitan Council, 1967. (Mimeographed.)

Referral Manual. Saint Paul: Metropolitan Coun-
     cil, 1968.

Resolution for Seven Counties. Saint Paul: Metro-
     politan Council, 1969.

Solid Waste Disposal Advisory Committee. *Recommen-
     dations for Solid Waste Disposal in the Twin
     Cities Area*. Saint Paul: Metropolitan Coun-
     cil, 1968.

Summaries of Acts. Saint Paul: Metropolitan Coun-
     cil, 1969.

Twin Cities Area Metropolitan Development Guide.
     St. Paul: Twin Cities Metropolitan Planning
     Commission, 1968.

Twin Cities Metropolitan Planning Commission. *An-
     nual Report, 1958*. St. Paul: Twin Cities
     Metropolitan Planning Commission, 1958.

_____. *Annual Report, 1959*. St. Paul: Twin
     Cities Metropolitan Planning Commission, 1959.

_____. *Annual Report, 1960*. St. Paul: Twin
     Cities Metropolitan Planning Commission, 1960.

_____. *Annual Report, 1962*. St. Paul: Twin
     Cities Metropolitan Planning Commission, 1962.

_____. 1965-1966 Biennial Report to the Minne-
sota Legislature. St. Paul: Twin Cities Metropolitan Planning Commission, 1967.

_____. Metropolitan Population Study: Part II.
Numbers and Distribution. St. Paul: Twin
Cities Metropolitan Planning Commission, 1961.

_____. Position Paper on Legislation for Metro-
politan Government. St. Paul: Twin Cities
Metropolitan Planning Commission, 1967.

PUBLICATIONS OF TWIN CITIES AREA
ORGANIZATIONS AND INDIVIDUALS

Agenda of the Twin Cities Seminar. Minneapolis:
Upper Midwest Council for Research and Development, 1966.

Barrett, Robert A. Metropolitan Inter-County Council: Organization Study. St. Paul: Metropolitan Inter-County Council, 1967.

Dunne, Dennis W. This is a Matter of Great Importance to you and to this Metropolitan Area.
Minneapolis: Minneapolis Chamber of Commerce,
1967. (Mimeographed.)

Excerpts from 1966 DFL Platform. Minneapolis:
Citizens League, 1966.

The Future Role of the Metropolitan Planning Commission. Minneapolis: Citizens League, 1965.

A Government Structure Program. Minneapolis: Metropolitan Section, League of Minnesota Municipalities, 1970.

Honsey, Milton C., and Bergstrom, Vernon. Report
on the Study of the Municipality of Metropolitan Toronto. Minneapolis: Hennepin County
League of Municipalities, 1964.

Kolderie, Ted. Governing the Twin Cities. Minne-
     apolis: Upper Midwest Research and Development
     Council, 1969.

LeVander, Harold. This Is Where I Stand. Minne-
     apolis: LeVander for Governor Volunteer Com-
     mittee, 1966.

A Metropolitan Council for the Twin Cities Area.
     Minneapolis: Citizens League, 1967.

Metropolitan Maze . . . The Council-Watcher's Guide.
     Minneapolis: Council of Metropolitan Area
     Leagues of Women Voters, 1967.

Metropolitan Policy and Metropolitan Development.
     Minneapolis: Citizens League, 1968.

Minnesota's Twin Cities Metropolitan Area. Minne-
     apolis: League of Women Voters, 1966.

Minutes. Minneapolis: Citizens League, January
     15, 1968.

Olson, Stan. Report of Government Structure Commit-
     tee. Minneapolis: Metropolitan Section,
     League of Minnesota Municipalities, February
     3, 1967. (Mimeographed.)

Once Over Lightly. Minneapolis: League of Women
     Voters, 1965. (Mimeographed.)

Peterson, Orville. Toward More Effective Home Rule.
     Minneapolis: League of Minnesota Municipali-
     ties, 1957.

Presentation of the Metropolitan Section of the
     League of Minnesota Municipalities Before the
     House Committee on Metropolitan and Urban Af-
     fairs. Minneapolis: Metropolitan Section,
     League of Minnesota Municipalities, February
     13, 1967.

Proposed Rosemont Site. Minneapolis: Upper Midwest
    Research and Development Council, 1965.

Recommendations of the Urban Study and Action Com-
    mittee for the Formation of a Multi-Purpose
    7-County Metropolitan District. Minneapolis:
    Urban Study and Action Committee, September,
    1966. (Mimeographed.)

Report of Metropolitan Government Study Committee.
    St. Paul: Ramsey County League of Municipali-
    ties, 1967. (Mimeographed.)

Report to Platform Committee. Minneapolis: Repub-
    lican Advisory Committee on Intergovernmental
    Relations, 1966. (Mimeographed.)

Report of the Republican State Task Force on Metro-
    politan Affairs, 1968.

Resolution of the Board of Directors. Minneapolis:
    Upper Midwest Research and Development Council,
    1969.

Summary of Comments and Proposals on Areawide Gov-
    ernmental Problems of the Twin Cities Metro-
    politan Area. Minneapolis: Citizens League,
    1966.

Upper Midwest Research and Development Council Re-
    port, 1967. Minneapolis: Upper Midwest Re-
    search and Development Council, 1967.

Wilson, John O. Regional Differences in Social
    Welfare. Kansas City: Midwest Research In-
    stitute, 1967. (Mimeographed.)

STATE OF MINNESOTA DOCUMENTS

Journal of the House, Sixty-sixth session. St.
    Paul: State of Minnesota, 1969.

LeVander, Harold. _Inaugural Address_. St. Paul:
    State of Minnesota, 1967.

Report of Bipartisan Reapportionment Commission.
    St. Paul: State of Minnesota, 1966.

_Report of the Commission on Municipal Annexation
    and Consolidation_. St. Paul: State of Minne-
    sota, 1959.

Report of the Commission on Municipal Laws. St.
    Paul: State of Minnesota, 1961.

_Report on Water Supply and Sewage Disposal in the
    Minneapolis-Saint Paul Metropolitan Area_.
    St. Paul: Minnesota Department of Health,
    1961.

The "Quality of Life" in Minnesota Growth. St.
    Paul: Minnesota Department of Economic De-
    velopment, 1967.

LEGISLATION

California Legislature Assembly Bill No. 1846,
    April 7, 1969.

State of Colorado Engrossed House Bill No. 1085,
    1969.

Demonstration Cities and Metropolitan Development
    Act, 1966, P.L. 89-754, 80 Stat. 1255, 1261.

Federal Aid Highway Act, 1962, P.L. 87-866, 76
    Stat. 1145.

Housing and Urban Development Act, 1965, P.L.
    89-117, 79 Stat. 451, 502.

Omnibus Crime Control and Safe Streets Act, 1968,
    P.L. 90-351, Sec. 522, 82 Stat. 197, 2081.

Urban Mass Transportation Act, 01964, P.L. 88-365, 78 Stat. 302.

Minnesota State Constitution.

1957, Minnesota Laws, Chapter 468.

1957, Minnesota Sessions Law, Chapter 833.

1967, Minnesota Sessions Law, Chapter 892 (codified as Chapter 473A).

_____, Chapter 896 (codified as Chapter 473B).

_____, 1966 extra session Chapter 1 at p. 14.

1969, Minnesota Sessions Law, Chapters 312, 449, 590, 625, 777, 847, 868, 879, 979, 1039, 1111, 1122, 1124, 1142.

1961, Minnesota Statutes, Sections 360.101-360.144; 445.01-445.21.

1967, Minnesota Statutes, Chapter 645.023, Subdivision 1.

Minnesota Statutes Annotated, Extra Session, 1959, Chapter 45, Sections 2.02-2.715.

Minnesota Statutes Annotated, 412 et al.

COURT CASES

Baker v. Carr, 369 U.S. 186 (1962).

Davis v. Mann, 377 U.S. 678 (1964).

Duxbury v. Donovan, 138 N.W. 2d 692, Minn. (1965).

Honsey et al. v. Donovan, 236 F. Supp. 8D Minn. (1964).

Lucas v. Colorado General Assembly, 377 U.S. 713
     (1964).

Maryland Committee v. Tawes, 377 U.S. 656 (1964).

Reynolds v. Simms, 377 U.S. 533 (1964).

Roman v. Sinock, 377 U.S. 695 (1964).

WMCA, Inc. v. Lomenzo, 337 U.S. 633 (1964).

                U.S. GOVERNMENT DOCUMENTS

Alternative Approaches to Governmental Reorganiza-
     tion in Metropolitan Areas. Washington, D.C.:
     Advisory Commission on Intergovernmental Rela-
     tions, 1962.

Comprehensive Planning Assistance, Handbook 1:
     Guidelines Leading to a Grant (MD6041.3).
     Washington, D.C.: U.S. Department of Housing
     and Urban Development, 1969.

Factors Affecting Voter Reactions to Governmental
     Reorganization in Metropolitan Areas. Washing-
     ton, D.C.: Advisory Commission on Intergovern-
     mental Relations, May, 1962.

Frieden, Bernard J. Metropolitan America: Chal-
     lenge to Federalism. Washington, D.C.: Ad-
     visory Commission on Intergovernmental Rela-
     tions, 1966.

Haar, Charles M. Metropolitan Development and Bud-
     geting: A Step Toward Creative Federalism.
     Washington, D.C.: U.S. Department of Housing
     and Urban Development, September 21, 1967.
     Speech delivered at Columbia University.
     (Mimeographed.)

_____. The Growth of the Federal Role in Plan-
     ning. Washington, D.C.: U.S. Department of
     Housing and Urban Development, January, 1967.
     Speech printed in Planning and the Federal

__Establishment__. Proceedings of the American
Institute of Planners, 4th Biennial Government
Relations and Planning Policies Conference,
Washington, D.C., January 27-29, 1967.

Martin, Roscoe C. __Metropolis in Transition: Local
Government Adaptation to Metropolitan Growth__.
Washington, D.C.: The U.S. Government Printing Office for Housing and Home Finance Agency,
1963.

__Performance of Urban Functions: Local and Areawide__.
Washington, D.C.: Advisory Commission on Intergovernmental Relations, 1963.

__State and Local Finance: Significant Features,
1956-1966__. Washington, D.C.: Advisory Commission on Intergovernmental Relations, 1966.

U.S. Bureau of the Census. __1967 Census of Govern-
ment, Vol. I, Governmental Organization__.
Washington, D.C.: U.S. Government Printing
Office, 1968.

_____. __County and City Date Book__. Washington,
D.C.: U.S. Government Printing Office, 1967.

_____. __Current Population Reports: Population
Estimates__. Series P. 25-411. Washington, D.C.:
U.S. Government Printing Office, 1968.

_____. __Current Population Reports: Special
Census__. Series P. 28, No. 420. Washington,
D.C.: U.S. Government Printing Office, 1966.

U.S. Department of Labor, Bureau of Labor Statistics, and U.S. Department of Commerce, Bureau
of the Census. __Social and Economic Conditions
of the Negro in the United States__. BLS Report
No. 332, Current Population Reports, Series
P. 23-45. Washington, D.C.: U.S. Government
Printing Office, 1967.

__Urban and Rural America: Policies for Growth__.
Washington, D.C.: Advisory Commission on
Intergovernmental Relations, 1968.

BOOKS

Altshuler, Alan A. The City Planning Process: A
    Political Analysis. Ithaca: Cornell Univer-
    sity Press, 1965.

_____. A Report on Politics in Minneapolis.
    Cambridge: Joint Center for Urban Studies of
    Massachusetts Institute of Technology and Har-
    vard University, 1959. (Mimeographed.)

_____. A Report on Politics in St. Paul. Cam-
    bridge: Joint Center for Urban Studies of
    Massachusetts Institute of Technology and Har-
    vard University, 1959. (Mimeographed.)

Banfield, Edward C., and Grodzins, Morton. Govern-
    ment and Housing in Metropolitan Areas. New
    York: McGraw-Hill Book Company, 1958.

Bollens, John C., and Schmandt, Henry J. The Me-
    tropolis: Its People, Politics, and Economic
    Life. 2nd ed. New York: Harper & Row, 1970.

Bonovetz, James M. Perspectives on the Future of
    Government in Metropolitan Areas. Chicago:
    Loyola University, 1968.

Connery, Robert H., ed. Politics of Mental Health.
    New York: Columbia University Press, 1968.

Elazar, Daniel J. American Federalism: A View
    from the States. New York: Thomas Y. Crowell
    Company, 1966.

Goldwin, Robert A., ed. A Nation of Cities.
    Chicago: Public Affairs Administration, Uni-
    versity of Chicago, 1966.

Greer, Scott. Governing the Metropolis. New York:
    John Wiley and Sons, Inc., 1962.

Gulick, Luther Halsey. The Metropolitan Problem
    and American Ideas. New York: Alfred A.
    Knopf, 1962.

Jacobs, Herbert, and Vines, Kenneth N., eds. Poli-
    tics in the American States: A Comparative
    Analysis. Boston: Little, Brown and Company,
    1965.

Mitau, G. Theodore. Politics in Minnesota. Minne-
    apolis: University of Minnesota Press, 1960.

Modernizing Local Government. New York: Committee
    for Economic Development, July, 1966.

Murphy, Thomas P. Metropolitics and the Urban
    County. Washington, D.C.: Washington Na-
    tional Press, 1970.

Reshaping Government in Metropolitan Areas. New
    York: Committee for Economic Development,
    February, 1970.

Senior, Derek, ed. The Regional City. Chicago:
    Aldine Publishing Company, 1966.

Spreiregen, Paul D. Urban Design: Architecture
    of Towns and Cities. New York: McGraw-Hill
    Book Company, 1965.

NEWSPAPERS

Bland, Jim. "Twin Cities Metro Council Carved
    Order Out of Chaos," Dayton Daily News, Novem-
    ber 21, 1968.

"Change Needed," West Saint Paul Sun, Editorial,
    June 1, 1969.

Eisele, Al. "Rosenmeier Asks Metro Fiscal Unit,"
    Saint Paul Dispatch, March 25, 1969.

Farrington, Ted. "Metropolitan Decisions on Trans-
    portation in Conflict," Minnesota Valley Sun,
    December 12, 1968.

"Metro Council's First Year," Anoka County Union,
    August 16, 1968.

"The Metropolitan Monster," Fridley News, Editorial, June 23, 1960.

Minneapolis Star, July 4, 1961, to June 19, 1969.

Minneapolis Tribune, February 6, 1966, to June 11, 1969.

"Mr. Robbie's Toughest Selling Job," Golden Valley Suburban Press, June 30, 1960.

"Newsmen Voice Protest Against Robbie 'Metro' Service Plan," Columbia Heights Record, June 30, 1960.

"Olson Group May Join Metro Group," St. Louis Post Dispatch, February 3, 1966.

Saint Paul Dispatch, February 14, 1967, to June 14, 1969.

Saint Paul Pioneer Press, November 11, 1966, to June 27, 1969.

Tilton, John. "An Experiment in Self-Government Unfolds," The Sun, February 10, 1969.

Wilson, Betty. "Commissioners Plan to Organize Area Council," The West Saint Paul Booster, October 6, 1965.

ARTICLES

Beckman, Norman. "How Metropolitan Are Federal and State Policies?" Public Administration Review, XXVI, 2 (June, 1966), 99.

"Business at Work in the Twin Cities," Fortune, LXXVI, 2 (August, 1967), 123-24, 128.

Dunne, Dennis W. "A Challenge for the 1967 Legislature," Greater Minneapolis, Minneapolis Chamber of Commerce (December, 1966), p. 7.

Fischer, John. "The Minnesota Experiment: How to
     Make a Big City Fit to Live in," Harper's Maga-
     zine, CCXXXVIII, 1427 (April, 1969), 12.

"Minnesota Model," Time, XCIV, 12 (September 19,
     1969), 64-65.

Woodward, Frank L., et al. "Experiences with
     Ground Water Contamination in Unsewered Areas
     in Minnesota," American Journal of Public
     Health, LI, 8 (August, 1961), 1130-36.

Wright, Phyllis, M.D., with Zimmerman, David R.
     "Medicine Today," Ladies' Home Journal,
     LXXXVI, 5 (May, 1969), 46.

                    MISCELLANEOUS

Albertson, Howard. Memorandum to Committee on
     Rules, Minnesota House of Representatives.
     St. Paul: Howard Albertson, 1967. (Mimeo-
     graphed.)

Bray, Martha Coleman. "Minneapolis," Encyclopaedia
     Brittanica, XV, p. 556, 1964 ed.

_____. "St. Paul," Encyclopaedia Brittanica,
     XIX, p. 852, 1964 ed.

Edman, F. Robert. Background Cases Prepared for
     the Subcommittee on State Departments. St.
     Paul, 1967. (Mimeographed).

Fischer, John. Innovations in Government. Speech
     delivered at 1969 National Planning Confer-
     ence of the American Society of Planning Offi-
     cials in Cincinnati, Ohio, April 21, 1969.

Head, Douglas M., and Hartfeldt, Will H. Letter
     to James Hetland, Jr., Chairman of Metropoli-
     tan Council, October 6, 1967.

Honsey, Milton. News Release. October 27, 1965.

A Prototype Regional Council. Washington, D.C.:
    National Service to Regional Councils, August,
    1969. (Mimeographed.)

Rosenmeier, Gordon, and Albertson, Howard. Concepts
    on a Metropolitan Council. St. Paul, 1967.

Wilensky, Alan J. "The Twin Cities Metropolitan
    Council: A Case Study of the Politics of
    Metropolitan Cooperation." Unpublished
    Senior's Thesis, Princeton University, Prince-
    ton, New Jersey, April, 1969.

ABOUT THE AUTHOR

Stanley Baldinger, who is an urban planner with Community Renewal Programs, Washington, D.C., has had ten years of experience in government and public administration. He has held the position of Assistant to the Director of Current Programs and Planning of the National Capital Planning Commission in Washington, D.C., and the position of Secretary of the Co-ordinating Committee, a body established by Federal law to co-ordinate plans and programs of common concern to Federal and District of Columbia agencies.

Mr. Baldinger has served with the U.S. Department of State as a Foreign Service Officer in Washington, D.C., and in Rome, and with the Social Security Administration in Washington. He has traveled extensively through Europe and the Middle East, observing various national approaches to urban problems.

Mr. Baldinger holds an M.A. in Political Science from the University of Minnesota and an M.S. in Urban Planning from Columbia University.